T0320509

C# Game Programming Cookbook for Unity 3D

C# Game Programming Cookbook for Unity 3D

Second Edition

Jeff W. Murray

CRC Press
Taylor & Francis Group
Boca Raton London New York

CRC Press is an imprint of the
Taylor & Francis Group, an **informa** business

Second Edition published 2021
by CRC Press
6000 Broken Sound Parkway NW, Suite 300, Boca Raton, FL 33487-2742

and by CRC Press
2 Park Square, Milton Park, Abingdon, Oxon, OX14 4RN

First Edition published by CRC Press 2014
CRC Press is an imprint of Taylor & Francis Group, LLC

ISBN: 978-0-367-32170-3 (hbk)
ISBN: 978-0-367-32164-2 (pbk)
ISBN: 978-0-429-31713-2 (ebk)

Typeset in Minion
by SPi Global, India

This book is dedicated to my
amazing wife, Tori, and to
my boys, Ethan and William.
Boys, be nice to the cat and
the cat will be nice to you!

Contents

Acknowledgments

Thanks to all of my family, friends and everyone who has helped me with my books, games and projects over the years: Brian Robbins, Chris Hanney, Technicat, Molegato, NoiseCrime, Quantum Sheep, Mickael Laszlo, Juanita Leatham, CoolPowers, Dave Brake, Sigurdur Gunnarsson, Kevin Godoy R., Lister, Wim Wouters, Edy (VehiclePhysics), IdeaFella, Liam Twose, RafaEnd, Lynxie, Alistair Murphy, McFunkypants, Dani Moss, Malcolm Evans, Vinh, Scott Wilson, Jon Keon, Dunky, Huck Z, Paradise Decay, Kryten, Silverware Games, Pete Patterson, Dr. Not Oculus VR, Say Mistage, Andy Hatch, Lydia, RT Warner, GermanRifter VR, Sylvain Demers, Kenneth Seward Jr, Dancer (Space Dad), Steve Fulton, Paul Bettner, Derek Scottishgeeks, Jonny Gorden, Edward Atkin, Ottawa Pete, Sam W., Dylan Stout, Shane McCafferty, Will Goldstone, Sanborn VR, Gary Riches, J. Dakota Powell, Mayonnaise Boy, Stephen Parkes, Ram Kanda, Alex Bethke, Itzik Goldman, Joachim Ante, Robert Scoble, Tony Walsh, Andreas 'BOLL' Aronsson, Cat, Darrel Plant, Mike Baker, Rimsy, Cassie, Christopher Brown, Phil Nolan, Pixel Hat Studio, Marcus Valles, Trev, Karyl, Tami Quiring, Nadeem Rasool, Dwayne Dibley, Liz and Pete Smyth, Isaac and Aiden, David Helgason, VR Martin, James Gamble, Vasanth Mohan, Simona Ioffe, Alexander Kondratskiy, Tim and Paul, The Oliver Twins, Jeevan Aurol, Rick King, Aldis Sipolins, Ric Lumb, Craig Taylor, Rob Hewson, Dani Moss, Jayenkai (JNK), Matthew Kirubakaran, Elliot Mitchell, Ethan and William, Pablo Rojo, Paul Bettner, AdrellaDev, Gordon Little, Ryan Evans, Sasha Boersma, Matt Browning at Perfect Prototype, Hermit, Dirty Rectangles and the whole Ottawa game dev community.

I would also like to sincerely thank Anya Hastwell, Thivya Vasudevan and the team at SPI Global, the whole team at Routledge/CRC Press/AK Peters, including Randi Cohen, Jessica Vega and Rick Adams, for making this book a reality.

Thank *you* for buying this book and for wanting to do something as cool as to make games. I wish I could tell you how awesome it feels to know that someone else is reading this right now. I cannot wait to see your games and I sincerely hope this book helps you in your game making adventures. Have fun making games!

Introduction

The overall goal of this book is to provide a library of C# code with which to jumpstart your projects and to help you with the overall structure of your games. Many development cookbooks focus on only providing snippets of code, but, here, we take a different approach. What you are holding in your hands right now (or on your screen) is a cookbook for game development that has a highly flexible core framework designed to speed up development of just about any type of Unity project.

You might think of the framework as a base soup and the scripting components as ingredients. We can mix and match script components and we can share the same core scripts in many of them. The framework takes care of the essentials and we add a little extra code to pull it all together the way we want it to work.

The framework is optional, however – you can use a lot the components individually. If you intend on using the components in this book for your own games, the framework could either serve as a base to build your games on or simply as a tutorial test bed for you to rip apart and see how it all works. Perhaps you can develop a better framework or maybe you already have a solid framework in place. If you do find a way to develop your own framework, I say do it. The key to game development is to do what works for you and your game projects – whatever it takes to cross the finish line.

I hope it helps you to make your games and tell your stories. I also hope you remember to try to have fun doing it!

Prerequisites

You can get up and running with the required software for the grand total of zero dollars. Everything you need can be downloaded free of charge with no catches. All you need is:

Unity Personal or Unity Pro version

C# programming knowledge.

This is *not* a book about learning how to program. You will need to know some C# and there are several other books out there for that purpose, even if I have tried to make the examples as simple as possible!

What this book doesn't cover

This is not a book about learning to program from scratch. We assume that the reader has some experience of the C# programming language. Know that I am a self-taught programmer and I understand there may be better or alternative ways to do things. Techniques and concepts offered in this book are meant to provide foundation and ideation, not to be the final word on any subject.

1 Making Games in a Modular Way

1.1 Important Programming Concepts

There are some things you will need to know to utilize this book fully. For a lot of programmers, these concepts may be something you were taught in school. As a self-taught coder who did not find out about a lot of these things until long after I had been struggling on without them, I see this section as a compilation of 'things I wish I'd known earlier'!

1.1.1 Manager and Controller Scripts

Sometimes, even I get confused about the difference between a manager and a controller script. There is no established protocol for this, and it varies depending on who you ask. Like some readers of the first edition of this book, I find it a little confusing and I will try to clear that up.

1.1.1.1 Managers

Managers deal with overall management, in a similar way to how a Manager would work in a workplace situation.

1.1.1.2 Controllers

Controllers deal with systems that the managers need to do their jobs. For example, in the racing game example game for this book, we have race controller scripts and a global race manager script. The race controller scripts are attached to the players and track their positions on the track, waypoints, and other relevant player-specific race information. The global race manager script talks to all the race controller scripts attached to the players to determine who is winning and when the race starts or finishes.

1.1.1.3 Communication between Classes

An important part of our modular structure is how scripts are going to communicate with each other. It is inevitable that we will need to access our scripts from different areas of the game code, so you will need to know how to do that in Unity.

1. Direct referencing scripts via variables set in the editor by the Inspector window.

The easiest way to have script Components talk to each other (that is, scripts attached to GameObjects in the Scene as Components) is to have direct references, in the form of public variables within your code. They can then be populated in the Inspector window of the Unity editor with a direct link to another Component on another GameObject.

2. GameObject referencing using SendMessage.

SendMessage sends a message to a GameObject or Transform and calls a function within any of its attached script Components. It only works one way, so it is only useful when we do not need any kind of return result. For example:

```
someGameObject.SendMessage("DoSomething");
```

Above, this would call the function DoSomething() on any of the script Components attached to the GameObject referenced by someGameObject.

3. Static variables.

The static variable type makes a variable accessible to other scripts without a direct reference to the GameObject it is attached to. This is particularly useful behavior where several different scripts may want to manipulate a variable to do things like adding points to a score or set the number of lives of a player, and so on.

An example declaration of a static variable might be:

```
public static GameManager aManager;
```

You can have private or public static variables:

1.1.1.4 Public Static

A public static variable exists everywhere and may be accessed by any other script.

For example, imagine a player script which needs to tell the Game Manager to increase the current score by one:

1. In our GameManager.cs Game Manager script, we set up a variable, public static typed:

```
public static gameScore;
```

2. In any other script, we can now access this static variable and alter the score as needed:

```
GameController.gameScore++;
```

1.1.1.5 Private Static

A private static variable is accessible only to any other instances *of the same type of class*. Other types of class will not be able to access it.

As an example, imagine all players need to have a unique number when they are first spawned into the game. The player class declares a variable named uniqueNum like this:

```
Private static int uniqueNum;
```

When a player script is first created, it uses the value of uniqueNum for itself and increases uniqueNum by one:

```
myUniqueNum = uniqueNum;
uniqueNum++;
```

The value of uniqueNum will be shared across all player scripts. The next player to be spawned will run the same start up function, getting uniqueNum again – only this time it has been increased by one, thanks to the player spawned earlier. This player again gets its own unique number and increases the static variable ready for the next one.

1.1.2 The Singleton

A *singleton* is a commonly used method for allowing access to an instance of a class, accessible to all other scripts. This pattern is ideal for code that needs to communicate with the entire game, such as a Game Manager.

1.1.2.1 Using the Singleton in Unity

The most straightforward way to achieve singleton-like behavior is to use a static variable and, when Unity calls the Awake() function, set the instance variable to become a reference to the script instance it represents. The keyword 'this' refers to the instance of the script it is a part of.

For example:

```
public class MyScript : Monobehaviour
{
    private static MySingleton instance;
    void Awake()
    {
        if (instance != null)
            Destroy(this);

        instance = this;
    }
}
```

The singleton instance of our script can be accessed anywhere, by practically any script, with the following syntax:

```
MySingleton.Instance.SomeFunctionInTheSingleton();
```

1.1.3 Inheritance

Inheritance is a complex concept, which calls for some explanation here because of its key role within the scripts provided by this book. Have a read through this section but don't worry if you don't pick up inheritance right away. Once we get to the programming it will probably become clearer.

The bottom line is that inheritance is used in programming to describe a method of providing template scripts that may be overridden, or added to, by other scripts. As a metaphor, imagine a car. All cars have four wheels and an engine. The types of wheels may vary from car to car, as will the engine, so when we say 'this is a car' and try to describe how our car behaves; we may also describe the engine and wheels.

These relationships may be shown in a hierarchical order:

Car–

–Wheels

–Engine

Now try to picture this as a C# script:

Car class.

Wheels function

Engine function

If we were building a game with lots of cars in it, having to rewrite the car class for each type of car would be silly. A far more efficient method might be to write a base class and populate it with virtual functions. When we need to create a car, rather than use this base class, we build a new class, which inherits the base class. Because our new class is inherited, it is optional whether we choose to override wheels or engine functions to make them behave in ways specific to our new class. That is, we can build 'default' functions into the base class and if we only need to use a default behavior for an engine, our new class doesn't need to override the engine function.

A base class might look something like this:

```
public class BaseCar : MonoBehaviour {

        public virtual void Engine () {
                Debug.Log("Vroom");
        }

        public virtual void Wheels () {
                Debug.Log("Four wheels");
        }
}
```

There are two key things to notice in the above script. One is the class declaration itself and the fact that this class *derives* from MonoBehaviour. MonoBehaviour is itself a class – the Unity documentation describes it as "the base class every script derives from" – this MonoBehaviour class contains many engine-specific functions and methods such as Start(), Update(), FixedUpdate(), and more. If our script didn't derive from MonoBehaviour it would not inherit those functions and the engine wouldn't automatically call functions like Update() for us to be able to work with. Another point to note is that MonoBehaviour is a class that is built into the engine and not something we can access to edit or change.

The second point to note is that our functions are both declared as *virtual* functions. Both are public, both are virtual. Making virtual functions means that the behavior in our base class may be overridden by any scripts that derive from it. The behavior we define in this base class could be thought of as its default behavior. We will cover overriding in full a little further on in this section.

Let's take a look at what this script actually does: if we were to call the Engine() function of our BaseCar class, it would write to the console "Vroom." If we called Wheels, the console would read "Four wheels."

Now that we have our BaseCar class, we can use this as a template and make new versions of it like this:

```
public class OctoCar : BaseCar {
    public override void Wheels () {
        Debug.Log ("Eight wheels");
    }
}
```

The first thing you may notice is that the OctoCar class derives from BaseCar rather than MonoBehaviour. This means that OctoCar inherits functions and methods belonging to our BaseCar script. As the functions described by BaseCar were virtual, they may be overridden. For OctoCar, we override Wheels with the line:

```
public override void Wheels () {
```

Let's take a look at what this script actually does: In this case, if we were to call the Engine() function on OctoCar, it would do the same as the BaseCar class; it would write "Vroom" to the console. It would do this because we have inherited the function but have not overridden it, which means we keep that default behavior. In OctoCar, however, we have overridden the Wheels() function. The BaseCar behavior of Wheels would print "Four wheels" to the console but if we call Wheels() on OctoCar, the overridden behavior will write "Eight wheels," instead.

Inheritance plays a huge part in how our core game framework is structured. The idea is that we have basic object types and specific elaborated versions of these objects inheriting the base methods, properties, and functions. By building our games in this manner, the communication between the different game components (such as game control scripts, weapon scripts, projectile controllers, etc.) becomes universal without having to write out the same function declarations over and over again for different variations of script. For the core framework, our main goal is to make it as flexible and extensible as possible and this would be a much more difficult if we were unable to use inheritance.

1.1.4 Coroutines

Unity lets you run a function known as a coroutine, outside of the regular built in functions like Update, FixedUpdate, LateUpdate, and so on. A coroutine is self-contained code that will just go off and do its own thing once you have told it to run. As it is running on its own, you can do some cool stuff like pause it for a set amount of time and then have it start again, and coroutines are ideally suited to time-based actions like fade effects or animations.

Here is an example of a coroutine (this example code comes from the Unity engine documentation):

```
IEnumerator Fade()
{
    for (float ft = 1f; ft >= 0; ft -= 0.1f)
    {
        Color c = renderer.material.color;
        c.a = ft;
        renderer.material.color = c;
        yield return null;
    }
}
```

This code loops the value of ft from 1 to 0 and sets the alpha value of a color on a material to that value. This will fade out whatever renderer this script is attached to, fading more as the alpha channel gets closer to 0. Notice the strange line:

```
yield return null;
```

Do not be alarmed by this odd code above! All it does is tell the engine that, at this point, the coroutine is ready to end this update and go on to the next one. You need this in your code, but don't worry too much about why at this stage. I will go into some more detail below, but for now let us continue by looking at how you would start this coroutine running:

```
StartCoroutine("Fade");
```

StartCoroutine() takes the name of the coroutine as a string. Once called to start, the coroutine will do its thing and you do not need to do anything else. It will either run until we tell it to stop, or it will run until the object is destroyed.

A key thing to note here is that the function is declared as type IEnumerator. At first, I found this confusing, but it turns out that Unity coroutines use C#'s built in system for iterator blocks. IEnumerator (Iterator Enumerator) was intended to be a method for iterating through collections of objects. Coroutines instead use IEnumerator to iterate through your coroutine code, starting or stopping it between updates.

Another key point is that statement:

```
yield return null;
```

You can think of IEnumerator like a cursor making its way through your code. When the cursor hits a yield statement, that tells the engine that this update is done and to move the cursor on to the next block.

Another thing you can do with coroutines is to pause the code inline for a certain amount of time, like this:

```
yield return new WaitForSeconds(1.0f);
```

Using WaitForSeconds(), you can quite literally pause the coroutine script execution inline. For example:

```
IEnumerator DebugStuff()
{
    Debug.Log("Start.");
    yield return new WaitForSeconds(1.0f);
    Debug.Log("Now, it's one second later!");

}
```

Earlier in this section, I mentioned that the yield statement is used to tell Unity the current update is done and to move on to the next. In the code above, rather than just telling Unity to move on to the next bit of code, it tells Unity to wait for the specified number of seconds first.

1.1.5 Namespaces

Namespaces compartmentalize chunks of code away from each other. You can think of a namespace as a box to put your own scripts in, so that they can stay separated from other code or code libraries. This helps to prevent possible overlaps between code libraries (APIs and so on) and your own code, such as duplicate function names or variables.

To use namespaces, you wrap the entire class in a namespace declaration like this:

```
namespace MyNamespace
{
        public class MyClass() : Monobehaviour
        {
        }

}
```

When you want to refer to the code from another class, you need to be either wrapped in the same namespace or to have the using keyword at the top of the script, like:

```
using MyNamespace;
```

1.1.6 Finite State Machines (FSM)

A finite state machine is a commonly used system for tracking states. In video games, they are used to track game states. Example states might be GameLoaded, GameStarting, LevelStarting, and so on. The term *finite state machine* sounds a lot more complicated than it usually is. The actual code often takes the form of a long case statement that will execute code or call functions based on the current game state. For example:

```
Switch(currentGameState)
{
        Case GameStates.GameLoaded:
        GameLoaded();
        Break;
        Case GameStates.GameStarting:
        GameStart();
        Break;

}
```

Having code in each case statement can get unruly. To counter this, I like to split all of the code out into individual functions. This keeps the code tidy, easier to manage, and easier to debug when things do not go to plan.

▌█ 1.2 Naming Conventions

Naming conventions vary from programmer to programmer and even between companies. Some games companies have strict guidelines on how code is constructed and how to name variables, where they can and cannot be used, and so on, which is mostly in place to make it easier for other programmers to be able to understand the code and pick it up when they might need to. You may not need to take it that far, but I do feel that some organization of your naming helps. In this book, I follow a very loose set of rules for naming variables – just enough to make it easier for me to know quickly what type of variable I am looking at or what its purpose might be. Those are:

Object references (Transforms, Components, GameObjects, and so forth) are prefixed by an underscore (_) symbol. For example, a variable to hold a reference to a Transform might be named _TR. A variable used to talk to a Game Manager might be named _GameManager.

Most of the objects in this book (players, enemies, and more) derive from the ExtendedMonoBehaviour class, which contains a few variables that are used more commonly than others:

_RB   Used to reference a Rigidbody attached to this object.

_RB2D   For a 2D Rigidbody reference.

_TR   The Transform of the object.

_GO   The GameObject.

Where scripts need to be initialized before they can be used, in this book we always use a Boolean variable named didInit which gets set to true after initialization. You can use didInit to make sure initialization has completed.

Many programmers frown on the idea of declaring temporary variables, but I like to have _tempVEC and _tempTR variables available for whenever I need to refer to a quick Vector3 or another Transform inline. Having these variables already declared is just a little quicker than having to declare a new Vector3 each time, or to make a new Transform variable.

▉ 1.3 Where to Now?

Think about how your objects work together in the game world and how their scripts need to communicate with each other. I find it helps to make flow diagrams or to use mind-mapping software to work things out beforehand. A little planning early on can reduce a whole lot of code revisions later. That said, it is perfectly O.K. for your structure to grow and evolve as you develop it further. The framework shown in this book went through many iterations before reaching its final form.

Try to break up your scripts into smaller components to help debugging and flexibility. Also try to design for re-useability; hard-coding references to other scripts reduces the portability of the script and increases the amount of work you will need to do in the future when you want to carry it over into another project.

2 Making a 2D Infinite Runner Game

This chapter is different from the rest of the book and a dramatic diversion from what you may have seen in its first edition. Elsewhere in the text, I focus mainly on the code behind the games. This chapter offers up a step by step tutorial to using the framework to make a 2D infinite runner game. The goal of this chapter is to demonstrate two things: 1) How quickly you can turn around a game when you have a framework in place that takes care of a lot of the repetitive tasks. 2) The basics of how this books framework fits together to give you some background knowledge before we get down into nitty gritty of the framework code in Chapter 3.

This infinite runner (Figure 2.1) has a character that can move left, right, and jump. Platforms are spawned off-screen and moved to the left to create the illusion of movement.

I have already set up animations and imported the required graphics into the example project to get things going quickly. As the focus of this book is more toward code, project structure, and programming, I want to avoid using up too many pages on making graphics or on Unity editor-specifics. The Unity documentation features plenty of content on this.

Players jump and move to stay on the platforms if possible, with the score incremented at timed intervals. If the player falls off the bottom of the screen, the game ends.

To accomplish this, we will need:

1. The C# Game Programming Cookbook (GPC) framework, which is included as part of this book as a download from Github at https://github.com/psychicparrot/CSharpUnityCookbookExampleFiles

2. A platformer character capable of running left, right, and jumping

3. Platforms (auto moving to the left) and a method to spawn platforms off screen

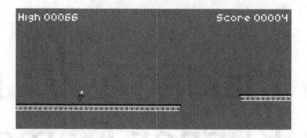

Figure 2.1 In the Infinite Runner example game, players jump and run to try to stay on the platforms for as long as possible.

4. A Game Manager script to keep track of game state and deal with scoring and so forth

5. Sounds for jumping and the game ending

6. An animated character

With just the framework and assets, by the end of this chapter, we will have a working game.

2.1 Anatomy of a Unity Project

Unity projects are made up of lots and lots of files. A game is made up of Scenes full of GameObjects. GameObjects are all the objects that make up a game. GameObjects may take the form of anything from an empty placeholder to a fully animated 3d model. Every GameObject has something called a Transform, which holds information on the rotation, position, and scale of the GameObject.

Scenes are essentially just files that hold information about which objects to load at runtime. They can contain GameObjects, or they can contain Prefabs. Prefabs are essentially files containing information about one or more GameObjects to load as though they are combined. By using Prefabs, you can reduce the time it takes to build multiple Scenes by combining multiple GameObjects into one, single, Prefab. Think of Prefabs as templates you make yourself by arranging GameObjects in the Scene and then creating Prefabs from them as templates to load and use elsewhere. When you drag a Prefab into a Unity Scene, it will appear as one or more GameObjects – replicating the original structure you created when you made the original Prefab. Since game projects are made up of many files, a lot of your time in Unity will be spent manipulating files, turning them into GameObjects, and Prefabs and then organizing and laying them out in Scenes. In the next section, we look at how Unity helps you to do this and how the editor is structured for exactly these kinds of tasks.

2.2 Open Unity, Then the Example Project for This Chapter

Open Unity. At the splash screen, choose to open an existing project and browse to the folder named Chapter2_UnComplete_ProjectFiles, which contains the example project for this chapter. Open the project. If you have any trouble along the way, or you just want to try out the completed game, you can find the

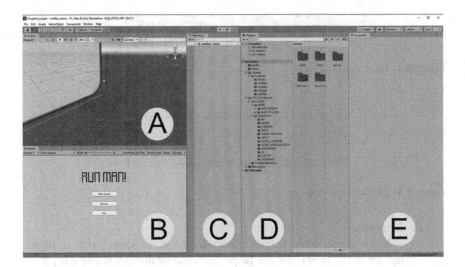

Figure 2.2 The Unity editor as seen in a 2 by 3 layout.

complete example as a part of the other example project found in the folder named All_Completed_ProjectFiles.

To keep everything in line with the information in this section, you should change the editor layout. In the top right of the editor, find the Layout dropdown button. Click on it and choose 2 by 3. After a short delay, the editor should arrange its panels into the default 2 by 3 layout.

Now that we have the editor laid out in similar ways, let's look through each panel to make sure we are using the same terminology. Check out Figure 2.2 – outlined below are the different sections shown in the figure, what those sections are and what they are for:

A. Scene

The Scene panel is your drag and drop visual window into a Unity Scene. You can manipulate GameObjects directly inside the currently loaded Scene.

B. Game

The Game panel shows a preview of the game. When you press Play, the editor runs the game inside the Game panel as if it were running in a standalone build. There are also a few extra features, such as Gizmos, that the Game preview offers to help you build out and debug your games.

C. Project

The Project panel is very similar to a file browser, in that it lists out all the files that go up to make your project. You can click and drag them, right click, and access a menu, use shortcuts, and delete them – almost all the regular functionality of a Windows Explorer window right inside the editor.

D. Hierarchy

The Hierarchy works in a similar way to the Project panel, only instead of being an interface to manipulate project files, it's there to manipulate GameObjects inside the current Scene.

Figure 2.3 The Transform tools.

Figure 2.4 The playback tools.

E. Inspector

Whenever you have a GameObject selected in the Scene panel, or high-lighted in the Hierarchy, the Inspector window shows you editable properties of the GameObject and any Components attached to it. Whatever you can't do with the Scene panel, you can probably do here instead.

Another point of interest in the main Unity editor are along the toolbar across the top of the editor, below the menus.

In the top left, find the Transform toolbar (Figure 2.3). This toolbar is to manipulate objects in the Scene panel. Tools, from left to right:

The Hand Tool	Allows you to pan the view around the Scene.
Move	Selection and movement of GameObjects.
Rotate	Selection and rotation of GameObjects.
Scale	Selection and scaling of GameObjects.
Rect Transform	Modify a GameObjects boundaries as a Rect (combined scaling and movement).
Transform	A method to manipulate scale, position, and rotation in a single, combined tool.
Custom	This tool allows access to custom Editor tools and will not be covered in this book.

At the center of the toolbar, find the Play, Pause and Step buttons (Figure 2.4) which are used to preview your game and to control what happens in the Game panel.

2.2.1 A Few Notes on the Example Project

Unity uses something called packages to extend the functionality of the editor in an officially supported and controlled way. To facilitate editing and set up of the 2D (two dimensional) sprites in this project, a package named 2D Sprite Package had to be imported. Accessing packages is done via the Package Manager – found in the menu Window/Package Manager. Check in Package Manager regularly, for updates to any libraries you download.

2.2.2 Sprites

2D sprites may be found in the projects Assets/Games/RunMan/Sprites folder. The sprites were made with a sprite editing program called Aesprite and exported as sprite sheets. Sprite sheets are groups of sprites which are split up into individual sprites by the engine. We tend to use sprite sheets for animations, exporting multiple frames of animation in a single image to save memory and having the engine take care of cutting them up to display. The import settings for all of the game images are set to their default values, the Sprite Mode is set to Multiple to accommodate the sprite sheets (Multiple allows you to slice up those images) and the Filter Mode has been set to Point (no filter) so that Unity does not try to filter images to make them smooth. For this type of visual style, we want the pixels to be defined and visible without filtering. The only other deviation from the defaults is the Compression level, which is set to None just to be sure to avoid any artifacts or anomalies that might stem from compressing small images.

2.2.3 Animation

Animation is a complicated subject and outside the scope of this book, but this section acts as a quick guide on how the animations for this game works.

Look out for RunMan_Animator in the Sprites folder. You can open it to view by double clicking on the RunMan_Animator file in the Project pane. An Animator contains a state machine graph (Figure 2.5) which controls the flow of animation. When an animated GameObject is initialized, the state machine graph begins in its Entry state and will transition to the default state. In Figure 2.5, you can see that RunMan_Animator has a default state of RunMan_Idle (that is, an arrow goes from Entry to RunMan_Idle) – this will play an idle animation for whenever RunMan is standing still. The animation is looped and there is no further flow (no more arrows pointing to boxes!) out from RunMan_Idle in the Animator graph; so, until told otherwise, the animation will stay in the idle state.

In the graph (Figure 2.5) look for the Any State state – this literally means any state in that this state can be triggered from any animation. The Any State has two arrows coming off it; one pointing to RunMan_Jump state and the other to a RunMan_Run state. So, how do we get the animation to change to run or jump when the Animator graph has no link from the endlessly looping RunMan_Idle state? Parameters are the answer! Parameters are variables that can be set and modified through code and used as Conditions by the Animator graph to control flow. In the case of Any State, whenever a Jump parameter is triggered the Animator will transition from Any State (that is, whatever state the graph is currently in) to RunMan_Jump. Whenever a Run parameter is triggered, the Animator will transition from Any State to RunMan_Run. RunMan_Run is a looping animation that, again, will play until the Animator graph is told to do otherwise.

In conclusion, the animation system for this game is set up to be as straightforward as possible. The Animator can be controlled by two parameters: Jump and Run. In our code, to transition to a run animation we just set the Run parameter. To play a jump animation, we set the Jump parameter.

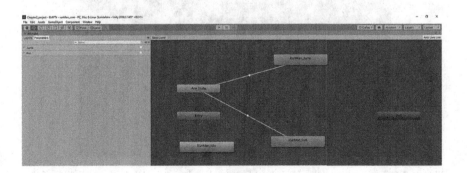

Figure 2.5 The Animator graph for the RunMan character.

▌ 2.3 Open the Main Game Scene

In the Project panel, there are a lot of folders. Most of them are sub-folders inside the GPC_Framework folder. We do not need to get into these just yet, but you should know that the files in GPC_Framework make up the framework and they are separated from everything else to keep framework files and your games files separated and neat.

Find the Games folder and click the little arrow next to it to expand out the folder to show its contents. It is intended that, whenever you build a game with the framework, you use the Games folder to put the assets that are specific to your game only.

The folder structure under Games looks like this:

Games

  RunMan

    Audio

    Prefabs

    Scenes

    Scripts

    Sprites

Stay as organized as possible as you move forward with game projects. This will help a lot as your project grows (and, often, they grow much bigger than you might expect!) to stay on course and to spend less time looking for lost assets.

In the Project panel, click on the Scene folder to show its contents. There is a single Scene inside that folder, named runMan_core. This is the Scene that will contain the main game. There will also be a main menu Scene, which we will add later in this chapter.

Double click on the runMan_core Scene in the Project panel, to open it. The Game panel will show the user interface already set up (Figure 2.6) but there's no other logic in the Scene yet, so pressing Play will do nothing. By using the framework, at the end of this chapter you will have a fun infinite runner game to play here instead. The books game framework takes care of most of the heavy lifting

Figure 2.6 To save time, the User Interface is already set up in the game Scene of the example project for this chapter.

and the bulk of the work is going to be to connecting existing scripts together to form the GameObject, logic, and physics for this game. You may be surprised to learn that it only takes four custom scripts.

◼ 2.4 The Game Manager

At the core of this game is the Game Manager. This is where the state of our game is tracked and the convergence point of all the game's objects and logic. We will be revisiting the Game Manager throughout this chapter, but what we need to do in this section is to set up the basic structure and a few variables for our other objects to access and use. For example, platforms will need to know how fast to move. We need all platforms to move at the same speed, so it makes sense to store the speed value in the Game Manager. Storing the platform speed also means that we can change the speed of the game easily from right inside the script that deals with game logic.

With the RunMan_core Scene open in Unity, click the plus sign at the top of the Hierarchy panel to show the Add menu. Choose Create Empty from the dropdown.

TIP: You can also access the Add GameObject menu by right clicking in an empty space in the Hierarchy panel or via the menu GameObject at the top of the editor.

In the Inspector, with the new GameObject selected, change the name from GameObject to GameManager.

Click Add Component. In the text box that appears after clicking that button, type RunMan_GameManager. Once you have finished typing, press enter on the keyboard. The Add Component window will automatically switch to show New Script (Figure 2.7). Click Create and Add. This creates a new C# script Component and adds it to the GameObject you just created. After a little time for the compiler to update, the Component should appear in the Inspector as a Component named (Script). The next step is to open the script and add some code to it.

Still in the Inspector, double click on the Script name inside the Component to open your default script editor (normally Visual Studio, unless you chose something different when you installed Unity). If you have any issues opening the script, you can get to it via the Project panel. Unity will have automatically placed the new script in the Assets folder. Click on the Assets folder in the Project panel and you should be able to see RunMan_GameManager on the right side of the split Project pane. Double click the script file to open it.

The default C# script Unity adds when you create new file looks like this:

```
using System.Collections;
using System.Collections.Generic;
using UnityEngine;

public class RunMan_GameManager : MonoBehaviour

{
    // Start is called before the first frame update
    void Start()
    {

    }
    // Update is called once per frame
    void Update()
    {

    }
}
```

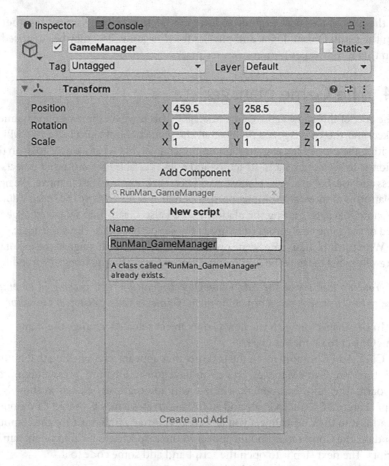

Figure 2.7 Naming and creating a new Component in the Inspector's Add Component panel.

The framework in this book exists within a namespace called GPC, so the first thing we need to do to be able to access everything inside the framework is to add a using statement to the top of the script. Below using UnityEngine, add the following line:

```
using GPC;
```

The framework includes a base version of a Game Manager script that we can inherit (see Chapter 1 for a brief guide to inheritance) to give this script some of the useful functionality we will need as the game grows. Let's change our new Game Manager script. The base script is called BaseGameManager. Change:

```
public class RunMan _ GameManager : MonoBehaviour
```

To:

```
public class RunMan _ GameManager : BaseGameManager
```

Press CTRL+S to save the script, or save the script via the menus File>Save.

Remember when we first created the GameManager through the Add Component button in the Inspector and the new Component appeared as something called (Script)? Flip back to the editor and you will see we now have a whole host of new things in the Inspector. The BaseGameManager script contains lots of useful things to help manage your game. We will go into the script in full detail in Chapter 3, Section 3.2.1.

In the Inspector now, there are three dropdown menu fields for Current Game State, Target Game State, and Last Game State. Below those, a whole lot of events that will be fired by our state machine entering states like loaded, game started, and so forth. We will deal with game states in full, further in this chapter in Section 2.7.1.

Before anything else, we do need to add a few variables. Place this code just after the class declaration, above void Start():

```
public float runSpeed = 1f;
public float distanceToSpawnPlatform = 2f;
public bool isRunning;
```

runSpeed will be used by platform movement code to determine how fast to move the platforms across the screen to simulate running.

distanceToSpawnPlatform contains a float value representing the gap (in 3d units) between platforms.

isRunning is a Boolean used by platforms to know whether they should be moving or not. The main use for isRunning is at the start of the game, before the player starts running as it sits in its idle animation state. We will use it again at the end of the game, just to stop the platforms moving when we show the final score game over messages.

Now that we have these variables set up in the Game Manager, we need to make this class accessible from everywhere so that other scripts can access it. To do that, we will take a basic Singleton approach. See Chapter 1, Section 1.4 for more information on this.

Beneath the variables you just added, right after the line:

```
public bool isRunning;
```

Add the following code:

```
public static RunMan_GameManager instance { get; private set; }

    // set instance in this script's constructor
    public RunMan_GameManager()
    {
        instance = this;
    }
```

What this does is to make a variable that is accessible from anywhere because it's public and static. As the constructor runs when a GameManager instance gets created, our public static variable gets populated with a reference to 'this' instance. Other scripts can now talk to this instance by referring to its static variable like this:

```
RunMan _ GameManager.instance
```

Going in via this instance variable, any other script in your game can call functions on RunMan_GameManager, access public variables, or set public variables. Just make sure that only one instance of RunMan_GameManager ever exists at any time, otherwise you may find a script trying to access the wrong object. If you do find yourself making more complicated scenarios that could lead to multiple instances you may want to add check to see if the instance variable is already populated before setting it. In the case of this game, we only ever need this single instance to be attached to a single GameObject in a single Scene and this is enough.

For now, that is as far as we need to take the Game Manager. There will be more later in the chapter, but this is enough to get going with and enough to provide the game platforms with the information they need to move.

▌ 2.5 Making Platforms to Run On

At the core of this game are platforms to run on, so that is a great starting point. As the platforms do not require any game specific code, we can go ahead, and figure out a method to spawn them and move them before adding game logic.

Right now, the user interface may get in the way of seeing everything clearly as you set up game elements. To hide the interface, look in the Hierarchy panel and find the UI_Canvases object. UI_Canvases is an empty GameObject with the actual user interfaces below, parented to it. If you cannot see the three Canvas GameObjects under UI_Canvases, click on the little arrow next to UI_Canvases to expand it out. Now, click the first one – the GetReadyMessageCanvas GameObject – to highlight it. Hold shift on the keyboard and click the GameUICanvas GameObject. This should select all three canvases at the same time. Over in the Inspector, find the Component named Canvas Group and set the value in the Alpha field to 0. All the user interface should now be hidden.

In the Project panel, find the Games/RunMan/Sprites folder. In Sprites, find the RunMan_Platform sprite. Left click and drag it into an empty part of the Hierarchy panel. If all goes well, you should see the platform appear in the center of the Game panel.

With RunMan_Platform GameObject selected in the Hierarchy, move the mouse so that it is hovering over the Scene panel. Press F on the keyboard. This will focus on the currently selected object, moving the Scene view to the center of the object to make editing easier. You may want to use the mouse wheel to zoom out a little at this point, too. Just enough so that there is space around the platform to move it around without it going off the edge of the screen.

In the Scene view, click and hold to grab the red arrow of the Gizmo Unity overlays on the platform. With the red arrow selected, you will only be able to move the platform along its X axis – left or right in the Game panel. Drag the platform to the left so that the left side of the platform is touching the left side of the Game panel.

Next, grab the green arrow of the Gizmo to move the platform on its Y axis. Hold down the mouse and move the platform so that the bottom of it touches the bottom of the Game panel.

This platform is going to be a starting platform for the player to stand on when the game first starts. To stop the player falling right through it, we need to add a Collider.

With RunMan_Platform still selected, look to the Inspector, and click Add Component. In the search box that appears after you click the button, type Edge and choose Edge Collider 2D from the dropdown to add an Edge Collider 2D Component to the GameObject.

With RunMan_Platform still selected in the Hierarchy, go back to hovering over the Scene panel and press F on the keyboard to focus the platform in the center of the view. Now that the Edge Collider 2D Component has been added to this GameObject, you should see a thin green line running lengthwise across the platform. This line will become the solid physics surface that the player will stand on. It needs to align with the top of the platform rather than where it is now. On the Edge Collider 2D Component, click the Edit Collider button (Figure 2.8).

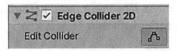

Figure 2.8 In Unity, some Colliders such as the Edge Collider 2D have an Edit button.

In the Scene panel, the green line can now be moved around. Hover the mouse over the green line and a small Gizmo block appears. By clicking and dragging the block, the green line will move. First, grab a point at the left side and move it up. Then, grab a point on the right and do the same so that the green line aligns perfectly with the top of the platform.

To complete the platform set up, just two more Components need to be added to it. In the Inspector, click Add Component, and find and add an Auto Destroy Object Component. In the field labeled Time Before Object Destroy, type 10. We want this object to delete itself after 10 seconds. The RunMan_ Platform Components should now look like those in Figure 2.8.

The second Component we are going to build ourselves. Click Add Component and type AutoTransformMove. Click New Script and then Create and Add to create a new C# script and add it to the GameObject.

Once the new script is attached to the GameObject and visible in the Inspector, double click on the name of the script to open it in your script editor. In your script editor, add the following line just above the class declaration and below the existing using statements:

```
using GPC;
```

To move the platforms, this script requires three variables. Add these just inside the class declaration:

```
public float moveSpeed;
public Vector3 moveVector;
private Transform _TR;
```

When the script first starts, we need to grab a reference to the GameObject's Transform. A Transform is a built-in Component we use for modifying position, rotation, and scale.

Scripts that derive from Monobehaviour (on any level) can contain functions that will be automatically called by the game engine. The Start() function will be called when the game starts. Change the Start() function to look like this:

```
void Start()
{
    // cache the transform ref
    _TR = GetComponent<Transform>();
}
```

The GetComponent will search for a Component, of whatever type is within the angled brackets, on the current GameObject. GetComponent() is a useful built in function, but it can be a little slow, so it is best to keep any calls to GetComponent() out of the main loop and called as least as possible.

Another Monobehaviour specific built-in function that will be called automatically by the engine is Update(). It will be called every frame (yes, 30 times per second when the frames per second speed is 30, or 60 at 60 fps and so on).

It is the ideal place to put our movement code. Replace the placeholder Update function already in your script with this:

```
void Update()
{
        // keep move speed updated from game manager
        moveSpeed = RunMan_GameManager.instance.runSpeed;

        // move the transform
        _TR.Translate((moveVector * moveSpeed) * Time.
deltaTime);

}
```

In the code above, moveSpeed gets its value from the runSpeed variable you made in RunMan_GameManager earlier in this chapter. It uses that Singleton variable instance, to gain access to it.

Beneath that, we use the Translate function (part of Transform) to move the platform. moveVector is a Vector3 typed variable which holds a direction vector used to define the direction of movement of the object. This gets multiplied by the moveSpeed to give us a Vector suitable for Translate that will change with the speed in RunMan_GameManager. It is then multiplied by Time.deltaTime. Unity provides some a helper class named Time to help track or manipulate how the engine deals with time. deltaTime is a variable holding the amount of time that has passed since the last frame Update, so we can use that deltaTime amount to make movement that adapts to time rather than being locked to framerates. This is a better idea than just move x amount each frame, because if the system does something in the background that causes the game to stall or if your game is running slower than it should on another system, the movement won't work as intended. By having movement that adapts to time elapsed, if things run slow or there are glitches it will move the same amount even if it needs to jump a bit.

Finally, add this function below the Update() function above the final curly bracket in the script:

```
public void SetMoveSpeed(float aSpeed)
{
        // provide method to adjust speed from other scripts
        moveSpeed = aSpeed;
}
```

Above, we just add a simple method for another script to tell this script how fast or slow to move. This will be used a little further in this chapter, called at the start of the game to tell the starting platforms to move once the game begins.

Press CTRL+S to save your script and go back to Unity.

With RunMan_Platform selected in the Hierarchy, look to the Auto Transform Move Component you made, leave Move Speed at 0 but change Move Vector so that X is –1, leaving Y and Z at 0.

Finally, we need to set up the Layer of the platform so that it can be detected as ground. In the top right of the Inspector, just below the name of the GameObject to the right, there is a dropdown menu labeled Layer (Figure 2.9). Click the dropdown and choose Ground from the list.

Press Play in the editor. The platform should zip off to the left of the screen. If it did, nice job! That is how it is supposed to behave. Stop playback by clicking the Stop button in the editor.

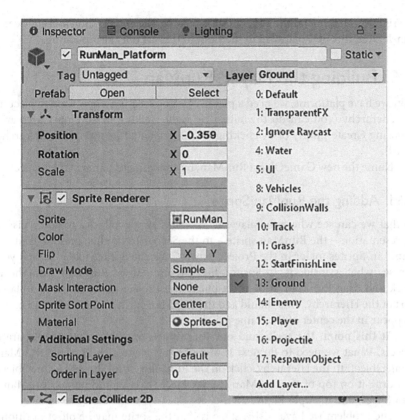

Figure 2.9 The Layer dropdown, in the Inspector, appears on all GameObjects in a Scene.

Now that the platform has everything it needs for the game, we need to turn it into a Prefab so that it can be spawned by another script whenever we need one. To turn the platform into a Prefab, click and drag RunMan_Platform from the Hierarchy into the Games/RunMan/Prefabs folder in the Project panel.

At the start of the game, RunMan should have three platforms to run across before the jumping starts so that the player has a chance to acclimatize to the environment. The last thing to do in this section is to duplicate the platform to make another two that will go alongside the one you already have in the Scene.

In the Hierarchy, right click on RunMan_Platform and choose Duplicate from the menu. A new GameObject should appear in the Hierarchy named RunMan_Platform (1) but you will not see any difference in the Scene or Game panels because it is currently in the exact same place as the original platform. Move it to the right by clicking on the red (X axis) arrow on the Gizmo shown in the Scene panel. Drag this duplicate platform to a position where the top of it is touching the original platform so there is no gap for the player to fall through (as Figure 2.10).

Now duplicate another platform to go to the right of the one you just added. In the Hierarchy, right click RunMan_Platform and choose Duplicate. Move it to

Figure 2.10 The three starting platforms are set up in the runMan_core Scene.

2.5 Making Platforms to Run On

the right by clicking on the red (X axis) arrow on the Gizmo shown in the Scene panel. Drag this new platform to the right of the last one, just touching.

■ 2.6 Building the Player, RunMan

Now we have platforms, we need a player. Start by creating a new GameObject in the Hierarchy (you can do this either by right clicking in an empty area and choosing Create Empty or by clicking on the + icon at the top of the Hierarchy panel).

Name the new GameObject RunMan, by changing its name in the Inspector.

2.6.1 Adding the RunMan Sprite

So that we can see where the player is, it would be a good idea to add a visual representation – the RunMan sprite – to the Scene. To do this, find the Games/RunMan/Sprites folder in the Project panel. Click the Sprites folder so that you can see what is inside it. In Sprites, find the file named RunMan_Run-Sheet. Click and drag RunMan_Run-Sheet out of the Project panel and into a blank part of the Hierarchy. This should add the RunMan sprite to the Scene and make it appear in the center of the Game panel.

At this point, the sprite and our RunMan GameObject are two separate objects. What we need to do next is to make the sprite a child of the RunMan GameObject. In the Hierarchy, click on the RunMan_Run-Sheet_0 GameObject and drag it on top of the RunMan GameObject. This should parent RunMan_Run-Sheet_0 to it, as per Figure 2.11.

The problem we have at this stage is that the sprite may be offset position-wise from the RunMan GameObject because Unity often spawns objects away from 0,0,0 world position. In Unity, all objects have world positions and local positions. You could say that a world position would be your street address and the local position might be where you are inside your house.

When you parent an object to another object it will inherit the parent's world position, but it will still hold whatever world position it had previously, now stored as a local position. That is, even though it moves with the parent GameObject it will be offset from it by whatever X, Y, and Z values are in its Transform box in the Inspector.

The RunMan GameObject will have all of the operational Components (movement code and collisions and so forth) attached to it which means that the sprites local position needs to be set to 0,0,0. This way, it will both move with the

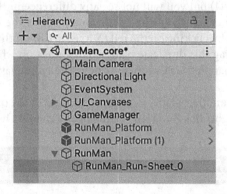

Figure 2.11 The RunMan sprite parented to a GameObject.

parent and be positioned in the exact same place – if we don't do that, collisions won't be happening where the sprite is and the game will make no sense.

Click on the RunMan_Run-Sheet_0 GameObject in the Hierarchy and set all three X, Y and Z fields of its Position (in the Transform section at the top of the Inspector) to zero, if they are not already. You may find that the sprite moves away from the center of the Game panel, but that is okay – we will set the exact player position after setting up physics.

2.6.2 Adding Physics and Collisions to RunMan

By the end of this section, RunMan will be able to fall and rest on a platform.

First, we need to add a Rigidbody to the RunMan GameObject to represent the player in the physics simulation. Click on the RunMan GameObject to get started. In the Inspector, click Add Component and find Rigidbody 2D (either scroll through to find it, or start typing Rigidbody into the search bar).

The gravity value needs changing on the Rigidbody 2D Component, to help give RunMan a jump style suitable for this game. In the Inspector, on the Rigidbody 2D Component, change Gravity Scale to 0.6

Next, find the Constraints field and click the little arrow to the left of it, to expand out the Constraints section. Next to Freeze Rotation, put a check into the Z box by clicking on it.

RunMan now has physics, but he has no Collision Components and will fall to infinity until we add a Collider. With the RunMan GameObject still selected in the Hierarchy, click the Add Component button in the Inspector. Find and add Capsule Collider 2D. Be careful not to add a regular Capsule Collider here, though. The standard Capsule Collider will only work in a 3D simulation and since Unity uses a separate physics engine for 2D physics than 3D, we need to be sure to use only 2D Components.

The Capsule Collider is a good way to represent a human in a physics simulation. You can elongate it from the head to the feet and it has a minimal contact surface to keep the friction levels down as it moves along the ground. As it has width, you can adjust a capsule to represent the body width too. In this section, you can either edit the Collider manually and try to get it to look like the shape in Figure 2.12, or you can enter the following numbers into the Inspector:

Offset:

X: 0
Y: 0.01

Size:

X: 0.04
Y: 0.15

Direction:

Vertical

Once you have entered in all the numbers via the Inspector, compare the shape of your capsule to the one in Figure 2.12 – if it looks good, move on to the next stage of adding player scripts.

Figure 2.12 The Capsule Collider is a good way to represent a simplified human form for collision calculations.

2.6.3 Player Scripts

The structure of players within the framework will be explained in depth in the next chapter. For this section, however, we will just focus on setting up a basic player and getting things ready for this specific game.

Make sure the RunMan GameObject is selected in the Hierarchy or click on it to highlight it. Click the Add Component button in the Inspector. Click New Script and type RunMan_CharacterController as the script name, and click Create and Add.

Double click on the RunMan_CharacterController name to open the script in your script editor. Replace the default script with this:

```
using System.Collections;
using System.Collections.Generic;
using UnityEngine;
using GPC;

public class RunMan_CharacterController :
BasePlayer2DPlatformCharacter
```

```
{
        public BaseSoundController _soundControl;
        public Animator _RunManAnimator;
        public bool isRunning;

        void Start()
        {
                Init();
        }

        public override void Init()
        {
                base.Init();

                isRunning = false;
                allow_jump = true;
                allow_right = true;
                allow_left = true;

                _soundControl = GetComponent<BaseSoundController>();
        }

        public void Update()
        {
                if (isOnGround && isRunning
&& !_RunManAnimator.GetCurrentAnimatorStateInfo(0).IsName("RunMan_Run"))
                {
                        StartRunAnimation();
                }
        }

        void OnTriggerEnter2D(Collider2D collision)
        {
                _soundControl.PlaySoundByIndex(1);
                RunMan_GameManager.instance.PlayerFell();
        }

        public void StartRunAnimation()
        {
                isRunning = true;
                _RunManAnimator.SetTrigger("Run");
        }

        public override void Jump()
        {
                base.Jump();
                _soundControl.PlaySoundByIndex(0);
                _RunManAnimator.SetTrigger("Jump");
        }
}
```

As a side note: Above, this script derives (meaning it inherits functions and variables from) another script named BasePlayer2DPlatformCharacter. This script is explained in full in Chapter 6, Section 6.4. 2D Platform Character Controller.

With this script Component in place, RunMan will be able to move left and right and jump. It will even play sounds. Save the script with CTRL+S or File/ Save, then return to Unity.

Look over in the Inspector and you will see that not only did it add the Run Man_Character Controller Component but it now has another Component called BaseUserManager. The BaseUserManager Component will be used to hold player-specific data such as scoring, but do not worry about this just yet – we will look at this is detail in Chapter 4, Section 4.3.

In the script above, notice that the class inherits from BasePlayer2DPlatformCharacter:

```
public class RunMan_CharacterController :
BasePlayer2DPlatformCharacter
```

The BasePlayer2DPlatformCharacter class provides the basics for controlling a platform character. It was originally intended for Mario-esque gaming but fits the needs of this game type just as well.

We will not be going into detail over how the rest of this script functions just yet. A more detailed description of BasePlayer2DPlatformCharacter will come later in the book, in Chapter 6, Section 6.4.

The player is going to need some form of input from the player. The framework has an input Controller that will watch for some regular key presses. We will add the input Component a little differently here – rather than using the Add Component button, go up to the Component menu at the top of the editor. There are quite a lot of different Components in there, but they are categorized. Find the CSharpBookCode category and choose CSharpBookCode>Base>Input Controller. The Input Controller Component should now be added to the player GameObject. Almost all of the classes in this book have a line of code to add them to these menus. Usually formatted something like:

```
[AddComponentMenu("CSharpBookCode/Base/Input Controller")]
```

The AddComponentMenu command above can add a script Component to any of Unity's menus. Having them in the menus makes it easier to find the Components you use regularly without having to type them into the search box under Add Component or to search for the Component you want. Thanks to the AddComponentMenu command, all the base classes from the framework can be found under the CSharpBookCode/Base menus.

Time to set up a few things on the Run Man Character Controller, now:

Find the Ground Layer Mask field. Click on it and choose Ground from the list. You may remember, when we set up the platforms in Section 2.5 of this chapter, that platforms are on the Layer named Ground. We will use this to identify a platform underneath the player so that we know when the player is on a ground surface and we can allow it to jump. Once the player is in the air, and no ground surface is detected, jumping will no longer be allowed.

2.6.4 RunMan Sounds

RunMan needs to make a little sound when he jumps, and we will also play a sound when he falls to his doom. The audio system, Audio Mixers, and how we deal with audio in the framework will be discussed in detail in Chapter 9.

Select RunMan in the Hierarchy, if it is not already highlighted. In the Inspector, hit Add Component, and add the Component named BaseSoundController. This Component holds a list of sounds, which may then be played by calling into the script and passing an index number of the sound we want to play. The code to do that is already contained in the scripts you have already added, so at this point it is a matter of adding sounds to this Component.

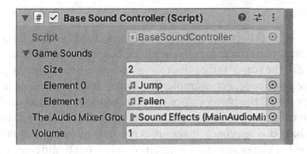

Figure 2.13 The Base Sound Controller Component holds a list of sounds to play.

In the Project panel, click on the Assets/Games/RunMan/Audio folder so that its contents show up in the Project panel.

Click and drag the audio file named Jump into the field named Game Sounds. The field should expand out to show the first item in the list. Next, click and drag the audio file named Fallen into the same Game Sounds field. You should now have something that looks like Figure 2.13 whereby the Game Sounds field has expanded to show its size (which is 2) and the Jump and Fallen items as element 0 and 1.

Beneath Game Sounds is a field named The Audio Mixer Group. An Audio Mixer is used to control volumes and effects in the Unity audio system. To the right of the field is a small target button (a circle with a smaller circle inside). Press that. A window should appear showing two groups of an Audio Mixer. Those are Sound Effects and Music. These act as channels for the audio to be routed through, so as this is a sound effect go ahead and select the Sound Effect group.

2.6.5 Animating RunMan

As I mentioned at the start of this chapter, all the animations and the Animator have been already set up ready to go but you will need to add an Animator Component to the sprite itself (not the RunMan GameObject, the actual sprite).

In the Hierarchy, click on RunMan_Run-Sheet_0 under the RunMan GameObject. Over in the Inspector, you should see that this sprite GameObject has a Sprite Renderer attached to it. Our Animator Component will take care of changing the sprite to whatever animation we need at the time, but it will need access to the Sprite Renderer which is why we add the Animator to this GameObject rather than its parent.

Click Add Component and add an Animator.

In the Project panel, find the folder Assets/Games/Sprites and click on it to show its contents. Click and drag RunMan_Animator out of the Project panel and drop it into the Controller field of the Animator Component you just added.

The final part of the puzzle is to tell the player script about this new Animator Component. Click on RunMan in the Hierarchy, then find the Run Man Animator field of the Run Man_Character Controller Component.

In the Hierarchy, click and drag RunMan_Run-Sheet_0 GameObject into that Run Man Animator field. Unity will automatically figure out that there is an Animator Component attached to the GameObject you just dropped into the field, and in turn will use the reference to the Animator rather than the GameObject.

Now, if you press Play to try out the game the player will fall down onto the platform and for the brief time that he is on a platform, you should be able to move left, right, and even jump by pressing the Space key. Next, we need to give RunMan some more platforms to run and jump on.

2.6.6 Scoring

The framework in this book includes something I call a User Data Manager. Essentially, every player manages its own data. Having score, health, lives, and so on belonging to the player rather than the game, we abstract out the player from the rest of the game code. For example, the Game Manager does not need to keep track of score for all the players since the players do that themselves. The Game Manager can tell a player to increase its score, but it does not have to do anything more than that. This approach makes it easier to implement things like multiplayer later, as the player structure is easier to switch out to different setups without affecting other code.

In the Hierarchy, click the RunMan GameObject to highlight it. In the Inspector, you should find that Unity has already added the BaseUserManager Component. This happens due to there being code – in one of the scripts that our RunMan_CharacterController script inherits from named BasePlayerStatsController – that tells Unity we require this Component to be attached to our GameObject.

The BaseUserManager contains a whole lot of helper functions to add score, reduce score, add health, or lives or levels. We will be looking at this system in detail further in this book, in Chapter 4, Section 4.3. For now, all you need to know is that everything we need to do with storing score for RunMan will be contained in that BaseUserManager Component.

▌ 2.7 The Game Loop and the Game Manager

A game loop usually refers to the a recurring core of game code, where logic exists that needs to be updated every frame or where game states are monitored and changed to control a games overall flow. The RunMan_GameManager script we have so far has no real game logic inside it, just a few variables and an instance variable, and this section adds in the game loop and supporting functions around it to do things like spawn platforms for the player to run on.

You might recall that when we made the RunMan_GameManager script back in Section 2.4, we programmed it so that the RunMan_GameManager class derives from BaseGameManager. BaseGameManager already has code in place to help us to deal with the state of the game.

2.7.1 Game States

The BaseGameManager includes 17 different states for larger, more complicated games, though for this project we only use 5 of them:

Game.State.loaded	This state is called when the main game Scene first loads.
Game.State.gameStarting	After initialization and set up of anything we need in the main game Scene, gameStarting will be set and we use this to display a message that will notify the player to 'get ready' to play.
Game.State.gamePlaying	Once the game is running, the states stays in gamePlaying.
Game.State.gameEnding	If the player falls off a platform and hits a hidden trigger, the game ends. The gameEnding state takes care of stopping movement and preventing any more score being earned. We also show the final 'game over' user interface as this state begins.
Game.State.gameEnded	When the gameEnded state occurs, we leave the main game Scene and load the main menu.

The BaseGameManager class deals with game states primarily through three functions: SetTargetState(), UpdateTargetState(), and UpdateCurrentState(). When a call to SetTargetState() is made, a new state is passed in which becomes the target state. BaseGameManager knows that the target state is different to the current state, so it makes a call to the UpdateTargetState() function. UpdateTargetState() will then check the target state and run any code that we want to run whenever that state begins (for example, during the gameStarting state we show a message to tell the player to get ready). At the end of UpdateTargetState() the current state is then updated to the desired new state.

Meanwhile, every frame from the Update() function in BaseGameManager, the function UpdateCurrentState() is called. Inside the UpdateCurrentState() we make calls to run any code that needs to run every frame, such as updating the user interface to show the current score and so on. These three functions are key to dealing with game states.

2.7.2 The Main Loop of RunMan_GameManager.cs

Open your RunMan_GameManager script in the script editor (to do this, go into Unity, find the GameManager GameObject in the Hierarchy, click to highlight it in the Hierarchy and then find the RunMan_GameManager Component in the Inspector. Double click on the script name to open it in the script editor).

As you work your way through the code in this chapter, always remember to stay above the final curly bracket at the very bottom of this script, otherwise the compiler will generate an error.

The new code will need some new variables to work, so we start by adding new variables to the top of the RunMan_GameManager script.

Just above the line:

```
public static RunMan _ GameManager instance { get; private set; }
```

Add the following variable declarations:

```
    public Transform _platformPrefab;

    public RunMan_CharacterController _RunManCharacter;

    private float distanceCounter;
    public RunMan_UIManager _uiManager;

    public float playAreaTopY = -0.4f;
    public float playAreaBottomY = 0.2f;
    public float platformStartX = 3f;
```

Next, replace the empty Start() function with this:

```
    public void Start()
    {
        SetTargetState(Game.State.loaded);
    }
```

When the game starts, the code above sets our current state to Game.State.
loaded so code can run that we need to run as soon as the Scene is done loading.

Below the new Start() function, add the code below:

```
public override void UpdateTargetState()
{
    Debug.Log("targetGameState=" + targetGameState);

    if (targetGameState == currentGameState)
        return;

    switch (targetGameState)
    {
        case Game.State.loaded:
            Loaded();
            break;

        case Game.State.gameStarting:
            GameStarting();
            StartGame();
            break;

        case Game.State.gameStarted:
            // fire the game started event
            GameStarted();
            SetTargetState(Game.State.gamePlaying);
            break;

        case Game.State.gamePlaying:
            break;

        case Game.State.gameEnding:
            GameEnding();
            EndGame();
            break;

        case Game.State.gameEnded:
            GameEnded();
            break;
    }
```

BaseGameManager already has the above function in it, but it was declared
as a virtual function. Having a virtual function like that means we can use the
override keyword to use a new version of the function – note that we override the
original function, not swap it out, or destroy the original. Any calls to
UpdateTargetState() will just be rerouted but, if we need to, we can always call the
original function too – it still exists – some times in this book, we will call the
original function as well as the overridden version, but not this time. Above, we
simply override the original function and use that.

Most of what we do in each state above is to call other functions to do the
actual work. For example, in the Game.State.loaded case statement, it just calls out
to Loaded(). I try as much as possible to keep code out of the state machine functions to make debugging easier. Calling out to separate functions is a good way to
avoid your game state code from getting out of hand – having code in each state
can soon get unruly and harder to debug, so it really is best if you try to keep
blocks of code in their own functions, instead.

There are a couple of calls to functions that we do not have in this script, such
as GameStarting() and GameStarted(). These are inherited functions and their
code can be found in BaseGameManager.cs. The reason we call out to those is

that they contain calls to invoke UnityEvents that we will be using to hide and show the user interface. We will get to setting up the UnityEvents further in the user interface further in this chapter, Section 2.9.

Now that our RunMan_GameManager class has everything it needs to deal with updates to the target state, we need to add in some of those new functions called out in the code, like Loaded(), StartGame() and so on.

Beneath the code you just added (note: staying above the final curly bracket in that script), add this function:

```
public override void Loaded()

{
        base.Loaded();

        // reset score
        _RunManCharacter.SetScore(0);

        SetTargetState(Game.State.gameStarting);
}
```

Above, Loaded() starts with a call to base.Loaded(), which tells Unity to run the original Loaded() function from the base class (BaseGameManager). Although here we are overriding that function, the original function still exists and we can still call it via base. This is useful when the base class has things in it that we don't want to replicate in an overridden function, but we still want to run. In this case, the base class only contains a call to invoke the UnityEvent OnLoaded. Again, we will get to the UnityEvents later in the chapter when dealing with user interface.

The next line resets our players score to zero at the start of the game:

```
_ RunManCharacter.SetScore(0);
```

Finally, now that we have finished everything that needs doing when the game first loads, there is a call to SetTargetState to move on to the new state Game.State.gameStarting.

Next, we add the function that will be called when UpdateTargetState() receives a call to change the state to gameStarting (from above, at the end of the Loaded() function). Add this code below the Loaded() function:

```
void StartGame()
{
        runSpeed = 0;

        // add a little delay to the start of the game, for
people to prepare to run
        Invoke("StartRunning", 2f);
}
```

Above, StartGame() sets the runSpeed to 0, so that RunMan does not start running right away. Remember when we added code to the platforms that used runSpeed from this Game Manager script? When the game starts, we hold everything in place – with runSpeed at 0, the platforms will not move.

Next, the StartGame() function schedules a call to a function named StartRunning() in 2 seconds, using Unity's built in scheduling function Invoke:

```
Invoke("StartRunning", 2f);
```

At this stage, after StartGame() has been called, the game sits in the Game. State.gameStarting state as we wait for the call to StartRunning to be made (by the above Invoke function call). There will eventually be a message on the screen to tell the player to get ready. The 2-second pause is for the player to read the message and to prepare to play the game (note that the message is currently hidden and we will not be adding it back in until Section 2.9 later in this chapter).

Once the 2 seconds are up, StartRunning() is called. Add this function to your script next, below the StartGame function you added previously:

```
void StartRunning()
{
        isRunning = true;

        runSpeed = 1f;
        distanceCounter = 1f;

        // start animation
        _RunManCharacter.StartRunAnimation();

        InvokeRepeating("AddScore", 0.5f, 0.5f);
        SetTargetState(Game.State.gameStarted);
}
```

StartRunning kicks the game to life! The first line sets the Boolean isRunning to true so that movement and animations can get started.

Below that, runSpeed is set to 1. The platform code we added earlier will use this variable to know how quickly to move the platforms across the screen, so now it is set to 1 the platforms will move.

The distanceCounter variable is used to keep a track of how far platforms move, which in turn is used to decide when to spawn new platforms for the player to jump on. As it is the start of the game, it is reset above to 1.

A call to StartRunAnimation() on the RunManCharacter object (an instance of the RunMan_CharacterController script Component attached to the player) gets the running animation started.

As well as the Invoke function, Unity provides another useful method for scheduling function calls. InvokeRepeating will call the specified function at regular intervals until either the Scene is unloaded or you use CancelInvoke() to stop it. In the code above, the AddScore() function is called every 0.5 seconds where the player will be awarded with score. The scoring system for this game is very simple, but it works well enough! Survive longer, get a higher score.

The last line of StartRunning() advances the game state:
SetTargetState(Game.State.gameStarted);

The UpdateTargetState() function you added earlier will deal with this change of state to Game.State.gameStarted, invoke the OnGameStarted() UnityEvent and change the state to Game.State.gamePlaying. From here on, the game just sits in Game.State.gamePlaying until the game ends.

Next, we need to add a function to deal with the end of the game. Add this code to your RunMan_GameManager class next:

```
void EndGame()
{
        // stop running
        isRunning = false;
        runSpeed = 0;

        // schedule return to main menu in 4 seconds
        Invoke("ReturnToMenu", 4f);

        // stop the repeating invoke that awards score
        CancelInvoke("AddScore");
```

```
              // update target state
              SetTargetState(Game.State.gameEnded);
      }
```

In the script above, we deal with what happens when the game is over. This will be called after the player falls off-screen. The first part of the script stops running and sets runSpeed to 0 so that the platforms stop moving.

The game is ending, so the next line schedules a call to ReturnToMenu in 4 seconds. We will get to this function further on in this section, but it may not come as a big surprise that ReturnToMenu() loads the main menu.

After setting up the call to return to the menu, the script above uses CancelInvoke to stop the AddScore() function from being called. Remember we set up the InvokeRepeating call for this in the StartRunning() function? This is how we stop it.

Finally, for the EndGame() function, we set the target state to gameEnded with this line:

SetTargetState(Game.State.gameEnded);

UpdateTargetState() has nothing specific for Game.State.gameEnded other than a call to Invoke the OnGameEnded UnityEvent, which will be used for user interface later in this chapter.

Add the following code to your RunMan_GameManager script next:

```
      void AddScore()
      {
              _RunManCharacter.AddScore(1);
      }

      void ReturnToMenu()
      {
              SceneManager.LoadScene("runMan_menu");
      }


      public void PlayerFell()
      {
              SetTargetState(Game.State.gameEnding);
      }
```

AddScore() tells the player to add one(1) to its score.

ReturnToMenu() uses Unity's SceneManager to load the main menu Scene. At this stage, we don't actually have a main menu Scene but we will be sorting that out in the user interface Section 2.9 of this chapter.

Lastly in the function above, the PlayerFell() function is where we set the target state to Game.State.gameEnding. This function will be called by the player whenever it hits trigger. A trigger is just a Unity Collider that does not try to resolve a collision, it just reacts to it. We will be adding a check to the player script further in this chapter, once the RunMan_GameManager class is complete.

The final part of RunMan_GameManager deals with spawning platforms for RunMan to run jump across. Right now, we only have two platforms which disappear off-screen soon after we hit Play. Let's fix that to make some real gameplay now. Add this near to the end of your RunMan_GameManager script, just above the final curly bracket:

```
      void SpawnPlatform()
      {
              runSpeed += 0.02f;
```

```
            distanceCounter = 0;

            float randomY = Random.Range(-0.4f, 0.2f);
            Vector2 startPos = new Vector2(3f, randomY);

            Instantiate(_platformPrefab, startPos, Quaternion.
identity);
            distanceCounter = Random.Range(-0.5f, 0.25f);
      }
```

New platforms are generated by the SpawnPlatform() function. The first line of SpawnPlatform() increases runSpeed by 0.02. This means that, over time, the game will gradually get faster and faster. It is a very simple way of increasing the difficulty over time so that the player should eventually concede.

When a new platform spawns, we reset the variable distanceCounter ready to measure the distance to the next spawn. A quick look to the Update() function you will tell you that we check distanceCounter against the variable distanceTo-SpawnPlatform, to decide how far to allow between platforms – but that's further down. Let's get back to SpawnPlatform().

The next line uses the built-in random number generator function Random. Range to ask the engine to come up with a number between playAreaTopY and playAreaBottomY:

```
float randomY = Random.Range(playAreaTopY, playAreaBottomY);
```

randomY can now be used as the height to spawn the next platform. We add it into a Vector2 on the next line:

```
Vector2 startPos = new Vector2(platformStartX, randomY);
```

Now that we have a Vector2 containing a position to spawn the new platform out (consisting of a nice random Y position and a start position held in platform-StartX that will be off-screen to the right of the play area), we can go ahead and spawn the platform on the next line:

```
Instantiate(_platformPrefab, startPos, Quaternion.identity);
```

Above, Instantiate takes a reference to a Prefab (_platformPrefab) followed by the starting position for the GameObject to be instantiated and finally a rotation value in Quaternions. Quaternion.identity is a zero rotation value, a default, meaning that the new platform will not be rotated.

The last line of SpawnPlatform() adjusts the distanceCounter variable by a small random amount:

```
distanceCounter = Random.Range(-0.5f, 0.25f);
```

The effect of this is that the next platform will have a random amount of space between it because we are changing where zero is in the distance counting system.

We finish this programming section with an Update() function. Update() is called every frame. In RunMan_GameManager, it is where we keep an eye on the distanceCounter to decide whether it is time to spawn a new platform.

Add this to your script above the final curly bracket:

```
void Update()
{
      if (isRunning)
      {
            distanceCounter += (runSpeed * Time.deltaTime);
```

```
                    // check to see if we need to spawn another
platform (based on distance travelled)
                if ((distanceCounter >= distanceToSpawnPlatform))
                {
                        SpawnPlatform();
                }
            }
        }
```

Above, Update() begins by checking that isRunning is true first. If the player is not running, we will never need to spawn any new platforms, so it makes sense not to run this code unless we are on the move.

distanceCounter is increased next by runSpeed multiplied by Time.deltaTime. We talked about Time.deltaTime in the platform movement script back in Section 2.5. By multiplying the runSpeed by deltaTime, we make movement time-based rather than frame based. This variable distanceCounter is essentially keeping stock of how far the player has run so that we know when to spawn the next platform. The check for that comes next in that Update() function:

```
        if ((distanceCounter >= distanceToSpawnPlatform))
        {
                SpawnPlatform();

        }
```

Whenever distanceCounter goes over our set distanceToSpawnPlatform, we make a call to spawn a new platform – remember that SpawnPlatform() also resets distanceCounter so that another platform will be spawned at the same distance again (give or take the small randomization adjustment made at the end of SpawnPlatform()).

And that's it for programming the game! We need to jump back to Unity and set up some references on the Component via the Inspector, but when it comes to programming, we have all the logic now to make the gameplay work. Save the script and return to Unity to set up the Component.

2.7.3 Setting Up the RunMan_GameManager Component in the Editor

In the Hierarchy, click on the GameManager to highlight it and show its properties in the Inspector. In the Inspector, scroll down to the bottom of the Components to show the groups of fields such as Run Speed, Distance to Spawn Platforms and so on as shown in Figure 2.14.

Run Speed	1
Distance To Spawn P	2
Is Running	
Platform Prefab	⚘RunMan_Platform (Transform ⊙
Run Man Character	RunMan (RunMan_Character ⊙
Play Area Top Y	-0.4
Play Area Bottom Y	0.2
Platform Start X	3

| Add Component |

Figure 2.14 The RunMan_GameManager fields reference other GameObjects in the main Scene that the Game Manager needs to create instances of or communicate with.

In the Project panel, find the Games/RunMan/Prefabs folder. This folder is where you should find the Prefab for the platform, we made back in Section 2.5. Click and drag the RunMan_Platform Prefab out of the Project window and drop it into the Platform Prefab field of the GameManager in the Inspector. This tells the Game Manager which Prefab to spawn when we tell it to spawn a new platform.

We now need to provide the Game Manager with a reference to the player. In the Hierarchy, find the RunMan GameObject then click and drag it into the Run Man Character field of the GameManager in the Inspector.

Make sure that the values in your Game Manager match up with those in Figure 2.14.

▌ 2.8 The Demise of RunMan

Now that we have platforms moving and a character ready to jump over them, we need to add a method to detect whenever the player misses a platform and falls off screen. To accomplish this, we use a Collider set to be used as a trigger (so that it does not resolve a collision, it only reports it) scaled across the entire width of the screen and positioned just below the bottom of the play area. Whenever the player hits the trigger, it will know that it has fallen outside of the play area and end the game.

When adding a trigger, I prefer to be able to see the object so that I can scale and place it easily. If this was a 3D game, I would just add a cube to the Scene and arrange it as necessary before disabling the renderer to hide it. Sadly, Unity does not have any 2D primitives (cubes, spheres and so on) but we can use a 3D primitive and add a 2D Collider to it. Bit of an odd mix, I know, but there it is.

Find an empty space in the Hierarchy and right click. Choose the 3D Object sub-menu and, from there, choose the Cube.

Next, click the Scale Transform button on the Toolbar (top left of the editor window) or press R on the keyboard to shortcut to scale mode. In the Scene panel, the Gizmo should now show some chunky squares instead of arrow heads. Click the red square and drag it to the right, to scale the cube out along its X axis. Stretch it so that it is about twice as wide as the Game panel area.

Now move the cube down, below the play area so that it is out of view of the Game panel. To switch back into move mode, click on the Move Transform button in the Toolbar or press W on the keyboard to shortcut. Grab the green arrow and move the cube down. It should look something like the one in Figure 2.15.

With the Cube GameObject selected in the Hierarchy, check out the Inspector. The Cube already has a Collider attached to it, but it is the wrong type. The Box Collider will only work with 3D physics, so we need to remove it and replace it with the 2D equivalent.

Right click on the Box Collider Component in the Inspector. Click Remove Component.

Click the Add Component button and start typing boxco to jump to the available Box Colliders. Choose the Box Collider 2D Component from the list (Figure 2.16). Once the new Component appears in the Inspector, check the box IsTrigger by clicking on it.

If you hit Play now and make RunMan fall off the bottom of the screen, you should now hear the sound effect that signals RunMan's demise. In the next section, we will be adding a game over screen that will go here as well as a main menu to return to after the game is over. Oh, and scoring. Phew! Sounds like a busy section.

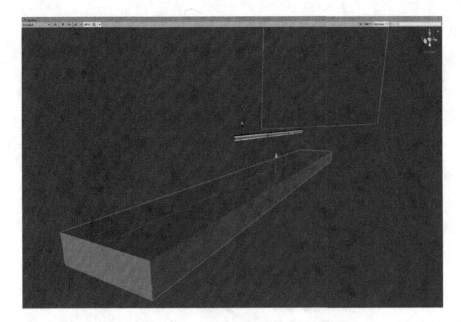

Figure 2.15 To detect falling players, we use a giant 3D cube hidden just off screen with a 2D Box Collider Component attached to it.

■ 2.9 Adding the User Interface

The game is all there, but it needs the following user interfaces:

1. A get ready message

2. An in-game UI to tell players the current score and high score

3. A game over message

4. A main menu to return to, after the game is over

There is a little more cheating going on here with the user interface – remember at the start of the chapter when we hid it all? Yeah, the user interface is already there but it needs some additional code to be shown and hidden as needed.

In the Hierarchy, click the GameManager GameObject to highlight it. In the Inspector, scroll down to the Add Component button and click it. Choose New Script and type RunMan_UIManager in as the name of the script. Click Create and Add to make the new template Component. Once the Component appears, double click on the script name to open the script up in your script editor.

Replace the code with this:

```
using UnityEngine.UI;
using GPC;

public class RunMan_UIManager : CanvasManager
{
        // we derive from canvas manager to give us the
functionality to fade canvas nicely

        public Text _scoreText;
        public Text _highText;
        public Text _finalScoreText;
        public Text _newHighScoreText;
```

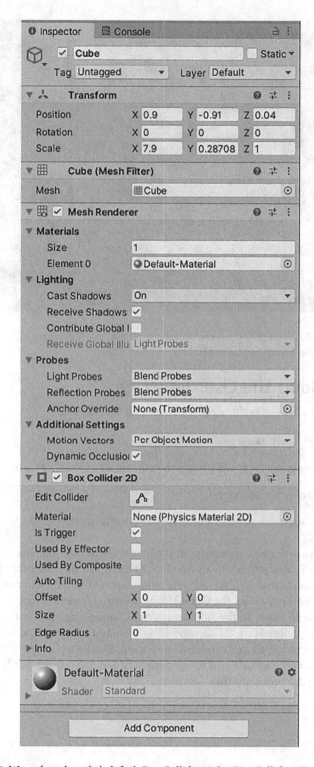

Figure 2.16 We replace the cube's default Box Collider with a Box Collider 2D Component, as the standard Box Collider will not work with 2D physics.

```
        void Start()
        {
                _scoreText.text = "Score 0";
                _newHighScoreText.gameObject.SetActive(false);

                // hide all ui canvas
                HideAll();
        }

        public void ShowGetReadyUI()
        {
                ShowCanvas(0);
        }

        public void HideGetReadyUI()
        {
                HideCanvas(0);
        }

        public void ShowGameOverUI()
        {
                ShowCanvas(1);
        }

        public void ShowGameUI()
        {
                ShowCanvas(2);
        }

        public void HideGameUI()
        {
                HideCanvas(2);

        }
        public void SetScore(int scoreAmount)
        {
                _scoreText.text = "Score "+scoreAmount.
ToString("D5");

        }
        public void SetHighScore(int scoreAmount)
        {

                _highText.text = "High " + scoreAmount.
ToString("D5");
        }

        public void SetFinalScore(int scoreAmount)
        {
                _finalScoreText.text = "Final Score " + scoreAmount.
ToString("D5");
        }

        public void ShowGotHighScore()
        {
                _newHighScoreText.gameObject.SetActive(true);
        }
}
```

The first thing to notice about the code above is that it derives from a class named CanvasManager. CanvasManager is part of the framework for this book, and it provides methods for showing and hiding Canvases. To use CanvasManager, each Canvas GameObject has a Component on it named Canvas Group. Canvas Group is a Component provided by Unity that allows you to control the alpha level of an entire UI Canvas and to enable or disable interactions with it. What my CanvasManager does is to use Canvas Group and a co-routine to fade in or out Canvases on demand. As you can see in the code above, showing, and hiding canvases can be done with the ShowCanvas() and HideCanvas() functions. All you pass in is an index number for the Canvas you want to show or hide and CanvasManager does the rest of the work for you. CanvasManager will be explained in detail further in this book, in Chapter 5, Section 5.9.1.

You may wonder where to get the index numbers referring to the Canvas you want to show or hide. This relates directly to an array of Canvases that you will find in the Inspector on this Component. Now that the script is set up, hit CTRL+S on the keyboard or File/Save to save the script. Return to the Unity editor and we will get started setting up the Component in the Inspector.

Back in the editor now, in the Hierarchy find the UI_Canvases GameObject and expand it with the little arrow if it is not already showing the three Canvases parented to it.

Click the GameManager GameObject now in the Hierarchy and look over to the Inspector. Scroll down to show the RunMan_UIManager Component. Right now, the Component will look something like Figure 2.17 in that we are missing the four text references it needs and it has an empty UI Canvas Groups array. UI Canvas Groups is the array we need to get those Canvas index numbers from, so the next step is to add references to the three UI Canvases you just looked at over in the Hierarchy.

Find the click on the little arrow to the left of UI Canvas Groups to expand out the array so you can see the Size field.

Make sure GameManager is still highlighted in the Hierarchy for this next step: Back in the Hierarchy, click and drag GetReadyMessageCanvas onto the UI Canvas Groups name (just above the size field) so that Unity adds it to the array automatically. As you hover over the name, to show you are in the right place the cursor will change to show a little plus sign and you can release the mouse to have Unity add the new item. Now, do the same for the GameOverMessageCanvas and the GameUICanvas GameObjects.

Now you need to set up the text fields. To do that, find GameOverMessageCanvas in the Hierarchy and click the little arrow next to it to expand it out and show child objects under it. Now do the same for the GameUICanvas GameObject – click the arrow to expand it out and show child objects under it. At this point, we have all the text fields we need on display in the Hierarchy and we will be able to drag and drop them into the corresponding fields of the RunMan_UIManager Component.

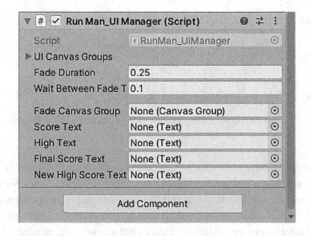

Figure 2.17 The RunMan_UIManager Component in the Inspector.

Get to the RunMan_UIManager Component again by clicking on GameManager in the Hierarchy and scrolling down in the Inspector to show it.

Under GameUICanvas in the Hierarchy, click and drag ScoreTextLabel out of the Hierarchy and into the Inspector, into the field labeled Score Text under the RunMan_UIManager Component.

Next, click and drag HighScoreTextLabel out of the Hierarchy and into the Inspector, into the field High Text.

Under GameOverMessageCanvas in the Hierarchy, click and drag FinalScoreTextLabel out of the Hierarchy into the Final Score Text field of the RunMan_UIManager Component in the Inspector.

Finally, under GameOverMessageCanvas again, click and drag NewHighScoreTextLabel out of the Hierarchy and into the New High Score Text field in the Inspector.

With all the user interface references set up, we can now use some of the UnityEvents on the GameManager to call functions on the script you just added and show or hide user interface as needed. When a UnityEvent is invoked (called by code) it can trigger a function call to a function within a script Component on any other GameObject. We just need to tell it which GameObject the script is on, and which function to call.

Click on GameManager in the Hierarchy, to show the GameManager's properties and Components in the Inspector.

Under the Game Events label find the OnLoaded() event. Right now, it will say List is Empty. Beneath that, to the right, find the little plus icon and click on it. The List is Empty message should now disappear to show two accessible fields and a grayed-out dropdown menu (Figure 2.18). The top left box reads Runtime Only – this refers to when this UnityEvent should be active. As we do not want it to do anything in any state other than when the game is running, we can leave it at its default state. Beneath that is an object box that starts with the default state of None. What we need to do here is to add a reference to a GameObject. In this case, however, we are going to be calling functions in the RunMan_UI Manager Component attached to the GameManager which means we need to reference the GameManager here.

To do that, keep the OnLoaded() UnityEvent visible in the Inspector, then from the Hierarchy drag out the GameManager GameObject and drop it into the None(Object) target field. The dropdown to the right of it should now be enabled. Click the dropdown and choose RunMan_UIManager from the list, followed by ShowGetReadyUI. When the game is started, the OnLoaded event will be invoked and our call to ShowGetReadyUI triggered, showing the get ready message to the player.

Let's set up the rest of the events.

Find the OnGameStarted() event in the Inspector. Click the plus sign (+) twice, to add two new events. From the Inspector, drag the GameManager GameObject and drop it into the target boxes for each event (currently populated by None (Object)).

In the first dropdown, choose RunMan_UIManager followed by ShowGameUI.

In the second dropdown, choose RunMan_UIManager followed by HideGetReadyUI.

This will show the main game user interface (showing score and high score) when the game starts, as well as hiding the get ready message. Now we just need to add the game over UI.

Find the On Game Ended () GameEvent (you may need to scroll the Inspector down a little to find this). Again, click the plus (+) button twice to add to references. drag the GameManager GameObject out of the Hierarchy and into the target fields (currently None (Object)). With the dropdowns now available to

Figure 2.18 Game Events on the Game Manager Component in the Inspector.

click on: for the top dropdown, choose RunMan_UIManager followed by ShowGameOverUI. For the bottom dropdown, choose RunMan_UIManager followed by HideGameUI.

OK, so we have set up all the Canvases now but there is a little code to add to get the Game Manager to update the in game score display.

In the Project folder, find the Games/RunMan/Scripts folder and RunMan_ GameManager script. Double click the file to open it in the script editor.

At the top of the script, just below the class declaration:

```
public class RunMan_GameManager : BaseGameManager
{
```

Add the following variable declaration just after the opening curly bracket:

```
public RunMan _ UIManager _ uiManager;
```

Now scroll down to find the Loaded() function:

```
public override void Loaded()
{
    base.Loaded();
```

Add this just after the code above:

```
// set high score
        _uiManager.SetHighScore(GetComponent<BaseProfileManager>().
GetHighScore());
```

Now find the EndGame() function and add this before the closing curly bracket at the end of the function:

```
        if (GetComponent<BaseProfileManager>().
SetHighScore(_RunManCharacter.GetScore())== true)
            {
                _uiManager.ShowGotHighScore();
            }

        // update final score ui
        _uiManager.SetFinalScore(_RunManCharacter.GetScore());
```

The last piece of the puzzle adds score during the Update() loop. Find the Update() function. Find this code:

```
        if ((distanceCounter >=
distanceToSpawnPlatform))
            {
                SpawnPlatform();
            }
```

And add the following right after that closing bracket for the If statement (so that it has three curly brackets after it, at the end of the function):

```
_uiManager.SetScore(_RunManCharacter.GetScore());
```

The final completed script for RunMan_GameManager looks like this:

```
using UnityEngine;
using UnityEngine.SceneManagement;
using GPC;

[RequireComponent(typeof(BaseProfileManager))]

public class RunMan_GameManager : BaseGameManager
{
        public RunMan_UIManager _uiManager;
        public float runSpeed = 1f;
        public float distanceToSpawnPlatform = 20f;
        public bool isRunning;
        public Transform _platformPrefab;
        public RunMan_CharacterController _RunManCharacter;
        private float distanceCounter;
        public float playAreaTopY = -0.4f;
        public float playAreaBottomY = 0.2f;
        public float platformStartX = 3f;

        public static RunMan_GameManager instance { get; private
set; }

        // set instance in this script's constructor
        public RunMan_GameManager()
        {
                instance = this;
        }
```

```csharp
        private void Awake()
        {
                // reset all of the user data we have stored in the
ScriptableObject
                gameObject.SendMessage("ResetAllPlayerStats");
        }
        public void Start()
        {
                SetTargetState(Game.State.loaded);
        }

        public override void UpdateTargetState()
        {
                switch (targetGameState)
                {
                        case Game.State.loaded:
                                Loaded();
                                break;

                        case Game.State.gameStarting:
                                StartGame();
                                break;

                        case Game.State.gameStarted:
                                // fire the game started event
                                OnGameStarted.Invoke();
                                SetTargetState(Game.State.
gamePlaying);

                                break;

                        case Game.State.gamePlaying:
                                break;

                        case Game.State.gameEnding:
                                EndGame();
                                break;

                        case Game.State.gameEnded:
                                OnGameEnded.Invoke();
                                break;
                }
        }

        public override void Loaded()
        {
                base.Loaded();

                // set high score

                _uiManager.SetHighScore(GetComponent<BaseProfileMana
ger>().GetHighScore());

                // reset score
                _RunManCharacter.SetScore(0);

                SetTargetState(Game.State.gameStarting);
        }

        void StartGame()

        {
                runSpeed = 0;

                // add a little delay to the start of the game, for
people to prepare to run
                Invoke("StartRunning", 2f);
        }
```

```csharp
        void StartRunning()
        {
                isRunning = true;
                runSpeed = 1f;
                distanceCounter = 1f;

                SetTargetState(Game.State.gameStarted);

                // start animation
                _RunManCharacter.StartRunAnimation();

                InvokeRepeating("AddScore", 0.5f, 0.5f);
        }

        void EndGame()
        {
                // stop running
                isRunning = false;
                runSpeed = 0;

                // schedule return to main menu in 4 seconds
                Invoke("ReturnToMenu", 4f);

                // stop the repeating invoke that awards score
                CancelInvoke("AddScore");

                // let's try to store the high score (profile
manager takes care of checking if it's a high score or not, we just
submit a score)
                if (GetComponent<BaseProfileManager>().
SetHighScore(_RunManCharacter.GetScore()) == true)
                        _uiManager.ShowGotHighScore();

                // update final score ui
                _uiManager.SetFinalScore(_RunManCharacter.
GetScore());

                // update target state
                SetTargetState(Game.State.gameEnded);
        }

        void AddScore()
        {
                _RunManCharacter.AddScore(1);
        }

        void ReturnToMenu()
        {
                SceneManager.LoadScene("runMan_menu");
        }

        public void PlayerFell()
        {
                SetTargetState(Game.State.gameEnding);
        }

        void SpawnPlatform()
        {
                runSpeed += 0.02f;
                distanceCounter = 0;
                float randomY = Random.Range(playAreaTopY,
playAreaBottomY);
                Vector2 startPos = new Vector2(platformStartX,
randomY);
                Instantiate(_platformPrefab, startPos, Quaternion.
identity);
```

```
                    distanceCounter = Random.Range(-0.5f, 0.25f);
        }
        void Update()

        {
            if (isRunning)
            {
                distanceCounter += (runSpeed * Time.
deltaTime);

                // check to see if we need to spawn another
platform (based on distance travelled)
                if ((distanceCounter >= distanceToSpawnPlatform))
                    SpawnPlatform();

                _uiManager.SetScore(_RunManCharacter.
GetScore());
            }
        }
}
```

Play the game now. At the start, there should be a message to say get ready and once the game is in play the score and high score will be shown. When RunMan falls off the screen, you should also get a nice game over message with a final score!

The only problem is that ending the game makes an error like "Scene 'runMan_menu' couldn't be loaded because it has not been added to the build

Figure 2.19 Unity's Build Settings panel.

settings or the AssetBundle has not been loaded" – and this is down to Unity not finding a main menu, so let's fix that next.

2.9.1 Main Menu Setup

In the Project panel, find the Scenes folder. Double click the runMan_menu Scene to open it. To save time, this Scene is already almost ready to go. It is based on the MenuTemplate Scene found in the GPC_Framework/TemplateScenes folder, which is provided as a basic template to help you build a menu Scene quickly. To finish setting up the menu, we need to tell Unity where to find the menu Scene, by adding it to Build Settings.

Click the File menu (top left of the editor) followed by Build Settings. With Build Settings open, click and drag runMan_menu out of the Project panel and drop it into the Scenes In Build area of Build Settings (Figure 2.19). Close the Build Settings window once you have done that.

The menu template Scene that you just copied over has everything you need for a main menu, but we do need to tell it where to find the game so that it can load the game Scene when a player hits the start button.

Find and click on the MenuManager GameObject in the Hierarchy to high-light it. In the Inspector, find the Menu With Profiles Component. In the Game Scene Name field, type runMan_core (case sensitive!).

Hit CTRL+S to save the Scene (or File/Save menu) and hit Play in the toolbar to play the game. The menu should appear.

Click the Start Game button to play the game. The main game should load, play, and even return to the main menu after the game ends.

3 Building the Core Game Framework

This chapter will give context to the design decisions made in the core framework as well as providing a good base for understanding how the individual code recipes work together and why they may sometimes have dependencies on other Components.

The framework for this book (as seen in Figure 3.1) features six main areas:

1. Game Manager
   The Game Manager acts like a central communication script for all parts of the game and oversees game state.

2. Players
   Players may already be present in the game scene or instantiated by the Game Manager. The players structure will be explored later in Chapter 4 of this book.

3. AI and enemies
   As with players, AI controlled characters, or enemies may already be present in the scene at load time or created at runtime. We look at AI in full in Chapter 10.

4. UI Manager
   The UI Manager draws all the main in game user interface elements, such as score display, and lives. We look at UI in Chapter 11.

5. Sound Manager
   The Sound Manager handles sound playback. Sound is in Chapter 9.

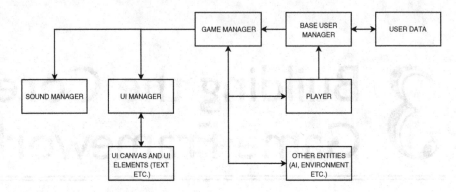

Figure 3.1 Diagram of the game framework.

To maximize flexibility, the base classes need to be able to accommodate different configurations. For example, a player controller should allow for input to be passed in from another script so that control systems can easily be switched out if we want to use, say, a controller vs. keyboard controls. The player script does not need to know where the input is coming from, but it needs to provide a common interface for an input script to communicate with. Just as a common interface is used to communicate with the player controller, it should not matter to the player controller as to where the input comes from.

▎ 3.1   Controllers and Managers

In this book, there are two terms I use to specify types of main classes; those are Controllers and Managers.

3.1.1 Managers

Managers are used in this book as a term to represent a script that specifically manages objects or data (dealing with players, audio or other game elements in a similar way to how a manager might manage staff in a company). For example, it could be a GlobalRaceManager class used to track and get information from a set of RaceController script Components attached to racing vehicles. The manager script uses information from the RaceController Components to calculate race positions of players as well as informing players as to the game's current running state, managing overall race logic.

3.1.2 Controllers

Controllers specialize in specific tasks such as helping scripts communicate with each other, holding game-specific player information or dealing with session data. For example, the players in this book have a player controller script. Enemies have an enemy controller. Controllers can be independent of other scripts or managed by manager scripts, depending on what it is they need to do.

▎ 3.2   Core Framework Scripts

There are several scripts in the Scripts/BASE folder that are intended to act as templates, or as classes to derive from, in your own games. In this section of the book we will be looking at the scripts that go to make up the main framework.

Core framework classes in the BASE folder that will be covered in this chapter are:

- 3.2.1. BaseGameManager

- 3.2.2. ExtendedCustomMonoBehaviour

- 3.2.3. BaseCameraController

Other base scripts will be covered in specific parts of this book. For example, the scripts found in GPC_Framework/BASE/PLAYER are covered in Chapter 4 when we look at the player structure.

3.2.1 BaseGameManager

The Game Manager is the core of gameplay, where overall game functions are described and dealt with and where current game state is held.

Core functions of the Game Manager are:

1. Tracking game state:

    a. Storage of the game state

    b. Providing functions for changing game state

    c. Changing the game state based on calls to functions such as EndGame(), StartGame(), or PauseGame()

2. Creating player(s)

3. Camera set up and specifics such as telling the camera what to follow

4. Communicating between session manager, user manager, and game actions

5. Any communications between scripts that we would like to keep as standalone and not have to recode to talk directly to each other

Keeping track of game state is important, as some elements will need to change their behavior. If the game is paused, for example, we may want to suspend all input, freeze game time, and show a pop up. When the game ends, we will need to disable player input and so on. Tracking game states is the job of the Game Manager script.

A typical game may have several different core states, such as:

1. Game running

2. Game paused

3. Loading

4. Game ended

There may also be several custom states, such as a state for showing a cutscene or perhaps a state for playing a special audio clip. I recommend creating a new state for any game action that affects the behavior of one or more of your scripts. That way, you can always have the scripts rely on the Game Manager to know how to behave.

Many of the key functions in BaseGameManager are virtual; put there to serve as an established protocol for dealing with different types of game activity. They contain little or no code in their default state and the intention is that you override them in your own derived versions of a Game Manager, later.

You can find BaseGameManager.cs script in the folder Assets/GPC_ Framework/Scripts/BASE/GAME. It looks like this:

```
using UnityEngine;
using UnityEngine.Events;
```

Above, the regular namespaces are imported, along with UnityEngine. Events. In my Game Manager classes, I like to have a set of UnityEvents for all or most game states. Next up in the code, we tell Unity that this code is part of a Namespace named GPC:

```
namespace GPC
{
    [AddComponentMenu("CSharpBookCode/Base/GameManager")]
```

Using namespaces provides scope to the code inside them. It is used to organize code and it is helpful to prevent your code from conflicting with others (such as duplicate class names and so forth). As we tend to use a lot of library C# code with Unity, I recommend using namespaces for all your classes.

Unity's AddComponentMenu function is used to make a menu item in the Unity editor. This is completely optional, but I like to have those menu items available.

We now move into the BaseGameManager class itself:

```
public class BaseGameManager : MonoBehaviour
{
```

The BaseGameController class derives from MonoBehaviour so that it can tap into automatically called system functions such as Awake(), Start(), Update(), FixedUpdate() and so forth.

Now, on to the variable declarations. The first variables declared are:

```
public Game.State currentGameState;
public Game.State targetGameState;
public Game.State lastGameState;
```

currentGameState, targetGameState, and lastGameState will be used to keep tabs on the overall state of our games. Notice that they are typed as Game.State, which is a custom class containing all the game states in an enum. It is intended that, as your games expand, the Game class may be expanded on to include other game states as required, though I have tried to include all the states needed for a range of different games.

We will get to how the states are used in the code chunk below:

```
private bool paused;

public void SetTargetState(Game.State aState)
{
    targetGameState = aState;
```

```
        if (targetGameState != currentGameState)
            UpdateTargetState();
}

public Game.State GetCurrentState()
{
        return currentGameState;
}
```

Above, a variable declaration of a Boolean to hold the paused state followed by a couple of functions to deal with the game states. That will come up later in the script, but for now focus on the game state functions. Whenever game state should change, a call to SetTargetState is made. This might be from a function within the Game Manager or it could come from one of your own scripts elsewhere in the project.

Rather than jumping in and setting a new current state right away, we use a target state first. After a call to SetTargetState(), the state that gets passed in goes into the variable targetGameState. By going through this process of having a target state before setting the current state, we can run any code that needs to be run at the start of a state change and then switch states after that code has run.

Here is an example of how having a target state before a current state is useful: Imagine the start of a game. When the game loads, we call out to SetTargetState to change state to Game.State.loaded. We do all the initialization needed to prepare for the game. After initialization, the current state becomes loaded and we can call again to SetTargetState(), to change the state to Game.State.Starting. With the target state of Game.State. gameStarting, a message telling the player to get ready is displayed and a timer starts. The current state is then set to Game.State.gameStarting and we stay in that state, until the timer finishes. Once the timer finishes, we call to SetTargetState() for a third time and this time pass in Game.State.gamePlaying. When the target state is gamePlaying, all the initialization to start the game begins (such as enabling player input or activating AI). Once the game is all ready to go, the current state shifts over to gamePlaying and we stay there, throughout gameplay, until game logic says otherwise.

The next block of code contains all the UnityEvents that will show up in the Inspector, ready to be populated with objects and calls to Components attached to them:

```
[Header("Game Events")]
public UnityEvent OnLoaded;
public UnityEvent OnGameStarting;
public UnityEvent OnGameStarted;
public UnityEvent OnLevelStarting;
public UnityEvent OnLevelStarted;
public UnityEvent OnLevelEnding;
public UnityEvent OnLevelEnded;

public UnityEvent OnGameEnding;
public UnityEvent OnGameEnded;
public UnityEvent OnGamePause;
public UnityEvent OnGameUnPause;
public UnityEvent OnShowLevelResults;
public UnityEvent OnShowGameResults;
public UnityEvent OnRestartLevel;
public UnityEvent OnRestartGame;
```

The advantage of having UnityEvents is that I can set up events in the editor, via the Inspector, to tell other scripts when state changes happen. As these are UnityEvents, I can add as many references to other Components via the Inspector and I do not need to know anything at all about them in the Game Manager script itself. An example of where this comes in useful is with user interface. In the running game example from Chapter 2, when the game enters its Loaded state, the OnLoaded() UnityEvent is fired. In the Inspector, I set up the event to call out to RunMan_UIManager.ShowGetReadyUI(). This shows a message to tell the player to get ready. By using events to call standalone Components, I take away any dependency on the UI scripts from the Game Manager. They can work completely independently, just so long as the UnityEvent has been set up correctly in the Inspector. The UnityEvents will be called by functions triggered through the game states:

```
    public virtual void Loaded() { OnLoaded.Invoke(); }
    public virtual void GameStarting() { OnLoaded.Invoke(); }
    public virtual void GameStarted() { OnLoaded.Invoke(); }
    public virtual void LevelStarting() { OnLevelStarting.Invoke(); }
    public virtual void LevelStarted() { OnLevelStarted.Invoke(); }
    public virtual void LevelEnding() { OnLevelEnding.Invoke(); }
    public virtual void LevelEnded() { OnLevelEnded.Invoke(); }
    public virtual void GameEnding() { OnGameEnding.Invoke(); }
    public virtual void GameEnded() { OnGameEnded.Invoke(); }
    public virtual void GamePause() { OnGamePause.Invoke(); }
    public virtual void GameUnPause() { OnGameUnPause.Invoke(); }
    public virtual void ShowLevelResults() { OnShowLevelResults.
Invoke(); }
    public virtual void ShowGameResults() { OnShowGameResults.
Invoke(); }
    public virtual void RestartLevel() { OnRestartLevel.Invoke(); }
    public virtual void RestartGame() { OnRestartGame.Invoke(); }
```

The above functions are here as placeholders. The intention is that Game Manager scripts for use in real game projects will derive from this class and override these virtual functions with real functionality. If you do override them, remember that you will be overriding the calls to corresponding UnityEvents. Just remember to either run Invoke() on those GameEvents or call the base class with base.(functionname).

Next, the UpdateTargetState function, which is called whenever SetTargetState() is called upon to change the game state:

```
public virtual void UpdateTargetState()
            {
                // we will never need to run target state
functions if we're already in this state, so we check for that and
drop out if needed
                if (targetGameState == currentGameState)
                    return;

                switch (targetGameState)
                {
                    case Game.State.idle:
                        break;

                    case Game.State.loading:
                        break;
```

UpdateTargetState() begins by checking that we are not already in the state being set. If the current state is the same as the target state, we drop out of the function. This is a precautionary measure, just in case duplicate calls are ever made to update the state.

A switch statement looks at targetGameState and below that we have code that will run whenever the state is set. Above, there is no code to run in idle or loading states and it is not until we reach the loaded state that other functions are called:

```
case Game.State.loaded:
    Loaded();
    break;

case Game.State.gameStarting:
    GameStarting();
    break;
```

Remember that big list of virtual functions a couple of pages back? Inside these case statements are where they are called. Above, Loaded() and GameStarting() are called respectively.

Below, I skip ahead past the rest of the case statements to reach the end of the UpdateTargetState() function:

```
        // now update the current state to reflect
the change
        currentGameState = targetGameState;
    }
```

The last line of UpdateTargetState() sets the current game state to the target state, as the target state has now been processed by the case statements above it.

UpdateCurrentState() follows on next, which follows a similar pattern of case statements:

```
public virtual void UpdateCurrentState()
    {
        switch (currentGameState)
        {
            case Game.State.idle:
                break;
            case Game.State.loading:
                break;
            case Game.State.loaded:
                break;
            case Game.State.gameStarting:
                break;
```

The UpdateCurrentState() function is called every frame, making up the 'main loop' of this class. This is where any recurring game logic should be called. It is expected that you will override this function and have your own version in any variants of the BaseGameManager class.

Other functions in BaseGameManager are there to help turn games around quickly. If there are things that you use in many different games, it may save time to included them all in a script like this that you can derive all other Game Managers from. It saves having to rewrite the same code repeatedly across multiple projects.

The final part of the BaseGameManager deals with the mechanics of pausing and unpausing a game:

```
public virtual void GamePaused()
    {
        OnGamePause.Invoke();
        Paused = true;
    }

public virtual void GameUnPaused()
```

```
                {
                    OnGameUnPause.Invoke();
                    Paused = false;
                }
```

GamePaused() and GameUnPaused() are the functions to call to change the paused state of the game. The two functions call out to the OnPause and OnUnPause UnityEvents (Invoking them) as well as changing the game state as required.

A Boolean variable named paused holds the game pause state. The code uses something called a Getter and a Setter here so that a little game logic will be triggered whenever the value of the Paused variable is changed:

```
public bool Paused
{
    get
    {
        return paused;
    }
    set
    {
        paused = value;

        if (paused)
        {
            // pause time
            Time.timeScale = 0f;
        }
        else
        {
            // unpause
            Time.timeScale = 1f;
        }
    }
}
```

The Get part simply returns the value of the Boolean variable paused.

The Set part sets the Boolean variable paused and goes on to set Time. timeScale to either 0 (paused) or 1 (unpaused). Setting Time.timeScale affects how time passes. For example, setting timescale to 0.5 would mean that time passes 2× slower than real time. The Unity documentation states:

> Except for realtimeSinceStartup, timeScale affects all the time and delta time measuring variables of the Time class. If you lower timeScale it is recommended to also lower Time.fixedDeltaTime by the same amount.
> FixedUpdate functions will not be called when timeScale is set to zero.

3.2.2 ExtendedCustomMonoBehaviour

Extending MonoBehaviour is a useful way to avoid repeating common functions or variable declarations. For example, most of the scripts in this book use a variable named _TR to refer to a cached version of a Transform. ExtendedCustomMonoBehaviour contains the declaration for it. Wherever a new class would use MonoBehaviour, we just derive from ExtendedCustom MonoBehaviour and, in the new class, we do not have to declare _TR or any of the other commonly used variables or functions we choose to put in ExtendedCustomMonoBehaviour.

For the scripts in this book, the ExtendedCustomMonoBehaviour.cs script extends MonoBehaviour to include:

1. _TR variable to hold a cached reference to a Transform

2. _GO variable to hold a cached reference to a GameObject

3. _RB variable for a cached reference to a rigidBody

4. _RB2D variable for caching a reference to a rigidBody2D

5. didInit is a Boolean to determine whether the script has been initialized

6. An integer called id to hold an id number

7. A Vector3 type variable to use for temporary vector actions, called tempVEC

8. _tempTR is a variable used for any temporary references to Transforms

9. A function called SetID(integer) so that other classes can set the variable id

10. A function named IsInLayerMask(Integer, LayerMask) to compare layers

You can find ExtendedCustomMonoBehaviour.cs in the folder Assets/GPC_Framework/Scripts/BASE/UTILITY and it looks like this:

```
using UnityEngine;
public class ExtendedCustomMonoBehaviour : MonoBehaviour
{
        [Header("Transform and RB references")]
        public Transform _TR;
        public GameObject _GO;

        public Rigidbody _RB;
        public Rigidbody2D _RB2D;

        [Header("Initialization and ID")]
        public bool didInit;
        public bool canControl;
        public int id;

        [System.NonSerialized]
        public Vector3 tempVEC;

        [System.NonSerialized]
        public Transform _tempTR;

        public virtual void SetID( int anID )
        {
                id= anID;
        }

        public virtual void GetComponents()
        {
                if (_TR == null)
                        _TR = transform;

                if (_GO == null)
                        _GO = gameObject;
        }
```

```
        public Transform Spawn(Transform spawnObject, Vector3
spawnPosition, Quaternion spawnRotation)
        {
                return Instantiate(spawnObject, spawnPosition,
spawnRotation);
        }

        public static bool IsInLayerMask(int layer, LayerMask
layermask)
        {
                return layermask == (layermask | (1 << layer));
        }
}
```

Above, there are four functions in ExtendedMonoBehaviour:

SetID() – provides a method to set the id variable.

GetComponents() – tries to find the Transform and GameObject this is attached to.

Spawn() – Provides a method for spawning new GameObjects into a Scene.

IsInLayerMask() – provides a method for checking whether a layer is within a LayerMask. Publicly declared LayerMask variables provide a dropdown menu in the Inspector where you can choose several layers. Unity does not provide functionality to easily check whether a layer is within a LayerMask, so this function does that for us. It can be called with:

```
IsInLayerMask( <the layers index number to check>, <the LayerMask
object> );
```

IsInLayerMask() will return true, if the layer is found in that LayerMask. We use this with collisions to find out what layer the colliding object is on and if we should be paying any attention to it and reacting to our collision with it. IsInLayerMask() is here as a helper function because I found that I used it a lot across player and enemy scripts.

Feel free to add your own code to ExtendedMonoBehaviour to make it your own – anything that you find yourself repeating across MonoBehaviour-derived classes – just add code to here and inherit the ExtendedMonoBehaviour instead!

3.2.3 BaseCameraController

Each camera script in the example games for this book derive from a class named BaseCameraController. BaseCameraController.cs can be found in the folder Assets/GPC_Framework/Scripts/BASE/CAMERA

```
using UnityEngine;
namespace GPC
{
        [AddComponentMenu("CSharpBookCode/Base/Camera Controller")]

        public class BaseCameraController : MonoBehaviour
        {
                public Transform _cameraTarget;
                public Transform _TR;
```

```
private void Awake()
{
        if (_TR == null)
                _TR = transform;
}
public virtual void SetTarget(Transform aTarget)
{
        _cameraTarget = aTarget;
}
    }
}
```

Above, the BaseCameraController contains a single function that all camera scripts can use. The intention is that – as your cameras grow more complicated – you can add any shared code into the BaseCameraController class. At the time of writing, all it contains is an Awake() function to grab a reference to the camera's Transform and a SetTarget() function that will be used by other scripts to specify which object a camera should follow. Camera classes that derive from BaseCameraController can then use the variable cameraTarget to access the object the camera needs to follow.

4 Player Structure

A player can take on any form – humans, aliens, vehicles, and so forth. Designing a structure that can deal with all of them is a challenge. The way we need to store data, the types of data we need to store, the various types of movement code and weapons and so on, can soon become complicated.

A basic player using the framework in this book would be made up of a GameObject containing Unity-specific physics or collision Components, then four additional script Components (as seen in Figure 4.1):

1. The player controller
   A controller specific to game requirements – this may have functions to deal with game-specific operations like opening doors or holding the player in place before the game starts and so on

2. A movement controller
   To move the player around (depending on the type of movement required this could be anything, such as a vehicle, or a humanoid)

3. An input controller
   To provide input to the player controller from the user

4. A user data manager
   The data manager is an interface between user data and the player. It takes care of the manipulation of player data and how it is stored and retrieved. Score and health values would be stored here, and the data manager would also hook up with a profile system to provide saving and loading.

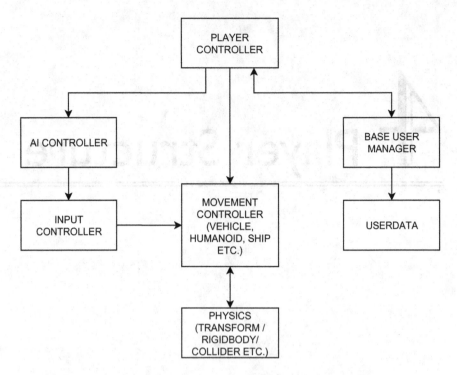

Figure 4.1 The Player GameObject has physics and collision Components attached to it, as well as Components to deal with data, sound, movement, and input.

▊ 4.1 A Player Controller

Things can be a little complicated when we look at the character controller class and its inherited scripts. As an example, a player might use a class name BlasterPlayerController that inherits a string of other classes:

ExtendedMonoBehaviour<BasePlayerStats<BaseCharacterController <ShootingPlayerCharacter<BlasterPlayerController

We are essentially layering classes on top of one another to provide the functionality we need for the specific game we are building. For example, if we wanted to change the character above to a player that could run around but did not need to use weapons, all it would take would be to remove one of the classes in the chain (changing the class declaration of BlasterPlayerController to derive from BaseCharacterController rather than ShootingPlayerCharacter) so that it looks like:

MonoBehaviour
<ExtendedMonoBehaviour<BasePlayerStats<BaseCharacterController <BlasterPlayerController

Let's say, this time, that we now want to replace the person with a vehicle. The new chain might look like this:

MonoBehaviour
<ExtendedMonoBehaviour<BasePlayerStats<BaseVehicleController <ShootingVehicleController<BlasterPlayerController

With a little caution in consideration of the order of inheritance, we can essentially plug and play different parts of the framework as needed.

When I developed this structure for the player controllers, I wanted something that could fit together in as much of a modular way as possible. Movement code should be kept separate from weapon code or code specific to a game like tracking waypoints in a racing game or something like that. You need to be a little extra cautious about how it all fits together, but the opportunity to reuse code is huge.

For examples of player controllers, look at the example racing game in Chapter 14. For a breakdown of a player controller script, see Section 4.5. later in this chapter.

▌ 4.2 Dealing with Input

Separate scripts provide input for the movement controllers to react to. They can be switched out for whatever input is required without having to change anything. The movement controller remains intact, regardless of what you 'feed' into it, which means you could use the exact same movement control script for a main player, AI players, and perhaps even remote players connected over a network – just using different inputs.

This system uses Unity's input system. It is currently being overhauled by Unity, with the big new update unfinished at the time of writing, so it may be that by the time you read this a new input system will be available for you to use. The principles shown in these scripts remain the same but if you want to use the new input system, you may need to change the point at which they get input. I expect that the current/ old input system will be around for a while before it will be deprecated, so if you do end up using these scripts they should still function without issue.

The BaseInputController class can found in the folder Assets/GPC_Framework/ Scripts/BASE/INPUT.

```
using UnityEngine;
namespace GPC

{
        [AddComponentMenu("CSharpBookCode/Base/Input Controller")]
        public class BaseInputController : MonoBehaviour
        {
                public enum InputTypes { player1, noInput };
                public InputTypes inputType;
                // directional buttons
                public bool Up;
                public bool Down;
                public bool Left;
                public bool Right;

                // fire / action buttons
                public bool Fire1;
```

Above, we provide two InputTypes by default, which can be used to enable or disable input. The first type is named player1 and the second, noInput. The intention here is that you could add extra input types such as layouts for other local players, devices, and so on.

```
        // weapon slots
        public bool Slot1;
        public bool Slot2;
        public bool Slot3;
        public bool Slot4;
        public bool Slot5;
        public bool Slot6;
```

```
public bool Slot7;
public bool Slot8;
public bool Slot9;

public float vert;
public float horz;
public bool shouldRespawn;

public Vector3 TEMPVec3;
private Vector3 zeroVector = new Vector3(0,0,0);
```

Above, the slot-based weapon system uses the keyboard buttons from 1 to 9 to directly select which weapon slot to use. For that reason, the input system has nine Boolean variables to take input from the number keys – though not implemented here, you can see how they are used in Chapter 7 when we look at a weapon system.

```
public virtual void CheckInput ()
{
        // override with your own code to deal with input
        horz=Input.GetAxis ("Horizontal");
        vert=Input.GetAxis ("Vertical");
}

public virtual float GetHorizontal()
{
        return horz;
}

public virtual float GetVertical()
{
        return vert;
}
```

Input provides an interface to Unity's input systems. According to the Unity documentation, Input.GetAxis returns the value of the virtual axis identified by axisName. The axis names are set in Unity's Input Manager (Edit>Project Settings>Input), although Horizontal and Vertical – the two we use above to set horz and vert – will be set up by default by Unity. After that, above, we have two functions that can return the horizontal and vertical input values.

```
public virtual bool GetFire()
{
        return Fire1;
}
```

Although the script includes a function called GetFire(), returning the value of the Boolean variable Fire1, the script does not include any code to do anything with Fire1. It is just there for consistency and it is expected that the player controller script handles firing as needed – for an example of this, please see Chapter 7 – Weapon Systems.

```
public bool GetRespawn()
{
        return shouldRespawn;
}
```

Again, the script contains GetRespawn() purely for protocol, with no actual functionality.

```
public virtual Vector3 GetMovementDirectionVector()
{
        // temp vector for movement dir gets set to
the value of an otherwise unused vector that always have the value
of 0,0,0
        TEMPVec3 = zeroVector;

        TEMPVec3.x = horz;
        TEMPVec3.y = vert;

        // return the movement vector
        return TEMPVec3;
}
```

For convenience, BaseInputController includes a simple system for returning a direction vector. The function will return a Vector3 with its x and y axis representing the levels of input.

▌ 4.3 User Data

It is not uncommon to store player information in a game controller or similar script removed from individual player objects. This approach may be well suited to single player games but moving to games that have more than one player may prove to be problematic. One solution may be for the game controller to have an array of classes containing player stats, manipulating them when other functions tell it to, but why not attach the player stats to each player and make it self-sufficient?

The framework for this book uses a data manager class for each player, consisting of everything we need to store for a single player:

1. Score

2. High score

3. Level

4. Health

5. Whether or not the player is finished (no longer active)

6. Name of the player

Each player has the BaseUserManager.cs script attached to its GameObject, giving each player its own set of stats. The game controller or other script elsewhere in the game structure can easily search for and access a player's information.

The BaseUserManager uses a static variable named global_userDatas to contain information about all the players in the game. As it is static, it persists across Scene loading and we keep player data wherever we are. The global_userDatas variable is typed as a List<UserData>, so it's a List containing UserData objects. You can easily modify or add new variables to the UserData class if you need to store more information about players.

The way BaseUserManager is intended to work is that you add players before the game starts – probably in the main menu when the player hits the start button. Just before the game begins, we add empty players to the global_userDatas List – however many players are going to be in the game – and that data persists until we go back and start the game again, at which point the players are wiped out and new ones made ready for a new game. Structuring your player data this way means that you keep player data away from Game Managers or player manager scripts – keeping code clean – and as an added bonus, it's easier to keep a track of your player data or multiple players data even if you are loading multiple Scenes along the way. Separating out the player data into a single List also makes saving and loading players states much easier, as you only need to save or load one List rather than each variable independently. There are some limitations to what you can save and load easily, due to serialization, but for most variable types – ints, strings, floats, and so on – the process for saving out the data is relatively straightforward.

4.3.1 The UserData Class

You can find this class in the folder GPC_Framework/Scripts/DATA.

UserData is a small data class used to store everything we need to keep track of, for players during a game. UserData is declared inside the script named UserData.cs:

```
namespace GPC
{
        [System.Serializable]
        public class UserData
        {
                public int id;
                public string playerName = "Anonymous";

                public int score;
                public int level;
                public int health;
                public int lives;
                public bool isFinished;
        }
}
```

You can easily add (or remove) variables to the UserData class, if you need to keep a track of other data. For ease of access, I use a class named Base PlayerStatsController that contains all the functions needed to 'talk' to the BaseUserManager. If you add new variables to the UserData class, you may also want to add methods to access them via BasePlayerStatsController. See Section 4.5. of this chapter for a full breakdown of BasePlayerStatsController.

4.3.2 The BaseUserManager Class

You can find this class in the folder GPC_Framework/Scripts/DATA.

The BaseUserManager class:

```
using UnityEngine;
using System.Collections.Generic;

namespace GPC
{
        [AddComponentMenu("CSharpBookCode/Base/Base User Manager")]

        public class BaseUserManager : MonoBehaviour
        {
```

After the using statements and declarations above, the first thing BaseUserManager contains is a static variable named global_userDatas:

```
public static List<UserData> global _ userDatas;
```

This global_userDatas List is used to hold a List of UserData objects – one per player in the game – and it is public static so that it can be accessed anywhere and retains its data regardless of Scene loading. We will look at the UserData class in the next:

```
public bool didInit;
public void Init()
{
        if (global_userDatas == null)
                global_userDatas =
new List<UserData>();

        didInit = true;
}
```

The Init() function checks to see if the global_userDatas List has already been initialized, if not we create a new List of type UserData.

```
public void ResetUsers()
{
        if (!didInit)
                Init();

        global_userDatas = new List<UserData>();
}
```

The ResetUsers() function is provided to wipe out all user information. This may be called at the start of the game, just before new players are added before the main game loads or perhaps at the end of the game to tidy everything up.

```
public List<UserData> GetPlayerList()
{
        if (global_userDatas == null)
                Init();

        return global_userDatas;
}
```

To process the List of players at the start of the game, you can grab it by using the above function, GetPlayerList() which will return a List containing everything in global_userDatas. In the games examples for this book, the Game Manager gets this List when the core Scene is loaded, and we iterate through the List to spawn one player into the Scene per entry in global_userDatas.

```
public int AddNewPlayer()
{
        if (!didInit)
                Init();
        UserData newUser = new UserData();
        newUser.id = global_userDatas.Count;
        newUser.playerName = "Anonymous";
        newUser.score = 0;
        newUser.level = 1;
        newUser.health = 3;
```

```
                           newUser.lives = 3;
                           newUser.highScore = 0;
                           newUser.isFinished = false;
                           global_userDatas.Add(newUser);
                           return newUser.id;
              }
```

AddNewPlayer() above, adds a new player (a UserData instance) to the global_userDatas List, populating the UserData object with default values for a player. Note that all of these values are declared in the UserData class from Section 4.3.1.

The rest of the class deals with getting and setting the player data:

```
              public string GetName(int id)
              {
                      if (!didInit)
                          Init();
                      return global_userDatas[id].playerName;
              }
              public void SetName(int id, string aName)
              {
                      if (!didInit)
                          Init();
                      global_userDatas[id].playerName = aName;
              }
              public int GetLevel(int id)
              {
                      if (!didInit)
                          Init();
                      return global_userDatas[id].level;
              }
              public void SetLevel(int id, int num)
              {
                      if (!didInit)
                          Init();
                      global_userDatas[id].level = num;
              }
              public int GetScore(int id)
              {
                      if (!didInit)
                          Init();
                      return global_userDatas[id].score;
              }
              public virtual void AddScore(int id, int anAmount)
              {
                      if (!didInit)
                          Init();
                      global_userDatas[id].score += anAmount;
              }
              public void ReduceScore(int id, int num)
              {
                      if (!didInit)
                          Init();
                      global_userDatas[id].score -= num;
              }
              public void SetScore(int id, int num)
              {
                      if (!didInit)
                          Init();
                      global_userDatas[id].score = num;
              }
              public int GetHealth(int id)
              {
```

```
                        if (!didInit)
                            Init();
                        return global_userDatas[id].health;
            }
            public int GetLives(int id)
            {
                        if (!didInit)
                            Init();
                        return global_userDatas[id].lives;
            }
            public void SetLives(int id, int num)
            {
                        if (!didInit)
                            Init();
                        global_userDatas[id].lives = num;
            }
            public void AddLives(int id, int num)
            {
                        if (!didInit)
                            Init();
                        global_userDatas[id].lives += num;
            }
            public void ReduceLives(int id, int num)
            {
                        if (!didInit)
                            Init();
                        global_userDatas[id].lives -= num;
            }
            public void AddHealth(int id, int num)
            {
                        if (!didInit)
                            Init();
                        global_userDatas[id].health += num;
            }
            public void ReduceHealth(int id, int num)
            {
                        if (!didInit)
                            Init();
                        global_userDatas[id].health -= num;
            }
            public void SetHealth(int id, int num)
            {
                        if (!didInit)
                            Init();
                        global_userDatas[id].health = num;
            }
            public bool GetIsFinished(int id)
            {
                        if (!didInit)
                            Init();
                        return global_userDatas[id].isFinished;
            }
            public void SetType(int id, int theType)
            {
                        if (!didInit)
                            Init();
                        global_userDatas[id].type = theType;
            }
            public int GetType(int id)
            {
                        if (!didInit)
                            Init();
                        return global_userDatas[id].type;
            }
            public void SetIsFinished(int id, bool aVal)
```

```
                    {
                        if (!didInit)
                            Init();
                        global_userDatas[id].isFinished = aVal;
                    }
            }
}
```

■ 4.4   The BasePlayerStatsController Class

You can find this class in the folder GPC_Framework/Scripts/BASE/PLAYER.

My player controllers derive from several other classes, one of which is BasePlayerStatsController, a class which gives the player controller access to a host of functions dealing with the user data. Okay, that is not the only function of BasePlayerStatsController. It is also there just to hold any variables that may be relevant to dealing with the players in the games, but BasePlayerStatsController mostly acts as a friendly interface between my player scripts and the user data. For example, I can call SetHealth(an amount) from my player controller without having to worry about identifying my player with the correct ID or anything like that. The functions I use to set UserData in BasePlayerStatsController already takes care of the ID and how the UserDataManager needs to be called.

The BasePlayerStatsController.cs script in full looks like this:

```
using System.Collections;
using System.Collections.Generic;
using UnityEngine;

namespace GPC
{
        [RequireComponent(typeof(BaseUserManager))]

        public class BasePlayerStatsController :
ExtendedCustomMonoBehaviour
        {
                public BaseUserManager _myDataManager;
                public int myID;

                public BaseInputController _inputController;
                public bool disableAutoPlayerListAdd;

                public virtual void Init()
                {
                        // cache the usual suspects
                        _RB = GetComponent<Rigidbody>();
                        _GO = GetComponent<GameObject>();
                        _TR = GetComponent<Transform>();

                        _inputController =
GetComponent<BaseInputController>();

                        SetupDataManager();
                }

                public virtual void SetPlayerDetails(int anID)
                {
                        // this function can be used by a game
manager to pass in details from the player list, such as
                        // this players ID or perhaps you could
override this in the future to add avatar support, loadouts or
```

```
                    // special abilities etc.?
                    myID = anID;
            }

            public virtual void SetupDataManager()
            {
                    // if a player manager is not set in the
editor, let's try to find one

                    if (_myDataManager == null)
                        _myDataManager =
GetComponent<BaseUserManager>();

                    if (_myDataManager == null)
                        _myDataManager =
gameObject.AddComponent<BaseUserManager>();

                    if (_myDataManager == null)
                        _myDataManager =
GetComponent<BaseUserManager>();

                    if (!disableAutoPlayerListAdd)
                    {
                            // add the player (set up data) to
the ScriptableObject we use to store player info
                            myID = _myDataManager.AddNewPlayer();
                            _myDataManager.SetName(myID, "Player");
                            _myDataManager.SetHealth(myID, 3);
                    }
            }

            public virtual void AddScore(int anAmount)
            {
                    if (!didInit)
                        Init();
                    _myDataManager.AddScore(myID, anAmount);
            }

            public virtual void AddHealth(int anAmount)
            {
                    if (!didInit)
                        Init();
                    _myDataManager.AddHealth(myID, anAmount);
            }

            public virtual void ReduceScore(int anAmount)
            {
                    if (!didInit)
                        Init();
                    _myDataManager.ReduceScore(myID, anAmount);
            }

            public virtual void ReduceHealth(int anAmount)
            {
                    if (!didInit)
                        Init();
                    _myDataManager.ReduceHealth(myID, anAmount);
            }

            public virtual void SetLives(int anAmount)
            {
                    if (!didInit)
                        Init();
                    _myDataManager.SetLives(myID, anAmount);
            }
```

```
public virtual void AddLives(int anAmount)
{
        if (!didInit)
                Init();
        _myDataManager.AddLives(myID, -anAmount);
}

public virtual void ReduceLives(int anAmount)
{
        if (!didInit)
                Init();
        _myDataManager.ReduceLives(myID, anAmount);
}

public virtual void SetScore(int anAmount)
{
        if (!didInit)
                Init();
        _myDataManager.SetScore(myID, anAmount);
}

public virtual void SetHealth(int anAmount)
{
        if (!didInit)
                Init();
        _myDataManager.SetHealth(myID, anAmount);
}

public virtual void SetName(string aName)
{
        if (!didInit)
                Init();
        _myDataManager.SetName(myID, aName);
}

public int GetLives()
{
        if (!didInit)
                Init();
        return _myDataManager.GetLives(myID);
}

public int GetHealth()
{
        if (!didInit)
                Init();
        return _myDataManager.GetHealth(myID);
}

public int GetScore()
{
        if (!didInit)
                Init();
        return _myDataManager.GetScore(myID);
}
    }
}
```

Right away, in the code above you may notice the similarities to the BaseUserManager class. A large portion of the script above is taken up with calls to the corresponding functions in BaseUserManager – by duplicating those functions here to call out to them, we are adding all of the functionality of BaseUserManager to the player script and simplifying how we need to call it. For example, I do not have to check that everything is set up and available every time I call to add score to the players score total. I also do not want to have to pass in the ID every time, so functions in the code above like GetHealth() and AddScore() simplify further interactions with BaseUserManager. If you added more variables to UserData, you would need to add ways to change them via both BaseUserManager and BasePlayerStatsController.

∎ 4.5 Managing Players

To manage players, add a BaseUserManager Component to the menu (or wherever you want to set up players initially) then set up a reference to it in your own script and call ResetUsers() to wipe out existing users, then AddNewPlayer to add a new player.

For a working example, look to the main menu section of the racing game example in Chapter 14.

5 Recipes
Common Components

■ 5.1 Introduction

The utility scripts and commonly used systems in this chapter may come in handy for a range of different types of game projects. In the Assets/GPC_ Framework/Scripts/COMMON folder you will find an eclectic bunch of reusable scripts like timers and camera controllers. In this chapter, we focus on those standalone scripts. You can easily take these and use them in any project, with or without using the GPC framework from this book.

Within the COMMON folder, there are several sub-folders. Those are;

AI

This contains scripts related to player or automatic control, such as a script to talk to the BaseAIController.cs script and act as a simple, functional bot moving around in a game environment.

CAMERA

Scripts related to the camera should go in here, such as third-person or top-down camera code.

GAME CONTROL

The scripts in this folder are about overall game state control. In the example files, you will find:

BattleController and GlobalBattleManager – used for deathmatch-style scoring and game state logic)

RaceController and GlobalRaceManager – containing the base logic for racing games, such as lap counting and position tracking

INPUT

Different player and game types require different control systems or input methods. Any common scripts dealing with input go in this folder.

LEVEL LOADING

Depending on the project, we may need to deal with loading differently. Place loading scripts in here.

SCRIPTABLE OBJECTS

All ScriptableObjects require files to define them and this is where you can find those files.

SPAWNING

Scripts related to spawning may be found here, which includes code to spawn objects when triggers are fired or to spawn paths for dynamic waypoint following objects.

USER INTERFACE

Anything related to user interface goes in here.

UTILITY

The Utility folder is home to small helper scripts, such as the timer class or a script to automatically spin a GameObject.

WEAPONS

Any weapons-related scripts outside of the base framework may be found here.

The scripts in this chapter are organized in order of how they appear in the respective folders, for ease of reference.

5.2 AI

You can also find more information about these scripts in Chapter 10, dedicated to AI.

5.3 Camera

The camera is the window into the game world, and it makes a huge difference to how the gameplay feels. Be sure to prototype, iterate, and put some time into finding the perfect camera set up! There are just two camera scripts for the example games in this book. Both cameras should provide a good starting point for camera systems in your own games.

The following scripts are found in example project, in the folder Assets/GPC_Framework/Scripts/COMMON/CAMERA.

5.3.1 Third-Person Camera

A third-person camera sits behind the player. It is not quite the same as a follow camera; a third-person camera usually orbits around the player rather than simply following it around. To visualize this, imagine that the camera is tied to a pole attached to the target player. As the player moves around, the camera remains to be the length of the pole away from it, but the camera is free to move around the player in a circle. The position of the camera is usually somewhere behind the player, with a little damping on its horizontal movement applied to it, to allow for a good sense of movement when the player turns. In some third-person camera setups, the camera may be allowed to move in or out from the target player.

```
using UnityEngine;
using System.Collections;

namespace GPC
{
    [AddComponentMenu("CSharpBookCode/Common/Cameras/Third
Person Cam Controller")]

    public class CameraThirdPerson : BaseCameraController
    {
        public float distance = 20.0f;
        public float height = 5.0f;
        public float heightDamping = 2.0f;

        public float lookAtHeight = 0.0f;

        public float rotationSnapTime = 0.3F;

        public float distanceSnapTime;

        public Vector3 lookAtAdjustVector;

        private float usedDistance;

        float wantedRotationAngle;
        float wantedHeight;

        float currentRotationAngle;
        float currentHeight;

        Quaternion currentRotation;
        Vector3 wantedPosition;

        private float yVelocity = 0.0F;
        private float zVelocity = 0.0F;

        void Update()
        {
```

The main update to the camera happens in Update(), rather than FixedUpdate(). The reason for this is that we prefer everything physics-wise to have been updated before moving the camera – which should have happened by Update() – and in doing so, there should be no discrepancies between the positions of our target objects between the end of the camera update and the drawing of the next frame. Drawing at the wrong time can cause a jittering effect as the objects we are following are updated after the camera positioning.

At the start of Update() is a null check to make sure that we have a target:

```
if (_cameraTarget == null)
    return;
```

Code from this script will eventually interpolate heights and rotation values, but it requires a little extra before we can do that:

```
wantedHeight = _cameraTarget.position.y + height;
currentHeight = _TR.position.y;

wantedRotationAngle =
_cameraTarget.eulerAngles.y;
currentRotationAngle = _TR.eulerAngles.y;
```

Before interpolation, we need to calculate target height and target rotations and we also need to find out what current height and rotation values are. The public variable height – which is our value set in the Inspector to tell this script how high to put the camera – gets added to wantedHeight along with the height of the target object we are following. With this new float value in wantedHeight, we now know exactly where the camera needs to be headed height-wise.

currentRotationAngle is a float representing the angle, in degrees, that we need to turn the camera at to try and reach the target rotation in wantedRotationAngle. It's an interpolation carried out by Mathf.SmoothDampAngle in the next line:

```
currentRotationAngle = Mathf.SmoothDampAngle(currentRotationAngle,
wantedRotationAngle, ref yVelocity, rotationSnapTime);
```

Mathf.SmoothDampAngle is an interpolation function designed specifically for easing between two angles. It will automatically cap the return value between 0 and 360 as well as choosing the correct way around (if your value is at 181 degrees, it would interpolate up rather than down so that the rotation has a natural flow and doesn't go back on itself).

The Unity documentation tells us that SmoothDampAngle takes the following parameters (in order of how they should be passed in):

current	The current position.
target	A Vector3 position we are trying to reach.
currentVelocity	The current velocity, this value is modified by the function every time you call it.
smoothTime	Approximately the time it will take to reach the target. A smaller value will reach the target faster.
maxSpeed	Optionally allows you to clamp the maximum speed.
deltaTime	Time since the last call to this function. Default is Time.deltaTime.

In this part of the code, the yVelocity variable holds the current velocity of the interpolated move, but it is not actually used anywhere else in the script. It's a required field for SmoothDampAngle, so we just provide it for the function to work right and forget about it. Note that one possible use for getting the velocity may be speed limiting the move, but SmoothDampAngle can take care of this with no extra code by providing a maxSpeed parameter. This is useful for limiting interpolation speeds without having to do it yourself with velocity.

The currentRotationAngle is, in effect, a portion of the rotation we need to make around the y-axis (hence using the name yVelocity to describe its speed). The variable rotationSnapTime decides how much time it should take for the rotation to happen, which is public and designed to be set in the Unity editor Inspector window on whichever GameObject the script is attached to, so that the rotation speed can be easily set in the editor.

Height is interpolated using Mathf.Lerp, which takes three parameters: the start amount, the target amount, and a time value clamped between 0 and 1.

We use the float heightDamping, multiplied by Time.deltaTime, to make the transition time based. Wondering why do we need to make the time parameter time based? Good question! How the time parameter of Mathf.Lerp works has been a very popular question on various forums and help pages. The time value represents how much of a portion, of the difference between the two values, that should be applied each time this line of code is executed. If the time value is zero, the return value will be the start amount. If time is 1, the return value will be the target amount.

By calculating the portion with Time.deltaTime, the transition from start value to target value is smoothed out over a repeatable, fixed amount of time rather than it being frame-rate dependent and based on how many times the Mathf.Lerp calculation line is called:

```
        currentHeight = Mathf.Lerp(currentHeight,
wantedHeight, heightDamping * Time.deltaTime);
```

Now that the script has calculated how much to rotate the camera and how high it should be on the y-axis, the script goes on to deal with positioning:

wantedPosition is a Vector3 that will hold the target position. The target position is made from the target Transform.position followed by setting its y position to the height calculated earlier in this section in currentHeight variable:

```
        wantedPosition = target.position;
        wantedPosition.y = currentHeight;
```

The next part of the code calculates how far behind the player we need to move the camera. For this, the script uses Mathf.SmoothDampAngle. zVelocity represents the speed of movement of the camera along its z-axis:

```
      usedDistance = Mathf.SmoothDampAngle(usedDistance,
distance, ref zVelocity, distanceSnapTime);
```

To place the camera at the correct position around the target using only a rotation angle, the solution lies within Quaternion.Euler. This rather frightening sounding function converts Euler angle vector3-based rotations into a vector. That is; you pass in Euler rotation values and you get back a direction vector instead. Multiply this by how far back we want the camera from the player; add that to the player's current position and we have the correct rotation, position and offset for the camera:

```
        wantedPosition += Quaternion.Euler(0,
currentRotationAngle, 0) * new Vector3(0, 0, -usedDistance);

    _TR.position = wantedPosition;
```

The final part of the function causes the camera to look at the target (player). It does this by using Unity's built-in Transform.LookAt() function. We pass in the position of the target object (as a Vector3) and add an extra offset to where the camera is going to look, via the lookAtAdjustVector variable. Note that you can also add an up vector to the LookAt() function, but in this case, we don't need to:

```
      _ TR.LookAt( _ cameraTarget.position);
_TR.Rotate(lookAtAdjustVector) ;
```

Above, in the last line we also add a small rotation adjustment. I like to use this so that the camera aims above the player as if it were looking forward, rather than looking right at the players vehicle or body. This can make the camera view more parallel to the ground level and keep good visibility, making the game easier to play in some situations. Of course, as with anything in this book, it is up to you to decide where the camera goes and how it moves to make your personal vision of your game. Try adjusting parameters and testing out the feel of different rotations or movement speeds.

5.3.2 Top-Down Camera

The TopDownCamera class is a very basic target following system from a top-down perspective:

```
using UnityEngine;
namespace GPC
{

        [AddComponentMenu("CSharpBookCode/Common/Cameras/Top Down
Cam Controller")]
        public class TopDownCamera : BaseCameraController
            {
            public Vector3 targetOffset;
            public float moveSpeed = 2f;
            public float maxHeight;
            public float minHeight;

            void LateUpdate()
            {
```

After the variable declarations, the LateUpdate() function checks to make sure that we have a target before it tries to position the camera:

```
                if (cameraTarget != null)
                    _TR.position = Vector3.Lerp(_TR.position,
                cameraTarget.position + targetOffset, moveSpeed *
Time.deltaTime);
                }
            }
        }
```

The single line controlling this camera uses the Vector3.Lerp function to interpolate the camera's Transform's position to that of the target stored in followTarget. We add an offset to the position (so that we end up above the target rather than inside it) and use the moveSpeed multiplied by Time.deltaTime to Lerp based on time.

▌ 5.4 Game Control

Game management and game control is central to every game project and often we need to break up these sections as much as possible to keep everything manageable and as easy to debug as possible. The Game Control folder contains a few helper scripts.

5.4.1 GlobalRaceManager

GlobalRaceManager.cs will be explained in Chapter 14, Section 14.4.3.

5.4.2 RaceController

RaceController.cs will be explained in Chapter 14, Section 14.4.4.

▌ 5.5 Input

Your games could take a variety of different inputs, or in some cases you may want to implement a third-party input solution like Rewired (made by Guaveman Enterprises) to provide extended detection of input hardware or force feedback effects.

In Chapter 4, we saw that the main player structure contained a single input script designed to take keyboard input. Adding input systems is case of building custom input scripts that follow a similar format, so that the existing player code need not be changed to accommodate different controls.

It may be required to take input from other methods than the keyboard, such as mouse, or joystick. You can easily set up alternate controls in the Unity editor via the Edit > Project Settings > Input menu.

Input scripts can be found in Assets/GPC_Framework/Scripts/COMMON/INPUT.

5.5.1 Mouse Input

Mouse_Input.cs calculates movement of the mouse between each frame and uses it for input. The script:

```
public class MouseInput : BaseInputController
{
        private Vector2 prevMousePos;
        private Vector2 mouseDelta;

        private float speedX = 0.05f;
        private float speedY = 0.1f;

        public void Start ()
        {
                prevMousePos= Input.mousePosition;
        }
```

The Start() function adds a default value to prevMousePos, which will be used to calculate the movement between each update. If prevMousePos was left at zero (its default) then the first time CheckInput() happens the script will incorrectly assume that the mouse has moved from 0,0 to the current mouse position.

Input provides an interface to Unity's input systems. It is used for everything from gyrometer input on mobile devices to keyboard presses. Input.mousePosition delivers the current position of the mouse in pixel coordinates as a two-dimensional vector, with the bottom left of the screen at 0,0 and top right at Screen.width, Screen.height.

The mouse input system uses mouse delta movement (the amount of movement since the last update) instead of mouse position. The delta amount is converted into a percentage value (a percentage of the screen width or height) and the resulting percentage value used as input.

```
        public override void CheckInput ()
        {
                // get input data from vertical and horizontal axis
and store them internally in vert and horz so we don't
                // have to access them every time we need to relay
input data out

                // calculate a percentage amount to use per pixel
                float scalerX = 100f / Screen.width;
                float scalerY = 100f / Screen.height;
```

CheckInput() starts by calculating a scale to work at. The floats scalerX and scalerY hold the equivalent of one percent of the screen's width and height respectively.

```
                        // calculate and use deltas
                        float mouseDeltaY = Input.mousePosition.y -
prevMousePos.y;
                        float mouseDeltaX = Input.mousePosition.x -
prevMousePos.x;
```

The delta amount of mouse movement is calculated in the code by taking the current mouse position and subtracting it from the position that the mouse was at the end of the last update.

```
                        // scale based on screen size
                        vert += ( mouseDeltaY * speedY ) * scalerY;
                        horz += ( mouseDeltaX * speedX ) * scalerX;
                        // store this mouse position for the next time we're
here
                        prevMousePos= Input.mousePosition;
```

When the mouse position is multiplied by the scale variables (scalerX and scalerY) we end up with a percentage amount. We say that the mouse is at a percentage amount across the screen and use that percentage amount as input.

```
                        // set up some Boolean values for up, down, left and
right
                        Up      = ( vert>0 );
                        Down    = ( vert<0 );
                        Left    = ( horz<0 );
                        Right   = ( horz>0 );
```

The mouse-based input script also populates the Boolean variables above, for directional movement, if required.

```
                        // get fire / action buttons
                        Fire1= Input.GetButton( "Fire1" );
                }
```

To make the fire button work properly, mouse button input must be set up correctly in the input settings of the Unity editor, under the Fire1 entry.

```
        public void LateUpdate()
        {
                        // check inputs each LateUpdate() ready for the next
tick
                        CheckInput();
        }
}
```

The script calls its own update function from LateUpdate(), which is where Unity recommends all input checking happen.

Note: To set up inputs correctly, open Unity's Input menu Edit > Project Settings > Input

▌ 5.6 Level Loading

There are two loading systems in this book. One uses Unity's SceneManager to just go ahead and load a Scene. Advanced level loading has its own chapter in this book, and you can find it in Chapter 13.

▌ 5.7 ScriptableObjects

ScriptableObjects are a great way to manage data that needs to persist across the entire game. There is just one script in the framework, ProfileScriptableObject.

5.7.1 ProfileScriptableObject

Saving and loading is covered, in full, in Chapter 12. For save profiles, this framework uses a ScriptableObject to store everything we want in the profile. This script needs to be serialized, so be aware of using any variable types that may not be easily serializable by the engine. It forms the basis of a save profile. You can find this script in the folder Assets/GPC_Framework/Scripts/COMMON.

The ProfileScripableObject.cs script looks like this:

```
using System.Collections;
using System.Collections.Generic;
using UnityEngine;
using System;

namespace GPC
{
        [CreateAssetMenu(fileName = "ProfileData", menuName =
"CSharpFramework/ProfileScriptableObject")]

        [Serializable]
        public class ProfileScriptableObject : ScriptableObject
        {
                public Profiles theProfileData;
        }

        [Serializable]
        public class Profiles
        {
                public ProfileData[] profiles;
        }

        [Serializable]
        public class ProfileData
        {
                [SerializeField]
                public int myID;
                [SerializeField]
                public bool inUse;

                [SerializeField]
                public string profileName = "EMPTY";
                [SerializeField]
                public string playerName = "Anonymous";

                [SerializeField]
                public int highScore;
                [SerializeField]
                public float sfxVolume;
                [SerializeField]
                public float musicVolume;
        }
}
```

▌ 5.8 Spawning

In many cases using Unity's built-in Instantiate function would be enough for creating objects for a desktop computer-based game, but instancing GameObjects in Unity can be an expensive process, particularly noticeable on mobile devices.

One common method of getting around the processor hit is to use pooling. Pooling is where you have a group of objects that you use and reuse without destroying them. Building a pool management system is beyond the scope of this book, although centralizing the spawning system will make it easy to switch out spawning for a better solution in the future.

Find these scripts in Assets/GPC_Framework/Scripts/COMMON/SPAWNING.

5.8.1 A Spawner Component

This Spawner class can either instantiate a prefab after an amount of time after the Scene starts, when the camera gets within a certain distance of the spawn point, or when the script is called to spawn by another script. It is used in this book for the example game Blaster, whereby each wave of enemies is stored in a separate Scene. The enemy prefabs are spawned automatically after the Scene finishes loading, and the player can get to blasting them.

```
using UnityEngine;

namespace GPC
{
        [AddComponentMenu("CSharpBookCode/Common/Spawn Prefabs (no
path following)")]

        public class Spawner : ExtendedCustomMonoBehaviour
        {
```

The class is added to the GPC namespace, then a menu item is added to the Unity editor via the AddComponentMenu tag. The class derives from ExtendedCustomMonoBehaviour so that we get access to its IsInLayerMask() function, if needed in future. For example, the TriggerSpawner class in Section 5.8.2 of this chapter derives from Spawner and makes use of IsInLayerMask().

```
                // should we start spawning based on distance from
the camera?
                // if distanceBased is false, we will need to call
this class from elsewhere, to spawn
                public bool distanceBasedSpawnStart;

                // if we're using distance based spawning, at what
distance should we start?
                public float distanceFromCameraToSpawnAt = 35f;
                public bool shouldAutoStartSpawningOnLoad;
                public float timeBetweenSpawns = 1;
                public bool startDelay;
                public int totalAmountToSpawn = 10;
                public bool shouldRepeatWaves;
                public bool shouldRandomizeSpawnTime;
                public float minimumSpawnTimeGap = 0.5f;
                public GameObject[] _spawnObjectPrefabs;
                private int totalSpawnObjects;
                private int spawnCounter = 0;
                private int currentObjectNum;
                private Transform _cameraTransform;
                private bool spawning;
                public bool shouldSetSpeed;
                public float speedToSet;
                public bool shouldSetSmoothing;
                public float smoothingToSet;
                public bool shouldSetRotateSpeed;
                public float rotateToSet;
```

The only variable declaration above of note is that the spawn objects are in an array. This means you can add more than one type of prefab to spawn.

```
void Start()
{
        // cache ref to our Transform
        _TR = transform;

        if(_cameraTransform==null)
                _cameraTransform = Camera.main.
transform;
```

Above, we cache the Transform and, if one has not been set in the Inspector, we try to find the Transform of the main Camera in the Scene with Unity's built-in Camera.main.

```
        if (shouldAutoStartSpawningOnLoad)
                StartSpawn();
}
```

We find out how many objects are in the spawn list array and store the result in a variable named totalSpawnObjects. This just makes it easier:

```
public void OnDrawGizmos()
{
        if (distanceBasedSpawnStart)
        {
                Gizmos.color = new Color(0, 0, 1,
0.5f);
                Gizmos.DrawSphere(transform.position,
distanceFromCameraToSpawnAt);
        } else
        {
                Gizmos.color = new Color(0, 1, 1, 1f);
                Gizmos.DrawSphere(transform.position, 1f);
        }                      }
```

A Gizmo is a shape that can be used to provide a visual aid to your Component or GameObject – a cube or a sphere – which gets displayed in the Scene view of the editor. Thanks to the code, whenever this Component is attached to a GameObject, Unity will draw a Gizmo around it to show you the distance at which our Spawner will activate. Drawing takes place in the function above, OnDrawGizmos(), which is called automatically by the game engine both when the game is playing and when it is idle, too.

Above, we check the Boolean variable named distanceBasedSpawnStart to see if we are using distance-based spawning. If it is true, we draw the sphere based on the spawn distance. If distanceBasedSpawnStart is false, we just draw the sphere with a fixed radius. This way, we always have a Gizmo to make it easier to see where spawning will occur.

To set the color of the Gizmo about to be drawn, you call Gizmos.color() with the parameters of red, green, and blue followed by an alpha value. All should be between 0 and 1. Once you have made a call to Gizmos.color() in your function, anything you draw after that point will be drawn with that color until you add another Gizmos.Color() call.

Drawing a sphere Gizmo is as simple as calling Gizmos.DrawSphere() and you pass in the position to draw it followed by the radius of the sphere. Above, we take our Transform's position, and in the first instance, we pass distanceFromCameraToSpawnAt as the radius so that the Gizmo exactly represents our spawn distance. In the second instance, when distanceBasedSpawnStart is false, we pass an arbitrary value as the radius instead.

```
public void Update()
{
        float aDist = Vector3.Distance(_TR.position,
_cameraTransform.position);
        if (distanceBasedSpawnStart && !spawning &&
aDist < distanceFromCameraToSpawnAt)
        {
                StartSpawn();
                spawning = true;
        }
}
```

The Update() function checks the distance between our Transform and the camera, by using Vector3.Distance(). This is not the most optimized thing to call every single frame, so be aware of this if you use it in a complicated project that may be impacted by this. An alternative might be to only check distance every few frames, instead, or perhaps on a timer.

Once we have the distance value in aDist we check that distanceBaseSpawnStart is true (indicating that we want to do distance-based spawning) and that we are not already spawning – spawning is false – then compare aDist to the distanceFromCameraToSpawnAt value. If these conditions are met, we can call StartSpawn() to spawn the prefab(s) and we set spawning to true to avoid any duplicate calls to spawn now that the process is in motion.

```
void StartSpawn()
{
        StartWave(totalAmountToSpawn,
timeBetweenSpawns);
}
```

To get the spawning process in motion, we call StartSpawn() above that will then call another function StartWave(). You will see below what StartWave() does, but note for now just that you pass in how many prefabs you want to spawn followed by the amount of time the system should wait before spawning another one.

Spawning is a process in this function, rather than a single action. StartWave() will continue to spawn as many objects as you tell it to, ultimately disabling its own GameObject once all prefabs have been added to the Scene.

```
public void StartWave(int HowMany, float
timeBetweenSpawns)
{
        spawnCounter = 0;
        totalAmountToSpawn = HowMany;

        // reset
        currentObjectNum = 0;
        CancelInvoke("doSpawn");
```

As StartWave() is the beginning of our spawn wave, we need to do a little set up first. spawnCounter is a variable we will use to keep tabs on how many prefabs this Spawner has added to the Scene. The value of spawnCounter will be compared to totalAmountToSpawn (set by the code above to the first parameter passed into this function, howMany) to know when to stop spawning.

currentObjectNum is an index number we can use to refer to the array holding all the prefabs. When there are more than one prefabs in that array (set in the

Inspector) then currentObjectNum will be increased every time a new prefab is spawned so that we get the next item from the array next time.

If there are more prefabs to spawn, a function named doSpawn() will be called repeatedly – until all prefabs are made. We use Unity's Invoke() function to schedule a call to doSpawn(), so whenever we run StartWave we make sure there are no outstanding Invoke calls to doSpawn() by using the CancelInvoke() function. If there any outstanding, CancelInvoke() will flush all of them out at once.

```
                        // the option is there to spawn at random
times, or at fixed intervals...
            if (shouldRandomizeSpawnTime)
            {
                    // do a randomly timed invoke call,
based on the times set up in the inspector
                    Invoke("doSpawn", Random.Range
(minimumSpawnTimeGap, timeBetweenSpawns));
            }
            else
            {
                    // do a regularly scheduled invoke
call based on times set in the inspector
                    InvokeRepeating("doSpawn",
timeBetweenSpawns, timeBetweenSpawns);
            }
        }
```

Above, we look to see if shouldRandomizeSpawnTime is true. If it is, we use a random amount of time between minimSpawnTimeGap and the value of timeBetweenSpawns (which was passed into this function as a parameter). Having a randomized spawn time can just make a game more interesting than having enemies spawning at fixed times all the time.

If shouldRandomizeSpawnTime is false, instead of using standard Invoke() to schedule the call to doSpawn(), the code here uses InvokeRepeating(). This will repeat call doSpawn() indefinitely – it takes two parameters, the first is the time before we do the first spawn, and the second parameter is the time between that and every other call after. We just use the value in timeBetweenSpawns for timing, passing its value in to InvokeRepeating() as both parameters.

```
    void doSpawn()
    {
            if (spawnCounter >= totalAmountToSpawn)
            {
                    if (shouldRepeatWaves)
                    {
                            spawnCounter = 0;
                    }
                    else
                    {
                            CancelInvoke("doSpawn");
                            this.enabled = false;
                            return;
                    }
            }
    }
```

As mentioned above earlier in the section, doSpawn() is called repeatedly until all of the prefabs we want to spawn have been added to the Scene. To accomplish that, spawnCounter counts up, and we compare it to totalAmountToSpawn to know how to proceed.

Above, if spawnCounter is greater or equal to totalAmountToSpawn then we need to end this wave of spawning and either start another wave by resetting spawnCounter to 0, or to cancel further calls to doSpawn() entirely with CancelInvoke(). If we are dropping out entirely and ending all spawning, the this.enabled = false line will disable the GameObject so that it no longer receives any calls to its functions from the engine (no more FixedUpdate(), Update(), or LateUpdate() calls and so on). We also know that enough spawns have been made, so we drop out of the function.

```
// create an object
Spawn( _spawnObjectPrefabs[ currentObjectNum ].transform,
_TR.position, Quaternion.identity);
```

Above, we call out to a function named Spawn() – a custom function from the ExtendedCustomMonoBehaviour class – to instantiate the prefab into the Scene. The parameters that Spawn() takes is a Transform for the prefab to spawn, a position, and a rotation.

```
        spawnCounter++;
        currentObjectNum++;
// check to see if we've reached the end of the spawn objects array

        if (currentObjectNum > _spawnObjectPrefabs.Length  - 1)
                currentObjectNum = 0;

        if (shouldRandomizeSpawnTime)
        {
                // cancel invoke for safety
                CancelInvoke("doSpawn");

                // schedule the next random spawn
                Invoke("doSpawn", Random.Range(minimumSpawnTimeGap,
timeBetweenSpawns));
        }
}
```

With the new prefab added to the Scene, our counters spawnCounter, and currentObjectNum are incremented. After that, we check currentObjectNum to see if it has been incremented too far – past the end of the _spawnObjectPrefabs array. If we tried to use this as an index number to access the prefabs array with, Unity would throw an error, so at this point if we find that currentObjectNum is too high it gets reset to 0.

Earlier in the class, we used the shouldRandomizeSpawnTime flag to decide whether to call this function with Invoke() or call it with InvokeRepeating(). Above, if we are using a randomize spawn time, we need to schedule the next call to doSpawn at a different, randomized period of time. For this, first any outstanding calls to doSpawn() are cancelled with CancelInvoke() – this is just a safety measure, as in the current state there should never be any duplicate calls. Again, we use Invoke() and Random.Range() to choose a random period of time. Random.Range() takes the minimum value of minimumSpawnTimeGap and the maximum value of timeBetweenSpawns.

5.8.2 Trigger Spawning

The TriggerSpawner class instantiates an object when another object enters the trigger that this script Component is attached to.

The easiest way to use this Component is to add a cube primitive to a Scene and set its Box Collider's IsTrigger property to true. Add this TriggerSpawner Component to your cube and then whenever your player enters the area outlined by the cube, it will trigger this script to spawn a prefab. Once you have the area worked out correctly, disable the cube's Mesh Renderer Component and you have a trigger spawn area.

One such use for this script would be to spawn an enemy when the player reaches an area in a level.

```
using UnityEngine;

namespace GPC
{
        [AddComponentMenu("CSharpBookCode/Utility/Trigger Spawner")]

        public class TriggerSpawner : Spawner
        {
                public GameObject ObjectToSpawnOnTrigger;
                public Vector3 offsetPosition;
                public bool onlySpawnOnce;
                public LayerMask triggerLayerMask;
```

We add this script as a menu item first, using Unity's AddComponentMenu tag. This class derives from the Spawner class from Section 5.8.1 of this chapter, so we can use its Spawn() function, have it draw a Gizmo so we can see where we will be spawning, and to get access to its base class, ExtendedCustomMonoBehaviour.

```
                void OnTriggerEnter(Collider other)
                {
                        if (IsInLayerMask(other.gameObject.layer,
triggerLayerMask))
                                return;

                        Spawn(ObjectToSpawnOnTrigger.transform,
_TR.position + offsetPosition, Quaternion.identity);

                        if (onlySpawnOnce)
                                Destroy(gameObject);
                }
        }
}
```

When an object with a Rigidbody and a Collider enter this GameObject's Collider (which MUST have its IsTrigger property checked in the Inspector), the prefab in objectToSpawnOnTrigger will be spawned at this GameObject's position.

5.8.3 Timed Spawning

This TimedSpawner Component will spawn a prefab in a set amount of time. In an arena blaster game, this might be used to delay the spawning of an enemy from the start of a level, using a random delay to make the start of the level more dynamic.

```
using UnityEngine;

namespace GPC
{
        public class TimedSpawner : Spawner
        {
                public float initialSpawnDelay;
                public bool shouldRandomizeSpawnTime = true;
                public float randomDelayMax = 0.5f;
```

```
[Space]
public bool waitForCall;
private Vector3 myPos;
private Quaternion myRot;

[Space]
public Transform _prefabToSpawn;
```

The class derives from Spawner, which provides a path to the Spawn() function in ExtendedCustomMonoBehaviour and the shouldRandomizeSpawnTime variable. Unlike the Spawner class, this script uses a single prefab rather than an array – the prefab reference should be placed into the 1_prefabToSpawn field via the Inspector in Unity.

```
public override void Start()
{
        base.Start();
        if (waitForCall)
                return;

        StartSpawnTimer();
}
```

The Start() function overrides the one found in our base class, Spawner. We still want to do everything that the base class does, which is remedied with a call to base.Start(). Above, Start() looks at waitForCall to see whether or not it should just get stuck in and start spawning. Whenever waitForCall is set to true, it is assumed that you will call StartSpawnTimer() from another script rather than have it called automatically in the Start() function above.

```
public void StartSpawnTimer()
{
        float spawnTime = initialSpawnDelay;

        if (shouldRandomizeSpawnTime)
                spawnTime += Random.Range(0,
randomDelayMax);

        Invoke("SpawnAndDestroy", spawnTime);
}
```

StartSpawnTimer() starts by calculating how much time we need to wait before running our SpawnAndDestroy(). It does this by declaring a local variable named spawnTime that starts out set to the value of initialSpawnDelay. We then check to see if we need to add a random amount of time to this, looking to see if shouldRandomizeSpawnTime is true. When it is, we use Unity's random number generator in Random.Range() to get a random number between 0 (the first parameter we pass it) and randomDelayMax (the second parameter). You can adjust the maximum random number by adjusting the value in randomDelayMax via the Inspector. The random number is added to our spawnTime variable, which will now be whatever initialSpawnDelay is set to plus the random number.

With spawnTime calculated, all that is left for this function to do above is to use Invoke() to schedule a call to SpawnAndDestroy() in spawnTime seconds.

```
void SpawnAndDestroy ()
{
        Spawn(_prefabToSpawn, _TR.position,
_TR.rotation);
        Destroy(gameObject);
}
    }
}
```

Above, SpawnAndDestroy() wraps up the class. The Spawn() function from ExtendedMonoBehaviour is used here to spawn a prefab from _prefabToSpawn at the same position and rotation as the Transform of the GameObject this script is attached to.

With the prefab spawned, this script (and this GameObject) has served their purpose so we remove them from the Scene with a call to Unity's Destroy() function. Destroy() takes a reference to the GameObject you want to destroy as a parameter.

5.9 User Interface

5.9.1 CanvasManager

CanvasManager will be covered in Chapter 11, Section 11.1.

5.9.2 ScreenAndAudioFader

The ScreenAndAudioFader class mixes the functionality from two other classes – BaseSoundManager and CanvasManager – to fade in or out both a Canvas and an audio mixer at the same time. In the Blaster example game in this book, I used this class to fade out the Scene at the end of each level. The audio and visual will fade out, the next level Scene is loaded, then the audio and visuals fade back in again.

We will be looking at Audio Mixers in detail in Chapter 9, when we look at the BaseSoundManager and how to deal with audio in your games. For that reason, we will avoid listing out the code for ScreenAndAudioFader in this section because all it does it call out to those other two classes to do all the work.

5.9.3 MenuWithProfiles

This script will be covered in detail in Chapter 12, when we look at save profiles.

5.10 Utility

The Utility folder in Assets/GPC_Framework/Scripts/COMMON/UTILITY holds a host of files that do not fit into a category but could serve to be useful all the same.

5.10.1 AlignToGround

The AlignToGround class uses raycasting to find out what angle the ground underneath is and align a Transform to it. Raycasting is the process of drawing an imaginary line and finding out which Colliders it hits. It uses Unity's collision systems, so if you want something to be detected by raycasting, the GameObject must have a Collider Component attached to it. Unity's raycasting system will return a whole host of information along with a reference to the Collider(s) it finds along the raycast, such as the exact point in 3d space the line intersects the object and more.

This script also uses Unity's Quaternion.Lerp function to smooth out the alignment. The alignment speed can be adjusted via the value in the variable named smooth.

```
using System.Collections;
using System.Collections.Generic;
using UnityEngine;

namespace GPC
{
        public class AlignToGround : MonoBehaviour
```

```
                    {
                            public LayerMask mask;
                            private Transform _TR;
                            RaycastHit hit;
                            Quaternion targetRotation;

                            private int smooth = 10;

                            void Start()
                            {
                                    _TR = GetComponent<Transform>();
                            }

                            void Update()
                            {
                                    RaycastHit hit;
                                    if (Physics.Raycast(_TR.position, -Vector3.
up, out hit, 2.0f))
                                    {
                                            targetRotation = Quaternion.
FromToRotation(_TR.up, hit.normal) * _TR.rotation;
                                            _TR.rotation = Quaternion.Lerp
(_TR.rotation, targetRotation, Time.deltaTime * smooth);
                                    }
                            }
                    }
```

Above, the script starts by grabbing a reference to the Transform in the Start() function and then we are into Update():

```
void Update()
        {
                RaycastHit hit;
                if (Physics.Raycast(_TR.position, -Vector3.up,
out hit, 2.0f))
```

The Physics.Raycast() function requires that you pass in a RaycastHit object as a place to put all the information it gathers, so we declare the variable hit first for this purpose.

There are a lot of different ways you can use Physics.Raycast() – 15 different overloads to be exact – so we will not be going through all of them, just how this line works. The Unity documentation is the place for that!

In this code, we pass in a position to say where to start the ray from, followed by a Vector3 to state the direction that the ray should be drawn. We then pass in that hit RaycastHit variable from above, followed by the length of raycast we want Unity to make, and finally we pass in a LayerMask variable named mask.

LayerMasks are used by Unity as a filter to decide which Layers should be included. When we pass in a LayerMask to Physics.Raycast(), the raycasting process will filter out any GameObjects that are not on the Layers specified in the LayerMask. In the editor, the LayerMask variable – when exposed as a public variable – will appear as a dropdown menu in the Inspector. The dropdown contains a list of all Layers set up via the Layers menu (at the top of the Inspector) and it allows you to choose one or multiple Layers for the mask.

Note: Using Physics.Raycast() will only return a single Collider, but if you need to detect more than one object along the ray you should look at RaycastAll().

After gathering information from Physics.Raycast(), we can align our Transform:

```
targetRotation = Quaternion.FromToRotation(_TR.up, hit.normal) *
_TR.rotation;
```

```
                            _TR.rotation = Quaternion.Lerp
(_TR.rotation, targetRotation, Time.deltaTime * smooth);
```

Quaternion.FromToRotation takes two parameters, which are vectors, from-Direction and toDirection. It takes these two vectors and creates a rotation that would rotate the first vector to match the second. This will be our target rotation.

In the next line above, we use Quaternion.Lerp to interpolate somewhere between our Transform's current rotation and toward the new rotation we just calculated and put into the variable targetRotation. Time.deltaTime multiplied by a float named smooth will provide us with the portion value to interpolate.

5.10.2 AutomaticDestroyObject

The main use for a script that automatically destroys its GameObject might be for special effects. Particle effects such as explosions will be instantiated, their effect will play out and then they need to be destroyed.

In the example games, a short and simple class called AutomaticDestroy Object.cs is attached to a GameObject. After a set amount of time, set in the Unity editor Inspector window, the GameObject is destroyed along with any associated child objects attached to it.

The full script:

```
public class AutomaticDestroyObject : MonoBehaviour
{
        public float timeBeforeObjectDestroys;

        void Start () {
                // the function destroyGO() will be called in
timeBeforeObjectDestroys seconds
                Invoke("DestroyGO",timeBeforeObjectDestroys);
        }

        void DestroyGO () {
                // destroy this gameObject
                Destroy(gameObject);
        }
}
```

The class, which derives from MonoBehaviour, is very simple. It uses Invoke to schedule a call to the DestroyGO() function at a time set by the public variable timeBeforeObjectDestroys. It probably goes without saying that DestroyGO() takes care of destroying itself, with Destroy(gameObject).

5.10.3 AutoSpinObject

One common action you may need to do is spin an object. This may be for several reasons, the most obvious being to draw attention to pickups. By spinning the pickups, they are more obvious to the player than static which could be easily missed or ignored.

Making an object spin in Unity may be very simple but having a script to take care of this is a useful little tool to keep in the toolkit.

```
using UnityEngine;
using System.Collections;

public class AutoSpinObject : MonoBehaviour
{
```

AutoSpinObject.cs derives from MonoBehaviour, so that it can use Unity's automatic calls to the Start() and Update() functions:

```
public class AutoSpinObject : MonoBehaviour
{
```

The function is derived from MonoBehaviour, so that we can update the object rotation in an Update() function.

```
public Vector3 spinVector = new Vector3(1,0,0);
private Transform myTransform;
```

The spinVector is a three-dimensional vector that we will use to spin the object with. By using a vector, we can spin the object in any direction in the 3d space simply by changing the values this script Component uses in the Inspector window of the Unity editor. Select the GameObject that has this script attached and change the value in the Inspector to change its behavior.

```
void Start ()
{
        myTransform=transform;
}
```

As per every other script, we cache a reference to this object's Transform in the Start() function. Caching this reference will save a lot of valuable processor time throughout the game.

The Update() function simply rotates the Transform, multiplying the spin-Vector variable by Time.deltaTime to ensure that the rotation is framerate independent and time based:

```
void Update () {
        myTransform.Rotate (spinVector*Time.deltaTime);
}
}
```

5.10.4 FaceCamera

The FaceCamera script Component uses Unity's built-in LookAt function to make a GameObject face toward the main Camera in the Scene. Note that this uses Camera.main to find the camera, which means it relies on the camera GameObject's tag being set to MainCamera for it to work.

5.10.5 LookAtCamera

The LookAtTransform script uses Unity's built-in LookAt function to make a GameObject face toward another Transform (set as target on the Component via the Inspector).

5.10.6 PretendFriction

The easiest way to move objects around in Unity is to simply apply forces to your rigidbodies. By using Rigidbody.AddForce and perhaps a multiplier based on Input.GetAxis or something similar, it is quite easy to get objects moving around but the only way to have them come to a stop is either to have them make friction against something else in the game world or to change drag values on the

Rigidbody. This may not always be an ideal solution and can present challenges when trying to control the turning behavior of objects floating in space or perhaps even character controllers. To help with controlling sideways slip, this simple PretendFriction.cs script can help.

```
using UnityEngine;
namespace GPC
{
        [AddComponentMenu("CSharpBookCode/Utility/Pretend
Friction")]

        public class PretendFriction : MonoBehaviour
        {
                private Rigidbody _RB;
                private Transform _TR;
                private float myMass;
                private float slideSpeed;
                private Vector3 velo;
                private Vector3 flatVelo;
                private Vector3 myRight;
                private Vector3 TEMPvec3;

                public float theGrip = 100f;
```

The script derives from MonoBehaviour, to tap into the Start() and FixedUpdate() system calls. Above, note that you can change the value of the variable theGrip to alter how much this script will control sliding.

```
        void Start ()
        {
                // cache some references to our RigidBody, mass and
transform
                _RB = GetComponent<Rigidbody>();
                myMass = _RB.mass;
                _TR = transform;
}
```

The Start() function caches the Rigidbody, amount of mass on the Rigidbody and the Transform.

```
                void FixedUpdate ()
                {
                // grab the values we need to calculate grip
                myRight = _TR.right;

                // calculate flat velocity
                velo = _RB.velocity;
                flatVelo.x = velo.x;
                flatVelo.y = 0;
                flatVelo.z = velo.z;

                // calculate how much we are sliding
                slideSpeed = Vector3.Dot(myRight, flatVelo);

                // build a new vector to compensate for the sliding
                TEMPvec3 = myRight * (-slideSpeed * myMass * theGrip);

                // apply the correctional force to the RigidBody
                _RB.AddForce(TEMPvec3 * Time.deltaTime);
                }
        }
}
```

The FixedUpdate() function will calculate how much an object is sliding – to do this, it finds how much sideways movement the object is making (to the right relative to the Transform's rotation) – to find out how much slip is happening.

5.10.7 TimerClass

Our timer system is named TimerClass.cs:

```
using UnityEngine;
using System.Collections;

namespace GPC
{
        [AddComponentMenu("CSharpBookCode/Common/Timer class")]

        public class TimerClass : ScriptableObject
        {
                public bool isTimerRunning = false;
                private float timeElapsed = 0.0f;
                private float currentTime = 0.0f;
                private float lastTime = 0.0f;
                private float timeScaleFactor = 1.0f; // <-- If you
need to scale time, change this!
                private string timeString;
                private string hour;
                private string minutes;
                private string seconds;
                private string mills;

                private int aHour;
                private int aMinute;
                private int aSecond;
                private int aMillis;
                private int tmp;
                private int aTime;

                private GameObject callback;

                public void UpdateTimer()
                {
```

In this script, we will only update time whenever the time is requested. Although there may be cases where the timer would need to be updated constantly, we only need to do this on demand for the games in this book. For the example games, we do not derive the class from MonoBehaviour and we call UpdateTimer() from another script; the Game Manager. If you want this script to update automatically, we will outline a method to modify the script to work like that at the end of this section.

The timer works by having a variable called currentTime that stores the amount of time since the timer was started. currentTime starts at zero, then UpdateTimer() calculates out how much time goes by between updates and adds it to currentTime. The value of currentTime can then be parsed into minutes, seconds, and milliseconds and returned as a nice, tidy formatted string in the GetFormattedTime() function of the TimerClass class.

UpdateTimer() will be the only function that updates the time system:

```
        public void UpdateTimer()
        {
                // calculate the time elapsed since the last
Update()
                timeElapsed = Mathf.Abs(Time.
realtimeSinceStartup - lastTime);
```

```
                // if the timer is running, we add the time
elapsed to the current time (advancing the timer)
                if (isTimerRunning)
                {
                        currentTime += timeElapsed *
timeScaleFactor;
                }


                // store the current time so that we can use
it on the next update
                lastTime = Time.realtimeSinceStartup;
            }
```

Above, the function works like this:

1. We calculate timeElapsed by taking the current time (Time.realtime-SinceStartup) and subtracting the value of lastTime from it – lastTime is set to the value of Time.realtimeSinceStartup at the end of this function, which means lastTime will keep its value until the next time UpdateTimer runs. As it keeps its value, it acts as a timestamp for the last time Unity reached the end of the function. By subtracting this time-stamp from the current time, we know exactly how much time has gone since UpdateTimer() last ran.

2. If the timer is running (i.e. The Boolean variable isTimerRunning is set to true) then we add timeElapsed to our currentTime variable. currentTime is the total amount of time that has passed since the timer started. When we add timeElapsed to currentTime, we also multiply it by a timeScaleFactor. This allows you to scale the time system, which is useful for when your game updates are set to run at a different time scale with Time.timeScale.

realtimeSinceStartup is used for good reason. By using realtimeSinceS-tartup, the game can do whatever it likes to the Time.timeScale value (speeding up or slowing down Unity physics updates) and realtimeSinceStartup will still provide unscaled time values. If Time.time were used, it would be affected by the timeScale and would fail to provide real time values if the physics timing (Time. timeScale) were set to anything other than 1.

Note: One commonly used method of pausing Unity games is to set Time.time Scale to 0, which would stop a timer that didn't use Time.realtimeSinceStartup. If you use Time.timeScale to pause the game, you will also need to be used to start and stop the timer as it will be unaffected by Time.timeScale.

Next, the StartTimer() function is used to start the timer:

```
public void StartTimer ()
    {
            // set up initial variables to start the timer
            isTimerRunning=true;
            lastTime=Time.realtimeSinceStartup;
    }
```

Above, the Boolean variable isTimerRunning is set to true when StartTimer() is called. isTimerRunning is used to say whether or not to update currentTime in the UpdateTimer() function earlier in the script. lastTime also needs to be reset when we start the timer, just in case the timer had previously been running. If the timer had been running, we do this to make sure that any time 'in-between' the timer being stopped and the timer starting up again, is not be counted.

```
        public void StopTimer ()
        {
// stop the timer
            isTimerRunning = false;

            // carry out an update to the timer
            UpdateTimer();
        }
```

In StopTimer() above, isTimerRunning is set to false, which stops UpdateTimer() from adding any extra time to the currentTime variable. To make sure we count the last bit of time correctly, a quick call to UpdateTimer() is made at the end of the function above.

If there is ever a need to reset the timer, we need to refresh the main variables to default states. In the ResetTimer() function; timeElapsed, lastTime and currentTime are reset:

```
public void ResetTimer ()
        {
            // resetTimer will set the timer back to zero
            timeElapsed = 0.0f;
            currentTime = 0.0f;
lastTime = Time.realtimeSinceStartup;

// carry out an update to the timer
            UpdateTimer();
        }
```

Above, we reset all the time variables to their starting states and call UpdateTimer() to start the timer process again.

Whenever we need to display the time on the screen, there is a good chance that we will need it to be formatted in a way like minutes: seconds: milliseconds. The GetFormattedTime function takes this value and breaks it up into the units we need, then puts together a nicely formatted string and returns it:

```
public string GetFormattedTime ()
        {
            // carry out an update to the timer so it is 'up to
date'
            UpdateTimer();
```

Above, GetFormattedTime() is called first. As mentioned earlier, the timer does not update itself – it is a lazy updater in that it only updates when we ask it so before providing the formatted time this ensures that the calculations are up-to-date.

From there on we are simply doing the math to get the minutes, seconds and milliseconds values from currentTime:

```
            // grab hours
            aHour = (int)currentTime / 3600;
            aHour = aHour % 24;
            // grab minutes

            aMinute = (int)currentTime / 60;
```

```
            aMinute = aMinute % 60;
            // grab seconds
            aSecond = (int)currentTime % 60;

            // grab milliseconds
            aMillis = (int)(currentTime * 100) % 100;
```

After minutes, seconds, and milliseconds values have been calculated and stored in the integer variables aMinute, aSecond, and aMillis, three new strings called seconds, minutes and mills are built from them:

```
            // format strings for individual mm/ss/mills
            tmp = (int)aSecond;
            seconds = tmp.ToString("D2"); // ToString()
formats .. in this case, D followed by how many numbers

            tmp = (int)aMinute;
            minutes = tmp.ToString("D2");

            tmp = (int)aHour;
            hour = tmp.ToString("D2");

            tmp = (int)aMillis;
            mills = tmp.ToString("D2");

            // pull together a formatted string to return
            timeString = minutes + ":" + seconds + ":" +
mills;
```

In C#, you can convert numbers to strings with the ToString() function. Something great about ToString() is that you can also pass in a format string. The format string takes the form of a letter followed by an integer number. Above, we use the format string D2 to tell ToString() to use two digits, which will convert our times into a neat format ready to display. Note that you can set as many digits as you like, simply by changing the number in the format string. For more information on format strings, you can find a full breakdown and a full list of all of the available formatting options online at Microsoft's .NET Standard numeric format strings page: https://docs.microsoft.com/en-us/dotnet/standard/base-types/standard-numeric-format-strings

Once the individual parts of the formatted time string are ready, we put them all together into a final timeString and return it at the end of the function, like this:

```
            // pull together a formatted string to return
            timeString=minutes+":"+seconds+":"+mills;

        return timeString;
    }
```

At the very end of the script, a GetTime() function provides a way for other scripts to process the value of currentTime:

```
public int GetTime ()
        {
            // remember to call UpdateTimer() before trying to
use this function, otherwise the time value will
            // not be up to date
        return (int)(currentTime);
        }
    }
}
```

GetTime() just returns the value of the variable currentTime so that you can take care of formatting or processing in another script.

5.10.7.1 Modifying the Timer to Update Automatically

If you want to use this and have the timer to update automatically, you could change the class declaration:

```
public class TimerClass
```

So that the class inherits from MonoBehaviour:

```
public class TimerClass : MonoBehaviour
```

Then, change the name of the UpdateTimer() function to Update(), which will be automatically called by the engine each frame.

5.10.8 WaypointsController

This script is so big and important that it gets its own chapter! Check out Chapter 8 to see how this script fits together and how it should be used in your own games.

▉ 5.11 Weapons

In the Weapons folder are four scripts: AutoShooter.cs, ProjectileController.cs, StandardSlotWeaponController.cs and ThreeWayShooter.cs. These scripts and how the weapons system can be used will be covered in full, in Chapter 7 of this book.

6 Player Movement Controllers

This chapter is all about movement. We build the scripts that will determine the way that a player moves and behaves in the physics world. It is entirely focused on movement.

In this chapter, we look at three different movement controllers:

1. 3D humanoid character
   It is assumed that this control script will be able to do humanoid things, such as run forwards, backwards and turn around.

2. Wheeled vehicle
   The vehicle controller utilizes Unity's Wheel Colliders to work toward a realistic physics simulation. There will be no gearing, but the vehicle will be able to accelerate, brake or steer left and right.

3. 2D Platform Player
   This 2D platform character controller offers left/right and jump functionality with basic ground detection.

You can find all of the scripts for this chapter in the folder Assets/GPC_Framework/Scripts/BASE/PLAYER/MOVEMENT.

▌ 6.1 Humanoid Character

The human control script uses Unity's character controller and is based on the third person character controller provided by Unity as a part of the game engine. This scripts original behavior was to move the player based on the direction of the camera and, here, it has been adapted to work either directionally or based on its own rotation by toggling the moveDirectionally Boolean variable to true or false.

The   BasePlayerCharacterController   class   derives   from ExtendedCustomMonoBehaviour, as described in Chapter 4 of this book.

```
using UnityEngine;
namespace GPC
{
        [AddComponentMenu("CSharpBookCode/Base/Character/Base Player
Character Controller")]

        public class BasePlayerCharacterController :
ExtendedCustomMonoBehaviour
        {
                [Header("Movement")]
                // The speed when walking
                public float walkSpeed = 7.0f;

                // after runAfterSeconds of walking we run with runSpeed
                public float runSpeed = 12.0f;
                public float speedSmoothing = 10.0f;
                public float rotateSpeed = 500.0f;
                public float runAfterSeconds = 3.0f;
                public bool moveDirectionally;

                // The current x-z move speed
                private float moveSpeed = 0.0f;

                // The current move direction in x-z
                private Vector3 moveDirection = Vector3.zero;

                // When did the user start walking (Used for going
into run after a while)
                private float walkTimeStart = 0.0f;

                // The last collision flags returned from
controller.Move
                private CollisionFlags collisionFlags;

                [Space]
                public float horz;
                public float vert;
                public bool isRespawning;
                public bool isFinished;
                public BaseInputController _inputController;

                private CharacterController _charController;
                private Vector3 targetDirection;
                private float curSmooth;
                private float targetSpeed;
                private float curSpeed;
                private Vector3 forward;
                private Vector3 right;

                public virtual void Start()
                {
                        Init();
                }
```

Above, the Init() function is called from Start(). As with many of the scripts in this book, Init() contains set up code.

```
                public virtual void Init()
                {
                        moveDirection = transform.
TransformDirection(Vector3.forward);
```

```
                        _charController =
GetComponent<CharacterController>();
                        GetComponents();

                        _RB = GetComponent<Rigidbody>();
                        _inputController =
GetComponent<BaseInputController>();
                }
```

·   Above, moveDirection is a Vector3 used later in the script to tell the character controller which direction to move in. Here in the Init() function, it is given the world forward vector as its default value.

    Init() then calls GetComponents(), which is a function in ExtendedCustomMonoBehaviour.cs (which this class derives from) that will grab references to the Transform and GameObject this script is attached to. We also grab the Rigidbody (as this script relies on physics to work) and stores the reference in the variable _RB. _inputController is populated with a reference to a BaseInputController Component (or a Component that derives from BaseInputController) so we can process input from the user.

    The BaseInputController class is used to provide input from the player to move the character around and it should be attached as a Component to the same GameObject as this script. BaseInputController.cs is provided as part of the framework for this book. You can use this script for input, or you could replace the input system with whatever you need just as long as you feed the variables named horz and vert with horizontal and vertical input values as floats.

```
        public void SetUserInput( bool setInput )
        {
                canControl= setInput;
        }
```

    Above, the SetUserInput() function is used to set the variable canControl, which is used to check whether user input should be disabled or not. This is just a nicer way of allowing other scripts to enable or disable user input.

    Having input separated into a single GetInput() function should make it easy to customize inputs if required. We deal with calling to update the input in the GetInput() function, next:

```
        public virtual void GetInput()
        {
                if (isFinished || isRespawning || !canControl)
                {
                        horz = 0;
                        vert = 0;
                        return;
                }
```

    Above, the start of GetInput() checks that we are supposed to be controlling the player. If not, the horizontal and vertical inputs for the character controller are locked at zero and we drop out of this function. Otherwise, we need to get the inputs from the BaseInputController Component:

```
                if (!canControl)
                        return;

                horz = _inputController.GetHorizontal();
                vert = _inputController.GetVertical();
        }
```

Above, before getting input from the user we make sure that canControl is true – meaning the user can control it – and drop out if this is not the case. Input scripts in this book will return values in the correct range so all we need to do is call the functions to return the input values into horz and vert.

```
public virtual void LateUpdate()
{
        if(canControl)
                GetInput();

}
```

LateUpdate() is used to call for an update to the input Boolean variables via the GetInput() script. Unity advises that LateUpdate as the best place to check for keyboard entry, after the engine has carried out its own input updates.

```
void UpdateSmoothedMovementDirection ()
{
        if(moveDirectionally)
                UpdateDirectionalMovement();
        else
                UpdateRotationMovement();

}
```

This script can function both to move directionally as well as rotationally, by setting moveDirectionally to true or false. Whenever moveDirectionally is set to false, pressing the left or right buttons will rotate the player left or right around its y axis. Pressing the up button will walk forwards along the player's z-axis and pressing down will move it backwards.

In the UpdateSmoothedMovementDirection() script, the moveDirectionally variable is checked to determine which type of movement function to call to update player movement:

The types of movement are split into two separate functions, which are called above depending on the state of moveDirectionally.

```
void UpdateDirectionalMovement()
{
        // find target direction
        targetDirection= horz * Vector3.right;
        targetDirection+= vert * Vector3.forward;
```

Directional movement uses the world x and z axis to decide which way to move; that is, the player moves along the world x or z axis based on the button pressed by the player. Above, the UpdateDirectionalMovement() function starts by taking the horizontal and vertical user inputs (from the variables horz and vert) and multiplying them by either a vector that points along the axis that we want horz or vert to affect. The targetDirection variable is a Vector3 that encompasses both vertical and horizontal movement into a single vector representing the direction our player will move in.

The targetDirection variable will be zero when there is no user input, so before calculating any movement amounts, we check that movement is intended first:

```
if (targetDirection != Vector3.zero)
{
        moveDirection =
Vector3.RotateTowards(moveDirection, targetDirection, rotateSpeed
* Mathf.Deg2Rad * Time.deltaTime, 1000);
        moveDirection = moveDirection.normalized;
}
```

Above, moveDirection will be used to move the player around. Its value comes from an interpolation between the current value of moveDirection and the targetDirection calculated earlier from the user inputs. This vector is then multiplied by rotateSpeed then converted into radians and again multiplied by Time.deltaTime to make the rotation speed time based. Vector3.RotateTowards is used to make the turn, which ensures that the rotation ends in the exact specified position.

The moveDirection vector is then normalized, to remove any magnitude from the equation.

The next part of the BasePlayerCharacterController class deals with speed:

```
            // Smooth the speed based on the current target
direction
            curSmooth= speedSmoothing * Time.deltaTime;
```

The variable curSmooth will be used further in the script, to decide how long it takes for the movement speed of the player to go from zero to max speed.

```
            // Choose target speed
            //* We want to support analog input but make sure
you can't walk faster diagonally than just forward or sideways
            targetSpeed= Mathf.Min(targetDirection.magnitude,
1.0f);
```

The variable targetSpeed is capped to a maximum of 1. To do this, Mathf. Min is fed the magnitude of the targetDirection and 1. Whichever is least will go into targetSpeed.

This script allows for two states of movement; running and walking. The transition between running and walking is timed – the character will begin walking and continue walking until vertical input is applied for more than (in seconds) the value of runAfterSeconds.

```
            if (Time.time - runAfterSeconds > walkTimeStart)
            {
```

Time.time is used above to keep track of how long the player has been walking, which means that Time.timeScale will affect it (if the game is paused or time is scaled, this timing will remain relative to the time scale).

```
                targetSpeed *= runSpeed;
            }
            else
            {
```

walkSpeed is a multiplier for the targetSpeed when the player is in its walking state:

```
                targetSpeed *= walkSpeed;
            }

        moveSpeed = Mathf.Lerp(moveSpeed, targetSpeed,
curSmooth);

            // Reset walk time start when we slow down
            if (moveSpeed < walkSpeed * 0.3f)
                walkTimeStart = Time.time;
```

moveSpeed was used earlier in the function, but it only gets calculated here because it relies on targetSpeed and curSmooth to have been worked out. moveSpeed is the result of an interpolation (using Mathf.Lerp) between its current value and the variable targetSpeed over an amount set by curSmooth.

When moveSpeed drops below the threshold set by walkSpeed (i.e. when the player releases the move input to slow movement down) walkTimeStart gets reset to Time.time to allow the walk to start again the next time the player moves.

The final part of the UpdateDirectionalMovement() function deals with move direction:

```
// Calculate actual motion
    Vector3 movement= moveDirection * moveSpeed;
    movement *= Time.deltaTime;

    // Move the controller
    collisionFlags = _charController.Move(movement);
```

The variable movement takes moveDirection and multiplies it by move-Speed, then on the next line the result is multiplied by Time.deltaTime to provide a time-based movement vector with magnitude suitable for passing into the character controller. When the controller is told to Move (with the movement vector passed in as a parameter) it will return a bitmask called CollisionFlags. When a collision occurs with the character controller, the collisionFlags variable may be used to tell where the collision happened; the collisionFlags mask represents None, Sides, Above or Below. Although the collision data is not used in this version of BaseTopDown.cs, it is implemented for future functionality.

```
    // Set rotation to the move direction
    _TR.rotation = Quaternion.LookRotation(moveDirection);
}
```

In the last line of the function above, Quaternion.LookRotation creates a rotation towards moveDirection and sets _TR.rotation to it – making the player face in the correct direction for the movement.

```
    void UpdateRotationMovement ()
    {
        _TR.Rotate(0, horz * rotateSpeed * Time.deltaTime, 0);
```

The second type of movement for this class is rotational. UpdateRotationalMovement() uses a combination of Transform.Rotate and the character controller's SimpleMove function to provide a control system that rotates the player on its y-axis and moves along its z-axis (in the case of the humanoid, this is forward and backward walking or running).

For horizontal input, the variable horz is multiplied by the variable rotateSpeed and multiplied by Time.deltaTime to be used as the rotation for the player's rotation around its y axis. Vertical input (stored in vert) is dealt with next, as vert multiplied by moveSpeed makes up the speed to traverse the player's z-axis at.

Note that moveSpeed is calculated further down in the function, so don't worry about that right away – just keep in mind that moveSpeed is the desired speed of movement:

```
    curSpeed = moveSpeed * vert;
```

CharacterController.SimpleMove moves a character controller; considering the velocity set by the vector passed into it. In this line, the vector provided to SimpleMove is the player's forward vector multiplied by curSpeed:

```
_ charController.SimpleMove( _ TR.forward * curSpeed );
```

targetDirection is a Vector3 type variable that determines how much, based on the vert input variable, we would like to move; even though its vector is only used in calculating for its magnitude later in the function:

```
        // Target direction (the max we want to move, used
for calculating target speed)
        targetDirection= vert * _TR.forward;
```

When the speed changes, rather than changing the animation instantly from slow to fast the variable curSmooth is used to transition speed smoothly. The variable speedSmoothing is intended to be set in the Unity inspector window and it is then multiplied by Time.deltaTime to make the speed transition time based:

```
        // Smooth the speed based on the current target direction
        float curSmooth= speedSmoothing * Time.deltaTime;
```

The next line of the script caps the targetSpeed at 1. Taking the target-Direction vector from earlier, targetSpeed takes a maximum value of 1 or, if it is less than 1, the value held by targetDirection.magnitude:

```
        // Choose target speed
        //* We want to support analog input but make sure
you can't walk faster diagonally than just forward or sideways
        targetSpeed= Mathf.Min(targetDirection.magnitude, 1.0f);
```

The rest of the function transitions between walking and running in the same way that UpdateDirectionalMovement() function did earlier in this section:

```
        // adjust move speed
        if (Time.time - runAfterSeconds > walkTimeStart)
        {
                targetSpeed *= runSpeed;
        }
        else
        {
                targetSpeed *= walkSpeed;
        }

        moveSpeed = Mathf.Lerp(moveSpeed, targetSpeed,
curSmooth);

        // Reset walk time start when we slow down
        if (moveSpeed < walkSpeed * 0.3f)
                walkTimeStart = Time.time;
    }
```

Above, we again change the targetSpeed to either runSpeed or walkSpeed.

moveSpeed lerps between the current speed and targetSpeed, and there is a check to see if the moveSpeed variable drops below a third of walkSpeed to tell us when the player is moving so slowly that we can reset walkTimeStart.

Next up, the Update() function:

```
    public void Update()
    {
        ApplyGravity();
```

```
            if (!canControl)
            {
                    // kill all inputs if not controllable.
                    Input.ResetInputAxes();
            }
            UpdateSmoothedMovementDirection();
    }
```

Above, Update() begins with a call to stop input when canControl is set to false. More than anything, this is designed to bring the player to a stop when canControl is set at the end of the game. When the game ends, rather than inputs continuing and the player being left to run around behind the game over message, inputs are set to zero.

UpdateSmoothedMovementDirection() calls one of two movement update scripts, based on the value of the Boolean variable moveDirectionally.

```
            void ApplyGravity()
            {
                    // apply some gravity to the character
controller
                    float gravity = -9.81f * Time.deltaTime;
                    _charController.Move(new Vector3(0, gravity, 0));
            }
```

Above, we apply gravity to the character controller – by default, Unity does not add gravity to this type of object. We do this just by calling Move() and passing in a Vector3 of the direction of gravity.

At the end of the class, GetSpeed(), GetDirection and IsMoving() are utility functions provided for other scripts to have access to a few of the character's properties:

```
      public float GetSpeed ()
      {
              return moveSpeed;
      }
              public Vector3 GetDirection ()
      {
              return moveDirection;
      }
              public bool IsMoving ()
      {
              return (Mathf.Abs(vert) + Mathf.Abs(horz) > 0.5f);
      }
      }
}
```

GetSpeed() and GetDirection() return their associated variables. IsMoving() takes the absolutes values of vert and horz to find out if the player is moving faster than 0.5f.

▌ 6.2 Wheeled Vehicle

The BaseWheeledVehicle.cs script relies on one of Unity's built-in WheelCollider system. WheelCollider components are added to GameObjects positioned in place of the wheels supporting the car body. The WheelCollider components themselves do not have any visual form and meshes representing wheels are not aligned automatically. WheelColliders are physics simulations; they take care of the physics actions such as suspension and wheel friction.

The math behind the friction system is beyond the scope of this book, though Unity documentation has coverage of the subject on the WheelCollider page of the online help.

BaseWheeledVehicle uses four WheelColliders for drive, and orientation of wheel meshes is dealt with by a script called BaseWheelAlignment.cs explained later in the chapter.

The class derives from ExtendedCustomMonoBehaviour (as discussed in Chapter 4 of this book) which adds a few commonly used variables.

BaseWheeledVehicle.cs starts like this:

```
using UnityEngine;
namespace GPC
    {
        [AddComponentMenu("CSharpBookCode/Base/Vehicles/Wheeled
Vehicle Controller")]
        [RequireComponent(typeof(Rigidbody))]
```

Above, we start the class with the usual reference to UnityEngine, and then add a menu item for this Component. Having a Rigidbody Component on the same GameObject this script is attached to is important. The next tag (those lines wrapped in square brackets are what Unity refers to as tags) is a RequireComponent. This will check to see if a Rigidbody is attached to our GameObject and will add one, if needed. We then set the namespace that all the framework comes under, our GPC namespace.

Now into the class:

```
    public class BaseWheeledVehicle : ExtendedCustomMonoBehaviour
        {
            public bool isLocked;

            [Header("Wheel Colliders")]

            public WheelCollider _frontWheelLeft;
            public WheelCollider _frontWheelRight;
            public WheelCollider _rearWheelLeft;
            public WheelCollider _rearWheelRight;
```

We use a Boolean variable named isLocked to hold a vehicle in place. In the example game, this is used to stop the play driving off before the 3,2,1 count completes at the start of the game.

Each WheelCollider variable is named based on its intended position; frontWheelLeft, frontWheelRight, rearWheelLeft and rearWheelRight. For the script to function correctly, WheelColliders need to be referenced (dragged and dropped) into the correct variables in the Unity Inspector window on the vehicle script.

```
    public BaseInputController _ inputController;
```

The default input system is set to use the BaseInputController class from this book's framework. You can, of course, switch out input for whatever you like. We use the _inputController variable to talk to BaseInputController and find out what is going on with the inputs each update, which happens further down in this class, in the GetInputs() function.

```
            [Header("Steer settings")]
            public float steerMax = 30f;
            public float accelMax = 5000f;
            public float brakeMax = 5000f;
```

```
[System.NonSerialized]
public float steer = 0f;
[System.NonSerialized]
public float motor = 0f;
[System.NonSerialized]
public float brake = 0f;

[Space]
public float wheelToGroundCheckHeight = 0.5f;

[Space]
public bool fakeBrake;
public float fakeBrakeDivider = 0.95f;

[Space]
public bool turnHelp;
public float turnHelpAmount = 10f;

public bool isGrounded;

[System.NonSerialized]
public float mySpeed;

[System.NonSerialized]
public Vector3 velo;

[Header("Audio Settings")]

public AudioSource _engineSoundSource;
public float audioPitchOffset = 0.5f;
```

Most of the other variables in here will be covered further on in the script, as we break it down, so we skip to the Start() function. Start()is called by the engine automatically. It calls the Init() function, which begins by caching references to commonly used objects:

```
public virtual void Start ()
{
        Init ();
}

public virtual void Init ()
{
        // cache the usual suspects
        _RB = GetComponent<Rigidbody>();
        _GO = gameObject;
        _TR = transform;
```

Next up, we grab a reference to the input controller Component attached to this GameObject and then set the center of mass of our Rigidbody:

```
_inputController = GetComponent<BaseInputController>();
_RB.centerOfMass= new Vector3(0,-1f,0);
```

The center of mass can be set on a rigidbody to change the way it behaves in the physics simulation. The further the center of mass is from the center of the rigidbody, the more it will affect the physics behavior. Setting the center of mass down at –1 helps make the vehicle stable and stops the vehicle from toppling over when going around corners.

```
// see if we can find an engine sound source, if we need to
if (_engineSoundSource == null)
{
```

```
        _engineSoundSource = _GO.GetComponent<AudioSource>();
    }
}
```

Above, if no engine sound source has been set up via the Inspector window of the Unity editor, the script tries to find it with a call to GameObject. GetComponent(). The sound source will be stored in engineSoundSource and used solely for engine sound effects.

As with all the movement controllers, SetUserInput (next) sets a flag to decide whether inputs should be used to drive the vehicle:

```
    public void SetUserInput( bool setInput )
    {
        canControl= setInput;
    }
```

Unlike other movement controllers from this book, this one introduces a lock state:

```
public void SetLock(bool lockState)
{
    isLocked = lockState;
}
```

The lock state is for holding the vehicle in place without affecting its y-axis. This differs from just disabling user input as it adds physical constraints to the physics object to hold it still (its purpose being to hold the vehicle during the counting in at the start of a race or other similar scenario).

```
    public virtual void LateUpdate()
    {
        if(canControl)
            GetInput();
        UpdateEngineAudio();
    }
```

Above, LateUpdate() starts by checking for input via the GetInput() function, when canControl is set to true. Next, UpdateEngineAudio() is called to update the pitch of the engine sound based on the engine speed.

```
public virtual void FixedUpdate()
{
        UpdatePhysics();
        DoFakeBrake();
        CheckGround();
}
```

All of the physics code is called, above, from a call to UpdatePhysics() in FixedUpdate(). We call out to a braking function DoFakeBrake() and CheckGround() to check to see if the vehicle is on the ground.

```
    public virtual void UpdatePhysics()
    {
    CheckLock();
```

CheckLock() is called first, which holds the vehicle in place when the lock is on (when isLocked is true) – ideal for holding vehicles in place at the start of a race!

```
                    // work out a flat velocity
                    velo = _RB.velocity;
                    velo =
transform.InverseTransformDirection(_RB.velocity);

                    // work out our current forward speed
                    mySpeed = velo.z;
```

Above, the variable velo is set to hold the velocity of our vehicle rigidbody. The next line converts that velocity to local coordinate space, so that we get values for how fast the vehicle is moving along each of its axis. Our vehicle's forward speed is along the z axis and sideways along the x. We take that z axis velocity and put into the variable mySpeed so that we know how fast our vehicle is moving.

mySpeed is used the next section, where we simulate a reverse gear when the vehicle is moving below an arbitrary speed:

```
                    // if we're moving slow, we reverse motorTorque and remove
brakeTorque so that the car will reverse
            if( mySpeed<2 )
            {
                    // that is, if we're pressing down the brake key
(making brake>0)
                    if( brake>0 )
                    {
                            rearWheelLeft.motorTorque = -brakeMax * brake;
                            rearWheelRight.motorTorque = -brakeMax * brake;
```

Above, bear in mind that this section of code is to simulate a reverse gear. mySpeed is checked to see if its value is less than 2. When the speed is this slow and the brake key is held down, brakeTorque is no longer applied to the wheels and instead of brake torque, a reverse amount of the maximum amount of brake torque (brakeMax) is applied to make the vehicle move backwards.

```
                    rearWheelLeft.brakeTorque = 0;
                    rearWheelRight.brakeTorque = 0;
```

In reverse mode, zero brakeTorque will be applied (by the code above) to the WheelColliders so that the vehicle is free to move backward. Although braking is dealt with above, we deal with the reverse motor further in the script.

```
                    frontWheelLeft.steerAngle = steerMax * steer;
                    frontWheelRight.steerAngle = steerMax * steer;
```

When the vehicle is reversing, steering is applied in reverse too, just like a real car.

```
                    // drop out of this function before applying the
'regular' non-reversed values to the wheels
                    return;
            }
}
```

If reverse conditions have been applied to the WheelColliders, this function drops out before the regular (forward) values are applied.

```
        if (turnHelp)
                _RB.AddTorque(Vector3.up * steer * turnHelpAmount *
_RB.mass);
```

6. Player Movement Controllers

Just using the wheels to steer the car is sometimes enough, but if you are working on something more arcade you will probably need to apply some extra turning force to get the car to feel less realistic and more fun. The turnHelp Boolean variable can be set on or off in the Inspector and you can adjust the turnHelpAmount to get a cool effect.

In the code above, Unity's AddTorque function is used to multiply an up vector by steer, turnHelpAmount and the rigidbody's mass. In the example racing game for this book, a turnHelpAmount of 2 is a good value for arcade physics.

Next up, we apply regular (forward) values to the WheelColliders:

```
    // apply regular movement values to the wheels
    rearWheelLeft.motorTorque = accelMax * motor;
    rearWheelRight.motorTorque = accelMax * motor;

    rearWheelLeft.brakeTorque = brakeMax * brake;
    rearWheelRight.brakeTorque = brakeMax * brake;

    frontWheelLeft.steerAngle = steerMax * steer;
    frontWheelRight.steerAngle = steerMax * steer;
}
```

Above, we tell the WheelColliders how to move. The motor, brake and steer values will be set by the GetInput() function later in this script.

```
    public void DoFakeBrake()
    {
        if (isGrounded && brake > 0 && fakeBrake && mySpeed > 0)
        {
            tempVEC = _RB.velocity;
            tempVEC.x = tempVEC.x * fakeBrakeDivider;
            tempVEC.z = tempVEC.z * fakeBrakeDivider;
            _RB.velocity = tempVEC;
        }
    }
```

Braking with WheelColliders relies on friction and the wheels relationship to the ground below them. The main issue with this is – without a lot of work – traction is easily lost, and it can be hard to get the vehicle to stop. Even more so if you are trying to make an arcade racer rather than a realistic simulation. To get around that, this script includes the DoFakeBrake() function above, which reduces the vehicles velocity values to slow down the vehicle faster. To adjust the effect, you can change the value of fakeBrakeDivider in the Inspector on the GameObject, or you can turn it on or off with the setting of the fakeBrake Boolean.

This enhanced braking system will only be applied when the vehicle is on the ground, so it relies on the isGrounded Boolean set by the CheckGround() function coming up next:

```
    public void CheckGround()
    {
        bool FLGrounded = false;
        bool FRGrounded = false;
        bool RLGrounded = false;
        bool RRGrounded = false;

        if (Physics.Raycast(_frontWheelLeft.
transform.position, Vector3.down, wheelToGroundCheckHeight))
            FLGrounded = true;
```

```
                        if (Physics.Raycast(_frontWheelRight.
transform.position, Vector3.down, wheelToGroundCheckHeight))
                                FRGrounded = true;

                        if (Physics.Raycast(_rearWheelLeft.transform.
position, Vector3.down, wheelToGroundCheckHeight))
                                RLGrounded = true;

                        if (Physics.Raycast(_rearWheelRight.
transform.position, Vector3.down, wheelToGroundCheckHeight))
                                RRGrounded = true;

                if (FLGrounded && FRGrounded && RLGrounded &&
                RRGrounded)
                {
                        isGrounded = true;
                }
                else
                {
                        isGrounded = false;
                }
        }
```

When wheels are off the ground, our enhanced braking and turn helper code needs to be disabled to avoid steering or braking in mid-air. To detect the ground, the function above uses Unity's Raycasting function to cast a ray straight down from the center of each WheelCollider. A raycast distance value is used, held in the float WheelToGroundCheckHeight. Individual Boolean flags are set for each wheel's grounded state. Those flags are checked at the end of the function to see if all of them are true – if so, we know that all four wheels are on the ground so isGrounded gets set to true. Otherwise, isGrounded is set to false.

```
        public void CheckLock()
        {
            if (isLocked)
            {
                // control is locked out and we should be stopped
                steer = 0;
                brake = 0;
                motor = 0;
                // hold our rigidbody in place (but allow the Y to move
so the car may drop to the ground if it is not exactly matched to
the terrain)
                Vector3 tempVEC = myBody.velocity;
                tempVEC.x = 0;
                tempVEC.z = 0;
                myBody.velocity = tempVEC;
            }
        }
```

The CheckLock() function, above, looks to see if the Boolean variable isLocked is set to true, then when it is it freezes all inputs to zero and zeroes x and z velocities of the vehicle's rigidbody. The y velocity is left as is, so that gravity will still apply to the vehicle when it is being held in place. This is important at the start of a race when the vehicle is being held until the 3,2,1 counting in finishes. If the velocity along the y-axis were zeroed too, the car would float just above its resting place against the ground until the race started when it would drop down some as gravity is applied.

steer, motor and brake are the main float variables used for applying to the vehicle to move it around. The function below, GetInput() gets values from the inputs set by the default input system:

```
public virtual void GetInput()
{
            // calculate steering amount
            steer = Mathf.Clamp(_inputController.GetHorizontal(),
-1, 1);
            // how much accelerator?
            motor = Mathf.Clamp(_inputController.GetVertical(), 0, 1);
            // how much brake?
            brake = -1 *
Mathf.Clamp(_inputController.GetVertical(), -1, 0);
}
```

Above, we grab input values from the Component referenced in _inputController (in this case, an instance of BaseInputController). Rather than relying on them being in the range we need, Mathf.Clamp is used to restrict our values between a start and end amount. For example, steer will only ever be between –1 and 1 thanks to the Mathf.Clamp statement above, where –1 is a turn to the left and 1 is a turn to the right. The motor variable will always be between 0 and 1 and brake between –1 and 0.

Braking works a little differently because it gets its input from the same axis used for the motor. The joystick axis used goes from 1, which would be up, to –1 which is down. Using the same axis but having two separate values for motor and brake means that we use positive values from GetVertical() to apply to motor but we also need to filter out any positive value coming back from GetVertical() to apply to the brakes. We only want the negative values of GetVertical() when it comes to breaking, because that is when the joystick is down rather than up. To do this, first of all the values are clamped between –1 and 0 by Mathf.Clamp. This will return a negative number, which is what we want but the WheelColliders will only take a positive number, so we have to reverse it by subtracting it from –1. What we end up with is that, whenever GetVertical() returns a negative value, the value of brake will be an inversed positive value of it ready to apply to the wheels back in the above UpdatePhysics() function.

```
public virtual void UpdateEngineAudio()
{
            _engineSoundSource.pitch = audioPitchOffset +
(Mathf.Abs(_frontWheelLeft.rpm) * 0.005f);
}
}
}
```

Changing the pitch of the engine AudioSource object makes a convincing motor sound. As it may be possible for the variable mySpeed to be negative, Mathf.Abs is used and an arbitrary multiplier to bring the number down to something that changes the pitch in a satisfactory manner. The number was decided by trial and error, adjusting its value until the motor sounded right.

As well as setting up WheelColliders, you may need a method to align the visual models to their physics counterpart like the BaseWheelAlignment class in the following section.

▌ 6.3 Wheel Alignment

WheelColliders will do a great job of acting like wheels, but if we want to see wheels there is still more work to be done; each wheel mesh needs to be positioned to match its WheelCollider counterpart. Quick shoutout to Edy (Vehicle Physics) for his public domain UnityScript wheel alignment, which served as the original basis for this class.

The BaseWheelAlignment class can be used to align the wheel meshes to the WheelColliders, as well as to provide a little extra functionality in spawning tire smoke as the wheel is slipping. The smoke is optional, of course, but it's here should you need it.

Each wheel should have a BaseWheelAlignment Component attached to it (that is, a wheel mesh for display, not the actual WheelCollider) and then a reference to a WheelCollider component. The wheels should be independent of the WheelColliders for them to move correctly; do not parent wheel meshes to the Colliders.

```
using UnityEngine;
namespace GPC
{
        public class BaseWheelAlignment :
ExtendedCustomMonoBehaviour
        {
```

Above, we only need access to the UnityEngine namespaces for this script, and then we are adding this class to the GPC namespace so that it acts as a part of theframeworkforthisbook.TheclassderivesfromExtendedCustomMonoBehaviour to use its Spawn() function and also one of its variables, _TR.

```
            public WheelCollider _correspondingCollider;
            public GameObject _slipPrefab;
            public float slipAmountForTireSmoke = 50f;
            private float suspensionDistance;
            private float RotationValue = 0.0f;
            private Transform _colliderTransform;
```

Skipping by the variable declarations (as they will become clearer as we work through the script), we move down to the Start() function:

```
        void Start()
        {
            _TR = GetComponent<Transform>();
            _colliderTransform = _correspondingCollider.
transform;
        }
```

_TR grabs a reference to the wheel Transform. This will be used to position the visual wheel. On the following line above, we grab _colliderTransform, which is a reference to the corresponding WheelCollider GameObject and will be used to find out where to position the visual wheel further down in the script.

```
        void Update()
        {
            RaycastHit hit;
            Vector3 ColliderCenterPoint = _colliderTransform.
TransformPoint(_correspondingCollider.center);

            if (Physics.Raycast(ColliderCenterPoint, -
_colliderTransform.up, out hit, _correspondingCollider.
suspensionDistance + _correspondingCollider.radius))
            {
```

Above, the Update() function works by casting a ray down from the center of the WheelCollider with the intention of positioning the wheel mesh based on where the ray finds a Collider hit. If nothing is picked up by the raycast, the wheel mesh is positioned at a point projected down from the center of the WheelCollider instead – representing a fully extended suspension distance.

The WheelCollider.center property returns a value from the WheelCollider's local coordinate space. Above, Transform.TransformPoint is used to convert it into a world space coordinate that we can use this point as the starting point for the ray cast. For a realistic representation of the structure of suspension, the ray cast length is limited to the length of the suspension add the radius of the wheel. Starting out from the center of the WheelCollider, the ray travels down the Collider Transform's negative up vector (i.e. down, as the WheelCollider's Transform describes it, is down from the bottom of our GameObject).

```
    _ TR.position = hit.point + ( _ colliderTransform.up *
_ correspondingCollider.radius);
        } else {
        _TR.position = ColliderCenterPoint - (_colliderTransform.up
* _correspondingCollider.suspensionDistance);
        }
```

Above, we deal with the positioning of the wheel based on whether Physics. Raycast finds a hit or not. If a hit is found, the position for the visual wheel is made up of the hit point, plus the wheel Collider's local up vector multiplied by the wheel radius. This should sit the wheel just above the hit surface.

The second statement above calculates the wheel position at a fixed distance from the WheelCollider's center, that distance made up of the Collider's local up vector multiplied by the suspension distance. This is how we get to that fixed, fully extended suspension distance mentioned earlier in this section.

```
    _ TR.rotation = _ colliderTransform.rotation * Quaternion.
Euler(RotationValue, _ correspondingCollider.steerAngle, 0);
        RotationValue += _correspondingCollider.rpm * 6 * Time.
deltaTime;
        RotationValue = RotationValue % 360;
```

In the code above, a rotation is calculated encompassing the steering angle turning the wheel about its Y axis, and a RotationValue variable used to turn the wheel on its X axis. The RotationValue variable is used to make our wheel look like it is rolling. RotationValue is made up of the WheelCollider's RPM (revolutions per minute) value multiplied by 6 – the 6 is 360 (degrees) multiplied by 60 (seconds) to convert RPM to radians – then again, multiplied by Time.deltaTime to make sure that the rotation is consistent, based on time since the last time Update() was called.

We then take the RotationValue variable and force it to loop around between 0 and 360 so that it does not keep accumulating the rotation to become a giant number. If a number gets too big, eventually it will cause floating point errors. Even though this is unlikely given that the average race does not take that much time, I prefer to fix it and anticipate the problem before it happens, so we just make RotationValue the modulus of RotationValue vs. 360 (modulus finds the remainder after dividing the first number by the second, giving a rotation between 0 and 360.

Next, we are into the tire slip calculations:

```
WheelHit correspondingGroundHit= new WheelHit();
```

To analyze detailed information from the WheelCollider and its contacts and relationships with the 3d world, Unity provides a structure called WheelHit.

A WheelHit object contains contact information like the magnitude of force being applied to the wheel, its forward vector and how much the wheel is slipping. Above, we declare a new variable named correspondingGroundHit with the specific purpose of getting to the sidewaysSlip value of the WheelCollider. With this, we can find out how much the wheel is slipping. If the sidewaysSlip value of correspondingGroundHit falls outside a specified threshold, the wheels must be sliding enough to merit some tire smoke to be instantiated.

```
            _ correspondingCollider.GetGroundHit( out
correspondingGroundHit );
            if ( Mathf.Abs( correspondingGroundHit.sidewaysSlip
) > slipAmountForTireSmoke )
            {
```

The first task above is to fill our GroundHit typed variable correspondingGroundHit with information from our wheel's WheelCollider. You do this by calling GetGroundHit on the WheelCollider and passing in a WheelHit object for it to populate on the way out.

Now correspondingGroundHit has data in it, in the next line we access that sidewaysSlip value. To always ensure we get a positive number back from it, we use Mathf.Abs and compare that value to the float variable slipAmountForTireSmoke.

```
            if ( slipPrefab ) {
                Spawn( slipPrefab, correspondingGroundHit.point,
Quaternion.identity );
            }
        }
}
```

If the condition above is met and sidewaysSlip is greater that slipAmountForTireSmoke, the line above instantiates a slipPrefab object into the Scene. It is assumed that slipPrefab contains a particle effect for tire smoke. The new prefab will be spawned at the point where the wheel meets the ground surface.

Note that the slipPrefab will be instantiated every step (every update) that the sidewaysSlip value is above the value of slipAmountForTireSmoke. If your tire smoke particle effect is complex you may need to change this to a timed system, instead.

■ 6.4 2D Platform Character Controller

In Chapter 2 of this book, we looked at building a basic infinite runner game where the player jumped between platforms. The runner games main character class from Section 2.6.3 – RunMan_CharacterController – derived from BasePlayer2DPlatformCharacter, which is used to control the player. It provides basic platformer / runner game functionality of running left or right and jumping. The script also detects platforms beneath the player, so that we know when it is grounded and able to jump.

This BasePlayer2DPlatformCharacter script Component should be attached to an avatar that already has a Rigidbody2D Component and 2D Collider like a Sphere Collider attached to it. Let's dig in:

```
using UnityEngine;
namespace GPC
{
        public class BasePlayer2DPlatformCharacter :
ExtendedCustomMonoBehaviour
```

```
{
        public float jumpPower = 2.5f;
        public float runPower = 0.6f;

        public bool canAirSteer;

        [System.NonSerialized]
        public bool allow_left;

        [System.NonSerialized]
        public bool allow_right;

        [System.NonSerialized]
        public bool allow_jump;

        public LayerMask groundLayerMask;
        public bool isOnGround;

        public BaseInputController _inputController;
```

Above, there is nothing particularly unusual about the variables or class declarations for this script until we reach the groundLayerMask declaration.

groundLayerMask is a LayerMask type variable that is used by this class to decide which collision layers to look for when trying to find ground underneath the player. When you see this Component attached to a GameObject, and the GameObject is selected, as the Component appears in the Inspector this variable will appear as a dropdown menu. The dropdown contains all the defined collision layers in your project, and you can choose one or multiple, if required. Layers in Unity are represented as bitmasks. A bitmask is used to access specific bits in a byte of data – you can think of a bitmask as a binary number that represents something else. Layers can be difficult to work with, but when you use a LayerMask, you avoid having to mess around with bit shifting. To help out, the class that this class derives from, ExtendedCustomMonoBehaviour, has a function in it called IsInLayerMask() that simplifies working with layers even more.

Above, _inputController is declared too. _inputController uses the BaseInputController class to read input from the player (in this case, keypresses) and we can access the values in _inputController to know what the user is asking our player to do and react.

```
        private void Awake()
        {
                Init();
        }

        public virtual void Init()
        {
                _RB2D = GetComponent<Rigidbody2D>();
                _inputController =
GetComponent<BaseInputController>();
                didInit = true;
        }
```

Above, we grab the Rigidbody2D component for _RB2D and populate the _inputController. Once we have those two variables set, didInit is set to true so that we know set up has completed.

```
        public virtual void LateUpdate()
        {
```

```
                CheckGround();
                UpdateMovement();
        }
```

LateUpdate() calls functions to update movement and check for ground.

```
        public virtual void UpdateMovement()
        {
                if (!didInit)
                        Init();

                _inputController.CheckInput();
```

Before doing anything in UpdateMovement(), there is a quick check that didInit is true.

Next, BaseInputController does not update itself! We tell it when to update. In this case, we call _inputController.CheckInput() from the UpdateMovement() function above.

```
        Vector2 moveVel = _RB2D.velocity;
        if (isOnGround || canAirSteer)
        {
```

You can decide whether to allow your player to steer in the air by enabling the canAirSteer Boolean (either set it in code, or via the Inspector on the Component). Above, we check to see that either the player is on the ground or air steering is enabled before grabbing inputs from _inputController for left and right movements.

```
                if (_inputController.Left && allow_left)
                {
                        moveVel.x = -runPower;
                }
                else if (_inputController.Right &&
allow_right)
                {
                        moveVel.x = runPower;
                }
                else
                {
                        if (allow_right || allow_left)
                        {
                                // stop if no left/
right keys are being pressed
                                moveVel.x = 0;
                        }
                }
```

moveVel is a Vector2 variable used to hold the target movement amount each step. Above, we set moveVel to either -runPower (running to the left), runPower (right) or zero it altogether to stop the player in place. As this script is intended to be used as a starting point for different types of games, it also contains the option to turn on or off left or right movement with the allow_left and allow_right Booleans. For the infinite runner example in this book, left and right movement is enabled but not all infinite runners allow the player to move left and right; some only require a jump button.

BaseInputController has both linear inputs in variables named vert and horz (standing for vertical and horizontal) which will return values between –1 and 1, as well as digital inputs in the variables Up, Down, Left and Right. Above, rather than use the linear inputs we use Left and Right. Either our player is moving, or it is standing still. There is no in-between!

```
                // jump key
                if (_inputController.Fire1 && allow_jump &&
isOnGround)
                {
                        // stop if no left/right keys are
being pressed
                        moveVel.y = jumpPower;

                        Jump();
                }
                _RB2D.velocity = moveVel;
        }
```

The last part of UpdateMovement() above is where we deal with jumping. By default, we use the input Fire1 as the jump key. The inputs can be modified and set up in Unity's Input Manager (Edit>Project Settings>Input Manager).

To make the player jump, we set its velocity along the y axis to the (float) value in the variable jumpPower. As this is only applied when the player is on the ground and the jump key has been pressed, it provides the right amount of thrust to seem like a jump. Above, we also call to a function named Jump() to take care of a few secondary tasks, which we will cover a little further on in the script.

```
        void CheckGround()
        {
                // assume we're NOT on the ground, first..
                isOnGround = false;

                // Cast a ray straight down.
                RaycastHit2D hit =
Physics2D.Raycast(transform.position, -Vector2.up, 0.3f,
groundLayerMask);

                // If it hits something...
                if (hit.collider != null)
                {
                        isOnGround = true;
                }
        }
```

To detect the ground beneath the player, this script uses the Physics2D. Raycast function. We pass in the start position, the direction (a down vector), the distance we want the ray to stop at and a LayerMask – groundLayerMask from the top of the script we discussed earlier in this section. A ray will be cast down from the player Transforms position and if the ray intersects with anything (if a Collider on the right layer is found), information about the Collider and the hit will be put into the RaycastHit2D variable hit.

All we need to do then is to check hit.collider. If no Collider was found during the raycast, Physics2D.Raycast returns null as the Collider. If we know a Collider was found, we know that there is ground underneath the player and we can set isOnGround to true.

```
        public virtual void Jump()
        {
                // use this function to trigger things that
happen when the player jumps
```

```
                }
        }
}
```

In this base class, there is only a virtual version of the Jump() function. This should be overridden by your own derived scripts if you need to do anything else when a jump happens. For example, the RunMan infinite runner game from Chapter 2 of this book uses an overridden version of the Jump() function to tell the player sprite to play its jumping animation.

7 Weapon Systems

To be as flexible as possible, in this chapter we build a weapon management system that will control individual weapon controllers. Those weapon controllers, in turn, will deal with spawning projectiles and finally projectiles will take care of themselves independently. Our weapon management system should function with a single weapon or we should be able to add many different weapons and switch between them.

The weapon controller deals with weapons and passes on messages to them. It contains an array containing all weapons and a method to activate and deactivate them as required.

Each weapon is a prefab with a script attached that derives from BaseWeaponScript.cs. The weapon should be self-contained other than when it receives a call to Fire() it should do whatever it is supposed to do. BaseWeaponScript contains the basics for a weapon (ammunition, reload time, and the ability to be disabled or enabled).

■ 7.1 Building the Scripts

For the weapon system, there are two main script Components and one for input:

1. BaseWeaponController
   This is the framework for our weapon control system. It offers everything the system requires and it is intended to be overridden for customization.

2. BaseWeaponScript
   This takes care of individual weapon types. If you were to think of the baseWeaponController as the arms of the player, the baseWeaponScript would be the design of the weapon it is holding.

3. StandardSlotWeaponController
This class provides a method for taking input from the player and changing the currently selected weapon.

All weapon-related scripts can be found in the folder Assets\GPC_Framework\Scripts\BASE\WEAPON.

7.1.1 The BaseWeaponController Class

The BaseWeaponController class derives from MonoBehaviour, to utilize the usual built-in Unity calls:

```
using UnityEngine;
using System.Collections.Generic;

namespace GPC
{
        [AddComponentMenu("CSharpBookCode/Base/Base Weapon
Controller")]

public class BaseWeaponController : MonoBehaviour
{
                public GameObject[] _weapons;
                public int selectedWeaponSlot;
                public int lastSelectedWeaponSlot;
                public Transform _weaponMountPoint;
                private List<GameObject> _weaponSlots;
                private List<BaseWeaponScript> _weaponScripts;
                private BaseWeaponScript _TEMPWeapon;
                private int ownerNum;
                public bool useForceVectorDirection;
                public Vector3 forceVector;
                private Vector3 theDir;

                public void Start()
                {
                        // default to the first weapon slot
                        selectedWeaponSlot = 0;
                        lastSelectedWeaponSlot = -1;
```

Default values are set for the currently selected weapon slot and the last selected weapon. When the lastSelectedWeaponSlot variable is set to –1, it just lets the weapon system know that it needs to set the weapon (to avoid duplicate calls later on, whenever the weapon slot is set it checks to make sure that the new weapon it is trying to set is different to the one currently set up – hence the –1 to make the values of selectedWeaponSlot vs. lastSelectedWeaponSlot different on initialization).

```
        // initialize weapon list List
        _weaponSlots = new List<GameObject>();

        // initialize weapon scripts List
        _weaponScripts = new List<BaseWeaponScript>();

        _TR = transform;
        if (_weaponMountPoint == null)
                _weaponMountPoint = _TR;
```

This script uses a List named _weaponSlots to hold different weapon(s) to spawn later in the function – this is a List of all of the available weapons even if ammo is not provide – above, we create a new empty List ready to populate. Along with storing the GameObjects of our weapons, we will be storing the BaseWeaponScript Components attached to each one. Our Transform is stored in _TR and the variable _weaponMountPoint is populated with _TR if it has not been set in the Unity editor Inspector window. The mount point should be an empty GameObject or similar Transform used to position and set the rotation of the weapons.

```
for (int i = 0; i < _weapons.Length; i++)
{
                GameObject _tempGO =
(GameObject)Instantiate(_weapons[i],
_weaponMountPoint.position, _weaponMountPoint.rotation);
                _tempGO.transform.parent = _weaponMountPoint;
                _tempGO.layer =
_weaponMountPoint.gameObject.layer;
                _tempGO.transform.position =
_weaponMountPoint.position;
                _tempGO.transform.rotation =
_weaponMountPoint.rotation;
```

Above, we loop through the _weapons array and instantiate each one. When the game starts and the above Start() function runs, the weapon prefab references from the _weapons List will be instantiated one by one and positioned at the weapon mount Transforms position. To make the weapon move around with the player, we set our new weapons parent to the weapon mount (you can only set the parent of a Transform, not a GameObject hence using .transform. parent). We copy the layer used by the weapon mount and set the new weapon to the same layer, before setting the position and rotation above.

```
weaponSlots.Add( TEMPgameObject );
```

These new objects are going to be the ones that the script manages, enabling and disabling them as required and calling on them to act as required. Each new weapon is added to a new List called weaponSlots:

```
// grab a reference to the weapon script
attached to the weapon and store the reference in a List
                _TEMPWeapon =
_tempGO.GetComponent<BaseWeaponScript>();
                weaponScripts.Add( TEMPWeapon );
```

The BaseWeaponScript instance attached to each weapon in those slots is found (using GameObject.GetComponent()) and stored in another List named weaponScripts:

```
// disable the weapon
                _tempGO.SetActive( false );
}
```

The weapons need to start out disabled, otherwise they will all appear on top of each other and all active. They are disabled here using the GameObject. SetActive() Unity function:

```
// now we set the default selected weapon to visible
                SetWeaponSlot(0);
}
```

Now that all the weapons are instantiated, set up, and hidden, the last thing needed for initialization is to set the default weapon slot to the first weapon (index of 0). To set the slot, use the SetWeaponSlot() function:

```
public void SetOwner(int aNum)
{
        // used to identify the object firing, if required
        ownerNum= aNum;

}
```

When a projectile hits an enemy or a player, the object being hit needs to know where the projectile came from to know how to react to it. Projectile identification can be done by layer. Set the layer on the gun mounting point object (the object that will be the parent to the weapon) and this weapon script will use the same layer for its projectiles.

Another method for checking where projectiles have come from is to assign each player with a unique ID number and to use the SetOwner() function to tell the projectiles who owns each one. The ID number is passed on to projectiles and stored in the script each projectile has attached to it:

```
public virtual void SetWeaponSlot (int slotNum)
{
        // if the selected weapon is already this one, drop
out!
        if(slotNum==lastSelectedWeaponSlot)
                return;
```

The function SetWeaponSlot() takes an integer to use as an index number to refer to the weapons stored in the List named weaponSlots. The weaponSlots List will be in the same order as weapons added to the original weapons array in the Unity editor Inspector window.

The SetWeaponSlot() function starts out making sure the weapon we are trying to set (in slotNum) is not the weapon already active (the lastSelectedWeaponSlot):

```
        // disable the current weapon
        DisableCurrentWeapon();
```

As a new weapon is about to be made active, the current weapon is disabled by a call to the function DisableCurrentWeapon():

```
        // set our current weapon to the one passed in
        selectedWeaponSlot= slotNum;
```

selectedWeaponSlot is an index used to store the currently active weapon slot. Here, it is set to the incoming parameter value of slotNum:

```
        // make sure sensible values are getting passed in
        if(selectedWeaponSlot<0)
                selectedWeaponSlot= weaponSlots.Count-1;

        // make sure that the weapon slot isn't higher than
the total number of weapons in our list
        if(selectedWeaponSlot>weaponSlots.Count-1)
                selectedWeaponSlot=weaponSlots.Count-1;
```

The new value of selectedWeaponSlot is then validated to make sure it is not less than 0 or more than the total number of occupied slots −1 (since the weaponSlots array of weapons starts at zero, we deduct 1 to find the last entry). During validation, if the value of slotNum is too high, it will be set to the nearest valid number – that way, the function will not fail in setting the weapon because of a bad value in slotNum:

```
            // we store this selected slot to use to prevent
duplicate weapon slot setting
            lastSelectedWeaponSlot= selectedWeaponSlot;
```

Now that selectedWeaponSlot has been set, lastSelectedWeaponSlot needs updating to the latest slot number:

```
            // enable the newly selected weapon
            EnableCurrentWeapon();
    }
```

A call to EnableCurrentWeapon() will take the value of selectedWeaponSlot and activate the currently selected weapon:

```
    public virtual void NextWeaponSlot (bool shouldLoop)
    {
```

The NextWeaponSlot() takes a Boolean parameter to tell the function whether or not to loop around from the last weapon to the first. If the shouldLoop parameter is false and the current weapon is already set to the last available weapon, it will return the same weapon instead of looping around to zero and returning the weapon from the first slot:

```
            // disable the current weapon
            DisableCurrentWeapon();
```

First, the current weapon is disabled in anticipation of setting a new one:

```
            // next slot
            selectedWeaponSlot++;

            // make sure that the slot isn't higher than the
total number of weapons in our list
            if(selectedWeaponSlot==weaponScripts.Count)
            {
                    if(shouldLoop)
                    {
                            selectedWeaponSlot= 0;
                    } else {
                            selectedWeaponSlot=
weaponScripts.Count-1;
                    }
            }
```

selectedWeaponSlot index number is incremented and validated to make sure that it now contains a valid index number (this is where the slot number will be looped back to zero if it goes over the total number of available weapons):

```
            // we store this selected slot to use to prevent
duplicate weapon slot setting
            lastSelectedWeaponSlot=selectedWeaponSlot;

            // enable the newly selected weapon
            EnableCurrentWeapon();
    }
```

The lastSelectedWeaponSlot gets updated before the new current weapon is enabled, completing the function:

```
public virtual void PrevWeaponSlot (bool shouldLoop)
{
        // disable the current weapon
        DisableCurrentWeapon();

        // prev slot
        selectedWeaponSlot--;

        // make sure that the slot is a sensible number
        if ( selectedWeaponSlot<0 )
        {
                if(shouldLoop)
                {
                        selectedWeaponSlot=
weaponScripts.Count-1;
                } else {
                        selectedWeaponSlot= 0;
                }
        }
        // we store this selected slot to use to prevent
duplicate weapon slot setting
        lastSelectedWeaponSlot=selectedWeaponSlot;

        // enable the newly selected weapon
        EnableCurrentWeapon();
}
```

PrevWeaponSlot works in almost exactly the same way as NextWeaponSlot(). It has a Boolean parameter to state whether to loop around if the current weapon slot drops below 0 and the most obvious difference is that the selectedWeaponSlot variable is decremented rather than incremented:

```
public virtual void DisableCurrentWeapon ()
{
```

Disabling the current weapon means that it will be both invisible and unable to fire:

```
if(weaponScripts.Count==0)
        return;
```

To disable the weapon, the script will need to talk to the BaseWeaponScript. cs attached to it. Since weaponScripts and weaponSlots Lists were created in the same order, the selectedWeaponSlot can be used as the index for either array.

To make sure that there are scripts in the weaponScripts array, its Count property is checked before going any further:

```
// grab reference to currently selected weapon script
TEMPWeapon= ( BaseWeaponScript )weaponScripts[select
edWeaponSlot];
```

A reference to the currently selected weapon slot's weapon class (BaseWeaponScript) is stored in the variable TEMPWeapon as it is retrieved from the weaponScripts List:

```
// now tell the script to disable itself
TEMPWeapon.Disable();
```

To tell the weapon to disable, it's a call to its Disable() function:

```
                // grab reference to the weapon's gameObject and
disable that, too
                GameObject _tempGO = (GameObject)_weaponSlots[select
edWeaponSlot];
                _tempGO.SetActive(false);
```

As well as disabling the actual weapon script, it now needs to be hidden from view. First, variable _tempGO receives a reference to the weapon's GameObject from the weaponSlots List. The _tempGO is then set to inactive by GameObject. SetActive():

```
        public virtual void EnableCurrentWeapon ()
        {
                if( weaponScripts.Count==0 )
                        return;

                // grab reference to currently selected weapon
                TEMPWeapon=
( BaseWeaponScript )weaponScripts[selectedWeaponSlot];

                // now tell the script to enable itself
                TEMPWeapon.Enable();

                GameObject _tempGO =
( GameObject )weaponSlots[selectedWeaponSlot];
                _tempGO.SetActive( true );
        }
```

Enabling the currently selected weapon is done by the EnableCurrentWeapon() function, which works almost exactly the same as DisableCurrentWeapon() except that it calls the Enable() function of the BaseWeaponScript instead of Disable():

```
        public virtual void Fire ()
        {
```

By default, the Fire() function will launch projectiles along the Transform's forward axis, but there is support for firing along a fixed vector by setting the useForceVectorDirection to true.

The function takes no parameters, making it easy to call from any other script:

```
                if(weaponScripts==null)
                        return;
                if(weaponScripts.Count==0)
                        return;
```

The weaponScripts List is checked to make sure that is has been properly initialized and that it contains entries (a quick count check):

```
                // find the weapon in the currently selected slot
                TEMPWeapon=
( BaseWeaponScript )weaponScripts[selectedWeaponSlot];
```

TEMPWeapon gets a reference to the currently selected weapon's script from the weaponScripts array:

```
        theDir = _ TR.forward;
```

By default, the firing direction is along our Transform's forward vector:

```
if( useForceVectorDirection )
        theDir = forceVector;
```

When useForceVectorDirection is set to true, theDir is set to the vector from the variable forceVector, which should be set in the Unity editor Inspector window on the GameObject:

```
// fire the projectile
TEMPWeapon.Fire( theDir, ownerNum );
        }
    }
}
```

The ownerNum was mentioned earlier in this section, where it is set by the SetOwner() function. When the call to the currently selected weapon's Fire() function goes out, it takes a Vector3, and the owner ID.

7.1.2 BaseWeaponScript

The BaseWeaponScript class derives from ExtendedCustomMonoBehaviour:

```
using UnityEngine;
namespace GPC
{
        [AddComponentMenu("CSharpBookCode/Base/Base Weapon Script")]

        public class BaseWeaponScript : ExtendedCustomMonoBehaviour
        {
                public bool canFire;
                public int ammo = 100;
                public int maxAmmo = 100;
                public bool isInfiniteAmmo;
                public GameObject _projectilePrefab;
                public Collider _parentCollider;
                public Transform _spawnPositionTR;
                public float fireDelay = 0.2f;
                public float projectileSpeed = 10f;
                public bool inheritVelocity;

                [System.NonSerialized]
                public Transform _theProjectile;

                private bool isLoaded;

                public virtual void Start()
                {
                        Init();
                }

                public virtual void Init()
                {
                        _TR = transform;
                        Reloaded();
                }
```

Start() calls Init(). Init() begins by grabbing a reference to the Transform. A call to Reloaded() ensures that the weapon will be loaded and ready to go from the start.

```
        public virtual void Enable()
        {
                canFire=true;
```

```
        }
        public virtual void Disable()
        {
                canFire=false;
        }
```

The Enable() or Disable() functions set the Boolean variable canFire to true or false, respectively. This will be checked elsewhere in the code before allowing any projectile firing. Note that the visual representation of the weapon is not hidden here; that task is left to the slot control script to deal with, rather than the weapon itself:

```
        public virtual void Reloaded()
        {
                // the 'isLoaded' var tells us if this weapon is
loaded and ready to fire
                isLoaded= true;
        }
```

When the weapon is fired, the assumption is made that it will not be loaded for a certain period (otherwise you could in theory fire out thousands of projectiles each second). To keep a track of when the weapon is in a loaded state, this script uses the Boolean variable isLoaded. A timed call to the Reloaded() function, after firing, will reset the weapon state again:

```
        public virtual void SetCollider( Collider aCollider )
        {
                _parentCollider= aCollider;
        }
```

SetCollider() is used to set a collider to be ignored by a projectile. For example, when the script is applied to a player it should ignore the player's collider to prevent the newly created projectile from exploding instantly. It should be set, using the Unity editor Inpsector window, to a collider that would likely destroy the projectile as it was spawned. If no parentCollider is set, the script will still work, but the projectile will not ignore any collider:

```
        public virtual void Fire( Vector3 aDirection, int ownerID )
        {
```

The Fire() function takes two parameters, a Vector3 to represent the direction of fire and an integer providing an ID number for its owner (which gets used primarily by collision code to know how to react):

```
            if( !canFire )
                    return;

            // if the weapon is not loaded, drop out
            if( !isLoaded )
                    return;
```

The Boolean variable canFire needs to be true (the weapon can fire) and isLoaded needs to be true (the weapon is ready to fire) before the function can progress to check the state of ammunition:

```
            // if we're out of ammo and we do not have infinite
ammo, drop out..
            if( ammo<=0 && !isInfiniteAmmo )
                    return;
```

If the integer variable ammo is less than zero and the Boolean isInfiniteAmmo has not been set in the Unity editor Inspector window, to true, then the function will drop out here too.

```
// decrease ammo
ammo--;
// generate the actual projectile
FireProjectile( aDirection, ownerID );
```

Since all of the criterion has been met, the function goes ahead, and decrements ammo in anticipation of the projectile about to be generated by the FireProjectile() function. The direction held by aDirection and the owner ID in the variable ownerID also get passed on to the FireProjectile() function as parameters:

```
// we need to reload before we can fire again
isLoaded= false;
```

This is where the Boolean variable isLoaded gets reset to false, to delay firing for a reasonable amount of time (set by the value held in the variable reloadTime):

```
        CancelInvoke( "Reloaded" );
        Invoke( "Reloaded", fireDelay );
}
```

CancelInvoke() is called to make sure that there is never more than one Invoke call to Reloaded() waiting to activate:

```
    public virtual void FireProjectile( Vector3 fireDirection,
int ownerID )
        {
```

The FireProjectile() function is where the projectile gets instantiated. It was called by that last function, Fire():

```
// make our first projectile
_theProjectile= MakeProjectile( ownerID );
```

The function MakeProjectile will do the work in getting a physical projectile into the scene, but it returns a Transform that this function can then use to set up with:

```
// direct the projectile toward the direction of fire
        _theProjectile.LookAt( theProjectile.position +
fireDirection );
```

Now theProjectile contains a Transform, the code uses the Transform. LookAt() function to align it along the target trajectory passed in via the parameter variable fireDirection. Since LookAt() requires a world position vector (as opposed to a direction vector), it takes the projectile's current position from theProjectile.position and adds the fireDirection vector to it. This will adjust the new projectile's rotation so that its z-axis is facing in the required direction of travel:

```
// add force to move our projectile
        _theProjectile.GetComponent<Rigidbody>().velocity =
fireDirection * projectileSpeed;
    }
```

To move the projectile, the projectile's Rigidbody has its velocity set to the required firing direction multiplied by projectileSpeed.

```
public virtual Transform MakeProjectile( int ownerID )
{
```

MakeProjectile() handles creation of a physical projectile, taking a parameter of the ownerID (to pass on to the projectile) and returning the instantiated projectile Transform:

```
// create a projectile
_theProjectile = Spawn(_projectilePrefab.transform,
_spawnPositionTR.position, _spawnPositionTR.rotation);
        _theProjectile.SendMessage("SetOwnerType", ownerID,
SendMessageOptions.RequireReceiver);
```

The Spawn() function in the ExtendedCustomMonoBehaviour class this script derives from is used to instantiate the projectile. Spawn() takes the exact same parameters as Unity's Instantiate function; the prefab reference to spawn, a Vector3 position and a rotation for the spawned object. It will return the Transform of the newly created object.

The projectile needs to know about the owner ID so that it can be identified during a collision. Above, once we have spawned the projectile and have its Transform, Transform.SendMessage() is used to pass the ownerID to the projectile.

```
if (_parentCollider != null)
{
// disable collision between 'us' and our projectile
so as not to hit ourselves with it!

        Physics.IgnoreCollision(_theProjectile.
GetComponent<Collider>(), _parentCollider);
            }
```

Physics.IgnoreLayerCollision() takes layers referring to which layers should ignore colliding with each other. This part of the code checks that parentCollider is not null, then as long as it contains something Physics.IgnoreCollision() is used to tell the engine to ignore collisions between the two colliders.

Whereas Physics.IgnoreLayerCollision() worked to disable all collisions between objects on two layers, the Physics.IgnoreCollision() function stops collision events on specified colliders.

```
        return _theProjectile;
        }
    }
}
```

Above, the newly created projectile needs to be returned to the function calling (especially when this is called from the Fire() function shown earlier in this section).

7.1.3 Switching between Weapons

Switching between different weapons is a case of either calling SetWeaponSlot() on your BaseWeaponController class from another script (possibly an input script) or derive a new class from BaseWeaponController that includes the switch functionality. In this section, we look at building a script to derive from BaseWeaponController and look for presses on the number keys 1 to 9 to choose the currently selected weapon. You can see this script in action in the Blaster game example from Chapter 15.

```
using UnityEngine;
namespace GPC
{
        [AddComponentMenu("CSharpBookCode/Common/Weapons/Standard
Slot Controller")]

        public class StandardSlotWeaponController :
BaseWeaponController
        {
                public bool allowWeaponSwitchKeys = true;
```

Above, our new script derives from BaseWeaponController. We include a Boolean variable, allowWeaponSwitchKeys, for toggling weapon switching on or off.

```
                public void Update()
                {
                        if (!allowWeaponSwitchKeys)
                                return;

                        // do weapon selection / switching slots
                        // ---------------------------------------
                        if (Input.GetKey(KeyCode.Less))
                                PrevWeaponSlot(true);
                        else if (Input.GetKey(KeyCode.Greater))
                                NextWeaponSlot(true);
```

Update() starts with a quick to check to see if weapon switching is allowed, dropping out if it is not. Next, when the greater than or less than keys are pressed, we call either PrevWeaponSlot() or NextWeaponSlot() to switch weapons.

```
                        // keys 1-9
                        string theKey = Input.inputString;
                        if (theKey == "")
                                return;
```

Input.inputString provides us with a string containing the most recent key pressed on the keyboard. Above, we store the value of Input.inputString in theKey and then check it to see whether it is empty. If the string is empty, no key has been pressed so we drop out.

```
                        var val = (Char.ConvertToUtf32(theKey, 0)-49);
                        if(val>-1 && val< _weapons.Length)
                                SetWeaponSlot(val);

                }
        }
}
```

Rather than checking input for every key from 1 to 9, we take the string theKey and convert it into a number. Char.ConvertToUtf32 will convert a string into a Unicode code. The numbers 1–9 are represented by the numbers 49 to 58. If we take the code from Char.ConvertToUtf32 and subtract 49 from it, we get a number between 0 and 9 – perfect numbers to pass into the SetWeaponSlot() function for choosing which weapon slot to use. Char.ConvertToUtf32 takes two parameters; a String to convert followed by the index number of the character you want to convert.

With a converted value in the local variable val, we check that it is greater than –1 and less than _weapons.Length to be sure that the number coming in is valid for weapon selection. If it is, we pass the value in to SetWeaponSlot() to choose the weapon.

NOTE: This is not actually a great way of doing this. Unfortunately, although it minimizes the amount of code it has the trade-off of inefficiency. Checking strings is expensive, in terms of processing, so although it works in simple situations it would not be optimized for more complex games. The best way to do this would be the simplest – to either just stick to using next/prev weapon buttons or to check each number on the keyboard with a set of if statements such as:

```
if (Input.GetKey("1"))
    {
            SetWeaponSlot(0);
    }
if (Input.GetKey("2"))
    {
            SetWeaponSlot(1);
    }
```

8 Waypoints Manager

▌ 8.1 Waypoint System

Waypoints can be used for more than just guiding AI objects or players around the game world. We can use them to guide a camera for cut scenes or a guided camera system, track who is winning a race, use them to make sure that the player is going in the right direction along a path, to reposition players in a safe location, for counting laps during a race and quite probably a whole other number of uses that don't immediately spring to mind. Waypoints are really useful for game developers.

For an example of this script in action, check out the racing game example in Chapter 14.

Our waypoints manager needs to be flexible enough to provide the functionality for all of these uses and then some, without going against the componentized methodology we are employing for this book. The functions it should provide are:

1. Produce a visual representation of the path we want our AI cars to take, to make manipulation of our waypoints in the editor a little easier

2. Provide an interface that can allow other scripts to search for the nearest waypoint to a given point in 3d space

3. Provide an interface that allows other scripts to get waypoint information from an index number: as our cars go around the track, they have a waypoint counter which could potentially be used with this function to establish where the current, next, or previous waypoints are.

4. Provide an interface that allows for other scripts to find out the total number of waypoints: as our cars hold their own waypoint counter numbers, they need some way to ensure that the counters stay within the boundaries of how many waypoints there actually are.

In the racing game example in this book, we use waypoints for the AI and for the main player;

1. To check that the main player is heading in the right direction: the car controller code will track the player's position on the track (based on which waypoint has been passed) and check its forward vector to make sure that it is facing the next waypoint along the track. If the player's forward vector is not within a certain tolerance angle, the game will display a wrong way message and eventually respawn the car facing the right way.

2. The respawning system uses waypoints to find a 'safe' place along the track to respawn the player as well as using its rotation to point the respawned car in the right direction along the track.

3. To find out how far the vehicle has traveled around the track, which is used to compare to the other players progress amounts to calculate race positions

The waypoints controller script:

```
using UnityEngine;
using System.Collections.Generic;
namespace GPC
{
        [AddComponentMenu("CSharpBookCode/Utility/Waypoints
Controller")]

        public class WaypointsController : MonoBehaviour
        {
                [ExecuteInEditMode]

                private List<Transform> _transforms;
                private Vector3 firstPoint; // store our first
waypoint so we can loop the path
                private float distance;
                private int totalTransforms;
                private Vector3 diff;
                private float curDistance;
                private Transform _closest;
                private Vector3 currentPos;
                private Vector3 lastPos;
                private Transform _pointT;

                public bool closed = true;
                public bool shouldReverse;

                void Start()
                {
                        GetTransforms();
                }
```

After the variable and class declarations, above, the Start() function calls a function called GetTransforms(). We will look at that in detail further down in the function.

Next, the OnDrawGizmos() function. If you have never dealt with Gizmos before, they are helper objects to make editing and/or visualization easier. Unity relies quite heavily on Gizmos for the editor and how you interact with it as well as providing a nice interface for you to build your own custom types.

All Gizmo drawing needs to be done in one of two functions (called automatically by the engine):

OnDrawGizmos	Called every frame. All Gizmos are pickable.
OnDrawGizmosSelected	Called only when the object with the script attached is selected.

The OnDrawGizmos() function is a runtime class (called automatically by the game engine) where we can draw our own Gizmos and do some editor-based manipulation. In this case, the OnDrawGizmos function of WaypointsController will render waypoint positions and draw lines between each one so that we have a simple visual representation of the path.

```
void OnDrawGizmos()
{                       GetTransforms();
        if (totalTransforms < 2)
                return;
```

At the start of the function, we call GetTransforms() to make sure that the information stored about all of the Transforms that make up our path are up to date (in case they have been moved or new ones added).

When you first build a path, obviously it will start with a single waypoint. With only one point, there is no end point for rendering a line to, so this function checks that there are enough waypoints to draw a line and drops out if the totalTransforms count is less than 2.

```
Transform _tempTR = (Transform) _transforms[0];
lastPos = _tempTR.position;
```

Above, we grab the first waypoint transform from the _transforms List, at index 0, and store it in _tempTR. We do this so that we have a starting point for drawing the lines that represent the path in the editor.

lastPos will act as the starting point for the next line, so at this stage we just need it to have a value:

```
        firstPoint = _tempTR.position;
        lastPoint = firstPoint;
_pointT = (Transform)_transforms[0];

        for (int i = 1; i < totalTransforms; i++)
        {
                _tempTR = (Transform)_transforms[i];
                if (_tempTR == null)
                {
                        GetTransforms();
                        return;
                }

                // grab the current waypoint position
                currentPoint = _tempTR.position;
```

Having all the Gizmos, lines, and editor helper graphics the same colors would make life harder. For that reason, Unity provides the Gizmos.color function to set their colors. It takes just one call to Gizmos.color (passing in a Color object) and everything after that point will be rendered using it.

```
        Gizmos.color=Color.green;
```

Gizmos.DrawSphere draws a sphere at a set position and radius like this:

```
Gizmos.DrawSphere(currentPoint,2);

// draw the line between the last waypoint
```
and this one
```
Gizmos.color=Color.red;
Gizmos.DrawLine(lastPoint, currentPoint);
```

Gizmos.DrawLine is another utility provided by Unity, to draw a simple line between two 3d vectors. The Gizmo drawing system has a few more options available to make editing easier.

According to the Unity documentation, the Gizmo interface provides;

DrawCube	Draw a solid box with center and size.
DrawFrustum	Draw a camera frustum using the currently set Gizmos.matrix for its location and rotation.
DrawGUITexture	Draw a texture in the scene.
DrawIcon	Draw an icon at a position in the scene view.
DrawLine	Draws a line starting at from toward to.
DrawRay	Draws a ray starting at from to from + direction.
DrawSphere	Draws a solid sphere with center and radius.
DrawWireCube	Draw a wireframe box with center and size.
DrawWireSphere	Draws a wireframe sphere with center and radius.

As stated earlier in this chapter, the waypoints are used at one stage as respawn points for vehicles that may be stuck or off-track. Their rotations are also used to ensure that the repositioned vehicle is facing in the correct direction; for that reason, we need the waypoints to face 'forward'. To make sure that the rotations of our waypoints are correct, we go through and point each one forward toward the next one:

```
pointT.LookAt(currentPoint);
```

You can easily rotate a transform so that its forward points toward another transform by using the transform.LookAt() function. It takes one or two parameters, the first being the transform you want to point toward and the second an optional up vector.

Note that having this functionality happening all the time during OnDrawGizmos() can make drag and drop editing difficult, as object pivots rotate around automatically when you drag waypoints. Comment out the line above if you find you are having trouble with automatically rotating points.

As the function continues, we continue to iterate through the waypoints and then close the path, if the Boolean variable closed is set to true (you can set that in the Inspector window of the editor when the gameObject that has this script attached is selected):

```
// update our 'last' waypoint to become this
```
one as we
```
// move on to find the next...
lastPos = currentPos;

// update the pointing transform
pointT=(Transform)transforms[i];
}

// close the path
if(closed)
```

```
                {
                        Gizmos.color=Color.red;
                        Gizmos.DrawLine(currentPoint, firstPoint);
                }
        }

        public void GetTransforms()
        {
                _transforms = new List<Transform>();
```

To make the waypoints control script easy to use, we need to make sure that our waypoints are set up in a way in the scene where we want to use them. This format is an empty GameObject with the WaypointsController.cs component attached to it, with all waypoints as child objects in the Hierarchy. All of the Transforms found in the GetTransforms() function are added to a List named _transforms like this:

```
        foreach(Transform t in transform)
        {
                // add this transform to our arraylist
                _transforms.Add(t);
        }

        totalTransforms=(int)_transforms.Count;

}
```

At the end of GetTransforms(), we store the total number of transforms in an integer for easy access later (so that we don't have to count the List each time we need to know how many Transforms it contains).

The rest of the class is made up of publicly accessible utility functions for other scripts to access:

SetReverseMode	SetReverseMode sets the value of a Boolean variable called shouldReverse, which determines whether the path should be reversed.
FindNearestWaypoint	Finds the nearest waypoint to a given position, within a given distance, and returns its index number as an integer.
	There are two implementations of the FindNearestWaypoint, one adds the extra parameter of exceptThis. The function will find the closest waypoint as normal, but when exceptThis is used it will ignore the specified transform.
GetWaypoint	Returns the transform of the waypoint at the index number passed in (as an integer).
GetTotal	Returns an integer value representing the total number of waypoints this class has control over.

```
        public void SetReverseMode(bool rev)
        {
                shouldReverse=rev;
        }

        public int FindNearestWaypoint ( Vector3 fromPos, float maxRange)
        {
                        if(transforms==null)
                                GetTransforms();

                        distance = Mathf.Infinity;
                        int tempIndex = 0;
```

To find the nearest waypoint to the 3d vector fromPos, the variable distance starts out at Mathf.Infinity (the computer equivalent of an infinite number!). We use this to compare distances during the iteration loop below. tempIndex is a local variable for storing the index of the closest waypoint during the comparison code below.

```
                        // Iterate through them and find the closest
one
                        for(int i = 0; i < _transforms.Count; i++)
                        {
                                Transform _tempTR =
(Transform)_transforms[i];

                                // calculate the distance between the
current transform and the passed in transform's position vector
                                diff = (_tempTR.position - fromPos);
                                curDistance = diff.sqrMagnitude;

                                if ( curDistance < distance )
                                {
```

As Mathf.Infinity is, well, infinity, this condition will always be satisfied at least once. There should always be something closer than infinity, meaning that as long as there are Transforms to compare, we should always get at least some kind of a return result no matter how far away they are in the 3d world.

```
                if( Mathf.Abs( _tempTR.position.y - fromPos.y ) < maxRange )
                {
```

In some cases, using Transforms that are too far away may not be so useful, so maxRange is provided to provide a distance limit, if needed.

```
                                // set our current 'winner' (closest transform) to
the transform we just found
                                _closest = _tempTR;

                                // store the index of this waypoint
                                tempIndex =i;

                                // set our 'winning' distance to the distance we
just found
                                distance = curDistance;
                        }
```

With the addition of the maxRange check, we can no longer be one hundred percent sure of a return result, so a quick check makes sure that closest has something other than a zero in it before returning the result:

```
                if(_closest)
                {
                        // return the waypoint we found in this test
                        return tempIndex;
                } else {
                        // no waypoint was found, so return -1 (this
should be acccounted for at the other end!)
                        return -1;
                }
```

It is possible to have two different implementations of the same function, each with its own set of required parameters. Here, a second version of the FindNearestWaypoint() function follows almost the same course as the first with the exception of a new transform passed in via the exceptThis parameter discussed earlier in this section.

```csharp
                    public int FindNearestWaypoint(Vector3 fromPos,
Transform exceptThis, float maxRange)
            {
                    if (_transforms == null)
                            GetTransforms();

                    // the distance variable is just used to hold
the 'current' distance when
                    // we are comparing, so that we can find the
closest
                    distance = Mathf.Infinity;
                    int tempIndex = 0;

                    // Iterate through them and find the closest
one
                    for (int i = 0; i < totalTransforms; i++)
                    {
                            // grab a reference to a transform
                            Transform _tempTR =
(Transform)_transforms[i];

                            // calculate the distance between the
current transform and the passed in transform's position vector
                            diff = (_tempTR.position - fromPos);
                            curDistance = diff.sqrMagnitude;

                            // now compare distances - making
sure that we are not
                            if (curDistance < distance &&
_tempTR != exceptThis)
                            {
                                    if (Mathf.Abs(_tempTR.
position.y - fromPos.y) < maxRange)
                                    {

                                            // set our current
'winner' (closest transform) to the transform we just found
                                            _closest = _tempTR;

                                            // store the index of
this waypoint
                                            tempIndex = i;

                                            // set our 'winning'
distance to the distance we just found
                                            distance = curDistance;
                                    }
                            }
                    }

                    // now we make sure that we did actually find
something, then return it
                    if (_closest)
                    {
                            // return the waypoint we found in
this test
                            return tempIndex;
                    }
                    else
                    {
                            // no waypoint was found, so return
-1 (this should be acccounted for at the other end!)
                            return -1;
                    }
            }
```

GetWaypoint() returns the transform of the waypoint at the index passed in via the integer 'index'.

```
public Transform GetWaypoint(int index)
{
        if( shouldReverse )
        {
```

This is the only place in the class where shouldReverse is used. GetWaypoint will reverse the index numbers of the waypoints when shouldReverse is true (i.e. Using GetWaypoint to get a waypoint with the index number of zero would return the last waypoint in the path, instead of the first).

To reverse the index passed into this function, the variable index is modified by subtracting it from the number of Transforms in totalTransforms.

```
                // send back the reverse index'd waypoint
                index = (totalTransforms - 1) - index;

                if(index<0)
                        index=0;
        }
```

Obviously, before trying to access the waypoint Transforms to send out as a return value, it is important to make sure that they have been set up; so, there is a quick check to make sure that Transforms is not null. If Transforms is null, we know that there will be no Transforms to work with so GetTransforms() is called to get everything set up:

```
        // make sure that we have populated the transforms
list, if not, populate it
                if(_transforms==null)
                        GetTransforms();
```

If the index being requested is too high, rather than return a wrong waypoint it will return a null value. The code on the requesting side can then check for a null return value and act accordingly:

```
        if(index>totalTransforms - 1)
                return null;
```

Now that everything has been set up correctly, the transforms List contains waypoints and the index number is within range, all that is left to do is return the transform from the array:

```
        return (Transform) _transforms[index];
}
```

The final piece in the waypoints controller script is GetTotal(), which is used by other scripts to find out how many waypoints there are:

```
public int GetTotal()
{
        return totalTransforms;
}
}
```

9 Recipe

Sound and Audio

In this chapter, we look at AudioMixers, build a script to act as a basic sound manager (BaseSoundManager) and discuss adding audio to the weapons system of the framework.

▮ 9.1 AudioMixers and Mixing Audio in Unity

Audio balancing is a huge part of making your game sound professional. It can be difficult to get the volumes of your sounds nicely balanced, so that you can hear everything important underneath the music or so that a laser doesn't sound louder than an explosion and so forth. Unity provides a great toolkit for balancing audio along with some effects to help get the kind of audioscapes your work needs.

Unity's AudioMixers allow you to organize sounds into groups and then manage those groups rather than dealing with individual sounds. For example, you might have a group for music, one for general sound effects and perhaps a third group for ambient background audio. Unity gives you a basic mixing desk where you can adjust the volumes of each group live, during gameplay, to balance them correctly. Another advantage of using an Audio Mixer is that you can use effects.

When you make an AudioMixer for your project, you can use the Audio Mixer window (Window>Audio>Audio Mixer) to see what is happening and adjust sliders (Figure 9.1).

9.1.1 Mixing Audio

To access the Audio Mixer in Unity, use the menu Window/Audio/Audio Mixer. The Mixer shows a list of mixers, snapshots, groups, and views down the left side. The main part of the window will show sliders for groups within the currently selected Mixer.

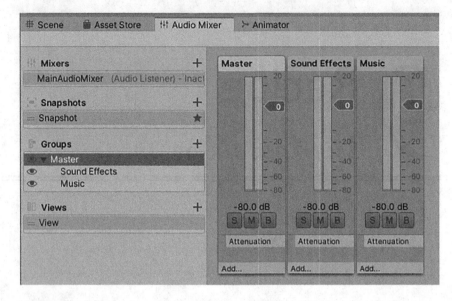

Figure 9.1 The Audio Mixer window allows you to change the balance between different audio groups.

9.1.2 Exposing Mixer Properties to Modify Them with Scripts

If you want to change properties of an AudioMixer, such as its audio levels, you need to expose them for them to be accessible via scripts. To do this, open the AudioMixer via the menu Window/Audio/Audio Mixer. Choose the Mixer you want to edit on the left, followed by the group you want to expose properties of. In the Inspector, right click on the name of the field you want to expose. For example, in Figure 9.2. we chose the Volume property under Attenuation of the Sound Effects group. A menu should appear, with the top option being to expose the property to script. Choose this option from the menu. The property will now

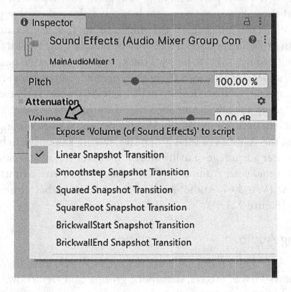

Figure 9.2 The Inspector shows properties of the currently selected Audio Mixer. You can click on a field to expose it to code.

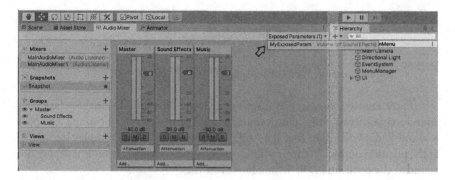

Figure 9.3 The Exposed Parameters menu shows exposed parameters and allows you to rename or unexpose them from scripts.

be exposed to script, but it will have a default name – MyExposedParam – which is not the most descriptive. To rename the exposed property, look to the Audio Mixer panel and find the Exposed Parameters button in the top right of it (Figure 9.3) – click on Exposed Parameters and Unity should show you any exposed parameters for the selected Mixer. To rename, right click the property you wish to rename and choose Rename from the menu.

If you ever want to unexposed a parameter, click on Exposed Parameters, and right click on the parameter you wish to unexposed. Choose Unexpose from the menu.

9.1.3 Audio Effects

Unity offers a variety of audio effects; you can add to AudioMixers to make your sounds more interesting or to help balance them dynamically. To add effects, first open the AudioMixer via the menu Window/Audio/Audio Mixer. Choose the Group you want to add effects to. In the Audio Mixer panel, there is an Add button at the bottom of each audio panel. Click Add to show the effects menu. At this point, let me draw your attention to the Duck Volume effect. Duck Volume will take input from another audio group and drop the volume of the group it is attached to. You may have already heard this effect in action in commercial videogames and tv shows during dialog, as it is most often used to drop the volume of music whenever dialog is played. To accomplish this, you would have your music and dialog channeled through two audio groups. Your music group would have the Duck Volume effect on it. Your dialog group would have the Send effect attached. In the Inspector with the dialog group selected, the Send effect has a field named Receive that lets you choose which group should receive audio levels. Setting this to the music channel would mean that the Duck Volume effect could get this groups levels and duck the volume of the music accordingly. Using audio ducking with notification sounds can also make the process of highlighting important sounds easier.

▉ 9.2 The BaseSoundManager Class

In this section, we build a basic sound management class named BaseSoundManager. Its specifications are:

- Must be able to manage multiple audio clips from a single class
- Ability to play an audio clip from a set position in 3d space

- Provide a function to set volume

- Provide a method to fade an AudioMixer group in and out

- To be accessible from other scripts

There are two ways to play a sound with the BaseSoundManager class. The sound manager can either play a sound at a set position, or you can tell it to play a sound and it will either find the AudioListener in the Scene and play the sound at the position of the Listener, or if it cannot find an AudioListener it will play the sound at the position 0,0,0. Syntax looks like this:

```
BaseSoundManager.Instance.PlaySoundByIndex( the index number from
the array of sounds );
```

Or

```
BaseSoundManager.Instance.PlaySoundByIndex( the index number from
the array of sounds, a Vector3 position );
```

AudioClips should be dragged in to the GameSounds array via the Inspector window in the Unity editor. Each AudioClip in the array will have its own AudioSource and GameObject instantiated when the BaseSoundManager class first runs. Think of each sound as having its own audio channel, to avoid overlaps, or too many different sounds playing on a single AudioSource. Internally, a class called SoundObject is used to store information about the audio sources and their GameObjects.

BaseSoundManager.cs starts like this:

```
using UnityEngine;
using System.Collections;
using System.Collections.Generic;
using UnityEngine.Audio;

namespace GPC
{
        [AddComponentMenu("CSharpBookCode/Base/Sound Controller")]
```

Above, we need System.Collections for the fading coroutine (see below, further down in the script) and System.Collections.Generic to be able to use Lists for storing SoundObject instances in. We also use UnityEngine.Audio for accessing Unity's audio classes. We use AddComponentMenu to make a menu item for this script in Unity and this script, like all the others in the framework, exists inside the GPC namespace.

The SoundObject class is declared next – and just in case you are wondering? Yes, it is okay to declare two functions in one script, in Unity:

```
        public class SoundObject
        {
                public AudioSource source;
                public GameObject sourceGO;
                public Transform sourceTR;
```

Unlike almost all of the other classes in this book, the SoundObject class does not derive from anything, as it is mostly used as a data container and its only function just calls out to play a sound via Unity's PlayOneShot() function.

```
            public SoundObject(AudioClip aClip, string aName,
float aVolume, AudioMixerGroup theMixer, Transform myParent)
        {
                sourceGO = new GameObject("AudioSource_" + aName);
                sourceGO.transform.parent = myParent;
```

Above, the constructor of the SoundObject class (a function that runs auto-matically when SoundObject is instanced) contains set up code to create a new GameObject in the Scene for its AudioSource Component to be attached to. When playing sounds, we do not call SoundObject directly – this is done further down, by the BaseSoundManager class. Note that the constructor for SoundObject has 5 parameters – when a SoundObject instance is created, each one will need these parameters passed into it. You will see how this is done further down in the BaseSoundManager class.

The constructor starts by creating a new GameObject with new GameObject(), which takes a name as a parameter – naming the new GameObject based on this. To make sure we know what this GameObject is, in the Scene's Hierarchy, it is named AudioSource followed by a name passed into this constructor as a param-eter. Next, we set the parent of the new GameObject here, too, or more specifi-cally the parent of its Transform. This is all about keeping sound GameObjects together in the Scene to keep it all neat and tidy and we get the parent Transform from a passed in parameter named myParent.

```
                sourceTR = sourceGO.transform;
                source = sourceGO.AddComponent<AudioSource>();
                source.outputAudioMixerGroup = theMixer;
                source.playOnAwake = false;
                source.clip = aClip;
                source.volume = aVolume;
                source.maxDistance = 2000;
        }
```

Every time we want to set the position of a sound, we will need to access the Transform of this GameObject and we store a reference to the Transform in the variable sourceTR, so that we do not have to look up the Transform repeatedly.

Next, we add an AudioSource to our new GameObject with GameObject. AddComponent(). We keep a reference to the AudioSource in the variable source for easy access later, and so that we can set the relevant properties on it, above. The properties we set on the AudioSource are:

outputAudioMixerGroup – This is the Audio Mixer for the sound to play through (passed in as a parameter).

playOnAwake – We set this to false, to prevent the AudioClip from playing automatically.

Clip – This is the AudioClip (the sample) that will be played by this AudioSource.

Volume – Our volume levels will usually be controlled by the AudioMixers, but having the volume available provides an extra method for individual audio volume control, if needed.

maxDistance – This is the maximum distance at which our sound should be heard.

After the constructor of our SoundObject, the function PlaySound():

```
public void PlaySound(Vector3 atPosition)
{
        sourceTR.position = atPosition;
        source.PlayOneShot(source.clip);
}
}
```

A position is passed in to PlaySound() as a parameter, as a Vector3. We use this to set the position of our AudioSource and AudioSource.PlayOneShot() is used to start the AudioClip playback. We use PlayOneShot() here, rather than just playing the AudioSource with Play(), so that any currently playing sounds will not be interrupted. If you just call AudioSource.Play() when you are playing sounds in close succession it will cut off the previous sound and sound broken. PlayOneShot() will play several sounds through the same AudioSource without interruption. It takes the AudioClip as a parameter, which we just get from the AudioSource already with source.clip – the AudioClip will never change for this AudioSource, so we know this is the correct sound to play.

On to the main BaseSoundManager class, next. It derives from MonoBehaviour so that it can use the Awake() and Start() functions called by the Unity engine:

```
public class BaseSoundManager : MonoBehaviour
{
        public static BaseSoundManager instance;
        public AudioClip[] GameSounds;
        public AudioMixerGroup theAudioMixerGroup;
        public Transform theListenerTransform;
        private List<SoundObject> soundObjectList;
        private SoundObject tempSoundObj;
        public float volume = 1;
```

There is nothing much to note about the variable declarations. Most of these should become clear as we work through the script below.

```
public void Awake()
{
        instance = this;
}
```

As this script does not check for multiple instances, care must be taken to ensure that there is only one instance per Scene.

```
void Start()
{
        soundObjectList = new List<SoundObject>();
        foreach (AudioClip theSound in GameSounds)
        {
```

SoundObjects are stored in a generic List. Above, we initialize the List soundObjectList ready to be populated by information about our sounds and their AudioSources and GameObjects.

To create the instances of SoundObjects, we then iterate through each AudioClip in the GameSounds array (which should be set up in the Inspector in the editor).

```
                        soundObjectList.Add(new
SoundObject(theSound, theSound.name, volume,
theAudioMixerGroup,transform));
            }
    }
```

Above, soundObjectList is populated by new instances of the SoundObject class. You may recall from earlier in this chapter that SoundObject takes 5 parameters. The first, the sound clip itself, comes from our GameSounds array we are iterating through. We then pass in a name for the sounds GameObject by using the name of the sounds from GameSounds. The volume is next, followed by the AudioMixer we want to use and, finally, our Transform to act as the object our sounds will be parented to. Note the Mixer needs to be set in the Inspector on this Component. In the example games, the AudioMixer will be set to use the Sound Effects Mixer.

```
            public void PlaySoundByIndex(int anIndexNumber,
Vector3 aPosition)
            {
                tempSoundObj =
(SoundObject)soundObjectList[anIndexNumber];
                tempSoundObj.PlaySound(aPosition);
            }
```

To play a sound, the function PlaySoundByIndex takes two parameters; an integer and a Vector3 position. We take a SoundObject instance from the soundObjectList array, using the passed in parameter anIndexNumber, and hold it in a variable named tempSoundObj. Next, calling PlaySound() on the SoundObject plays the sound at the passed in position, as we pass that to PlaySound() as a parameter. Passing in a position is optional here, however, and the next function deals with what happens when we do not pass in a position:

```
            public void PlaySoundByIndex(int anIndexNumber)
            {
                if (theListenerTransform == null)
                {
                    AudioListener theListener =
FindObjectOfType<AudioListener>();
                    if(theListener!=null)
                        theListenerTransform =
theListener.transform;
                }
```

When PlaySoundByIndex() is called without passing in a position, what we try to do above is to find the AudioListener in the Scene for positioning, instead. If we can find the Listener, the Transform gets stored in the variable theListenerTransform.

```
                tempSoundObj =
(SoundObject)soundObjectList[anIndexNumber];
                if (theListenerTransform != null)

    tempSoundObj.PlaySound(theListenerTransform.position);
                else
                    tempSoundObj.PlaySound(Vector3.zero);
            }
```

Again, as with the other implementation of PlaySoundByIndex(), we take a SoundObject instance from the soundObjectList array, using the passed in parameter anIndexNumber, and hold it in a variable named tempSoundObj. We then see whether or not theListenerTransform variable actually has anything in it – if it has, we use the position of theListenerTransform to position the sound by passing its position into PlaySound(). If there is nothing in theListenerTransform, we found no Listener in the Scene, and instead we pass Vector3.zero to PlaySound() to make the sound play at world space 0,0,0.

The audio fade functions are all similar but do different things with the volume levels. There are three functions for you to use:

StartFadeIn(AudioMixer audioMixer, string exposedParam, float duration)

This will fade in the exposed parameter in exposedParam of the AudioMixer, from –80 decibels to 0, in time duration x seconds.

Start FadeOut (AudioMixer, string exposedParam, float duration)

This will fade out the exposed parameter in exposedParam of the AudioMixer from 0 decibels to –80, in time duration x seconds.

StartFade (AudioMixer, string exposedParam, float duration, float targetVolume)

This will transition the exposed parameter in exposedParam of the AudioMixer from its current value to targetVolume, in time duration x seconds.

```
public static IEnumerator StartFadeIn (AudioMixer
audioMixer, string exposedParam, float duration)
{
    float targetVolume = 1;
    float currentTime = 0;
    float currentVol = -80f;
    currentVol = Mathf.Pow(10f, currentVol / 20f);
    float targetValue = Mathf.Clamp(targetVolume,
0.0001f, 1);

    while (currentTime < duration)
    {
        currentTime += Time.deltaTime;
        float newVol = Mathf.Lerp(currentVol,
targetValue, currentTime / duration);
        audioMixer.SetFloat(exposedParam,
Mathf.Log10(newVol) * 20f);

        yield return null;
    }
    yield break;
}

public static IEnumerator StartFadeOut (AudioMixer
audioMixer, string exposedParam, float duration)
{
    float targetVolume = -80;
    float currentTime = 0;
    float currentVol;
    audioMixer.GetFloat(exposedParam, out
currentVol);

    currentVol = Mathf.Pow(10f, currentVol / 20f);
    float targetValue = Mathf.Clamp(targetVolume,
0.0001f, 1);

    while (currentTime < duration)
```

```
                    {
                            currentTime += Time.deltaTime;
                            float newVol = Mathf.Lerp(currentVol,
targetValue, currentTime / duration);
                            audioMixer.SetFloat(exposedParam,
Mathf.Log10(newVol) * 20f);
                            yield return null;
                    }
                    yield break;
            }
            public static IEnumerator StartFade(AudioMixer
audioMixer, string exposedParam, float duration, float
targetVolume)
            {
                    float currentTime = 0;
                    float currentVol;
                    audioMixer.GetFloat(exposedParam, out
currentVol);
                    currentVol = Mathf.Pow(10f, currentVol / 20f);
                    float targetValue = Mathf.Clamp(targetVolume,
0.0001f, 1);
                    while (currentTime < duration)
                    {
                            currentTime += Time.deltaTime;
                            float newVol = Mathf.Lerp(currentVol,
targetValue, currentTime / duration);
                            audioMixer.SetFloat(exposedParam,
Mathf.Log10(newVol) * 20f);
                            yield return null;
                    }
                    yield break;
            }
        }
}
```

▉ 9.3 Adding Sound to Weapons

To add a sound to weapons, the easiest method is to add an AudioSource to the
projectile prefab and set its PlayOnAwake checkbox to true. Whenever a projectile is spawned, the sound will be played. By attaching the sound to the projectiles,
you can easily have different sounds for different projectile types just by changing
the clip on the AudioSource.

10 AI Manager

The AI controller in this book is a state machine. You may have heard of this before, but do we mean when we say state machine? Our AI system stores the current state of the AI and runs code according to whichever state it is. When the state changes, it runs different code. For example, when our state is set to chase, the AI should move toward an object. When the state is set to stopped, the AI should stand still. This is state machine AI.

In this book, the AI is split into several different scripts that fit together to add functionality. You can think of our main AI class, BaseAIController, as a class containing a set of utility functions for AI rather than a single all-encompassing script.

1. BaseAIController
   This contains base code for AI such as chase/follow behavior.

2. WaypointsController
   The code for dealing with waypoints: this is optional, depending on whether you want waypoint following.

3. AIBotController
   Using BaseAIController, this class can move a bot around, chase, and attack a target and stand on guard to look for a target to chase and attack. This is used by the Blaster game example in this book to move the bots around.

4. AISteeringController
   This uses the BaseAIController and WaypointsController to provide steering inputs that will follow a waypoint path (used in the example racing game in this book to drive the AI cars around the track).

We will be looking at the above scripts and breaking them down in this chapter, as well as a method for getting the weapon system firing with AI.

Note that this AI system is only intended for 3D games.

▪ 10.1 AI States

Before getting to the main BaseAIController.cs script, take a look at AIStates.cs below. It contains all of the AIStates from the previous section stored in an enumerator list similar to the one used by the character controller from Chapter 5 of this book. This list will be used by the AI to determine its current required behavior. The list is in its own file (the AIStates.cs file) and in a namespace called AIStates so that we can easily make it accessible from any script used by the game:

```
using UnityEngine;
namespace AIStates
{
        public enum AIState
        {
                moving_looking_for_target,
                chasing_target,
                backing_up_looking_for_target,
                stopped_turning_left,
                stopped_turning_right,
                paused_looking_for_target,
                translate_along_waypoint_path,
                paused_no_target,
                steer_to_waypoint,
                steer_to_target,
        }
}
```

▪ 10.2 The BaseAIController Class – Base AI Control

BaseAIController starts with the UnityEngine namespace as well as adding AIStates, as seen in the previous Section 10.1. By including AIStates as a namespace, it can be accessed as though it were part of the same script. We wrap the class in the GPC namespace, and it derives from ExtendedCustomMonoBehaviour:

```
using UnityEngine;
using AIStates;
namespace GPC
{
        [AddComponentMenu("CSharpBookCode/Base/AI Controller")]

        public class BaseAIController : ExtendedCustomMonoBehaviour
        {
                        public bool AIControlled;

                [Header("AI States")]
                public AIState currentAIState;
                public AIState targetAIState;

                [Header("Enemy input")]
                public float horz;
                public float vert;

                [Header("Enemy AI movement values")]
                public float obstacleAvoidDistance = 40f;
                public float modelRotateSpeed = 15f;
                public int _followTargetMaxTurnAngle = 120;
                public float minChaseDistance = 1f;
                public float maxChaseDistance = 10f;
                public float visionHeightOffset = 1f;
```

```
[Header("Waypoints")]
// waypoint following related variables
public WaypointsController _waypointsController;

public Transform _currentWaypointTransform;
public Transform _followTarget;
public Transform _rotateTransform;

[System.NonSerialized]
public bool reachedLastWaypoint;
public float waypointDistance = 5f;
public float pathSmoothing = 2f;
public bool shouldReversePathFollowing;
public bool loopPath;
public bool destroyAtEndOfWaypoints;
public bool startAtFirstWaypoint;

[Header("Layer masks and raycasting")]
public LayerMask obstacleAvoidLayers;
public string potentialTargetTag = "Player";
public LayerMask targetLayer;
public int obstacleFinderResult;

private int totalWaypoints;
private int currentWaypointNum;
private RaycastHit hit;
private Vector3 tempDirVec;
private Vector3 relativeTarget;
private float targetAngle;
private int obstacleHitType;
public int lookAheadWaypoints = 0;
```

There are a lot of variables to declare, so don't worry about those. We will see how they are used later in the breakdown. Other than ExtendedCustomMonoBehaviour, this script only uses one more script from the framework in this book – the WaypointsController class for using waypoints. Everything else is standalone and ready to be used in your projects regardless of whether you use the framework.

Once we get past the class declaration, we kick things off with a Start() function:

```
public virtual void Start()
{
        Init();
}
```

The Init() function takes care of making cached references to the GameObject, the Transform and its Rigidbody (this script assumes that there will always be a Rigidbody attached to the same GameObject it is attached to as a Component):

```
public virtual void Init ()
{
        // cache ref to gameObject
        _GO = GetComponent<GameObject>();

        // cache ref to transform
        _TR = GetComponent<Transform>();

        // cache a ref to our rigidbody
        _RB = _TR.GetComponent<Rigidbody>();
```

Above, Init() grabs references to other objects we will be needing further in the script.

```
        if( rotateTransform==null )
                _rotateTransform= _TR;
```

_rotateTransform is an optional parameter which may be set in the Unity editor Inspector window to provide a Transform for rotation which is different to the one that the script is attached to. This is used in cases where we do not wish to rotate the main Transform.

```
            didInit= true;
    }
```

As with all of the other scripts in this book, didInit is a Boolean variable used to determine whether or not the Init() function has successfully completed.

```
    public void SetAIControl( bool state )
    {
            AIControlled= state;
    }
```

Above, a Boolean variable named AIControlled is used to decide whether this script should take control. The SetAIControl() function just provides an easy way for other scripts to enable or disable AI control.

```
    // set up AI parameters --------------------
    public void SetobstacleAvoidDistance(float aNum)
    {
            obstacleAvoidDistance = aNum;
    }
    public void SetWaypointDistance(float aNum)
    {
            waypointDistance = aNum;
    }
    public void SetMinChaseDistance(float aNum)
    {
            minChaseDistance = aNum;
    }
    public void SetMaxChaseDistance(float aNum)
    {
            maxChaseDistance = aNum;
    }
    // -----------------------------------------
```

Above, functions to set several main parameters. Those are:

obstacleAvoidDistance(float) – In 3d units, how far the bot should look ahead in its attempts to avoid running into obstacles when it is patrolling.

wayPointDistance(float) – In 3d units, how close the bot will be allowed to get to a waypoint before it advances to the next waypoint.

minChaseDistance (float) – In 3d units, minChaseDistance determines how close the bot should get to its target, when chasing a target, before it stops moving toward it. This is to prevent the bot from getting too close and pushing the player around.

maxChaseDistance (float) – In 3d units, how far away from its target the bot can acknowledge a target.

```
    public virtual void SetAIState(AIState newState)
    {
            // update AI state
            targetAIState = newState;
            UpdateTargetState();
    }
```

There will be times when we may need to force the state of the bot from another script, such as telling it which state to start in when the game begins. Use the function SetAIState() for that, passing in an AIState.

```
public virtual void SetChaseTarget(Transform theTransform)
{
        // set a target for this AI to chase, if required
        _followTarget= theTransform;
}
```

At the end of the SetAIState() function, above, we call UpdateTargetState() to do anything that needs to be done before we can fully switch mode to the new state. For example, you could call out to your animation system to play an animation when the AI changes state between patrolling and chasing. In the base version of this script, there is no extra logic in UpdateTargetState() and the function is there to maintain protocol of having a target state and a current state with a good place to trigger action when the target state is changed. If chasing is required, the SetChaseTarget() function should be used to pass in a reference to the Transform that needs chasing. When you pass a Transform into SetChaseTarget() the Transform will be stored in a variable named followTarget.

```
public virtual void Update ()
{
        // make sure we have initialized before doing
anything
        if( !didInit )
                Init ();
```

The Update() function is called by Unity each frame update, but we need to be sure that the script has properly initialized before doing anything significant with it because it may be possible for Update() to be called before Init() has finished its run.

```
        if( !AIControlled )
                return;

        // do AI updates
        UpdateCurrentState();
}
```

Above, remembering that we are still in the main Update() function, if AIControlled is not set to true this function drops out before it has chance to do anything. The Boolean variable AIControlled makes it possible to turn on or off AI control. For an example of where this may come in handy, it is great for situations where we may want AI to take control of the player; such as at the end of a racing game when the race is complete and we want the car to continue driving but take the player out of the game. The AI script would be attached to all players, but in the case of the user's vehicle it is only activated after the race finishes. This is what happens in the example racing game in this book, in Chapter 14.

UpdateCurrentState() is right at the core of the script – it is called by the Update() function and deals with coordinating the bot to do what it should:

```
public virtual void UpdateCurrentState ()
{
```

In some cases, the AI script does not manipulate its GameObject's physics directly but instead acts as an input provider to another script which deals with the actual physics. The reason it works this way is so that AI can use the same movement controllers as the player without having to recode movement each time. For example, in the example racing game in Chapter 14, the AI cars use the exact same car physics as the user. When a car is set to use AI, the car physics controller script uses input from the AI script rather than a user input controller.

```
// reset our inputs
horz=0;
vert=0;
```

Above, the AI script uses horz and vert (both floats) to store horizontal and vertical input, which are the standard variable names used in other scripts in this book. Here in the UpdateCurrentState() function, they are reset to zero. This is centering the inputs before other functions change them.

```
switch (currentAIState)
{
        case AIState.paused_no_target:
        // do nothing
    break;

        default
        // idle (do nothing)
        break;
}
```

Above, if there is anything that needs to be done when the AI is in a particular state, this is the place. The switch statement above takes the variable currentAIState and we run the corresponding code for whatever the current state is.

In BaseAIController, the UpdateCurrentState() function is a placeholder – it is assumed that you will override this function in a derived version of this class to put your own logic into it. You can find examples of this in the AIBotController and AISteeringController scripts in GPC_Framework/Scripts/COMMON/AI.

Before the state is changed from targetAIState to currentAIState, we need to go through the UpdateTargetState() function:

```
public virtual void UpdateTargetState()
{
        switch (targetAIState)
        {
                default:
                        // idle (do nothing)
                        break;
        }
        currentAIState = targetAIState;
}
```

As we know that this will only happen when a new current state is about to be set, we can call code that only needs to be called when the AI enters the new state. Just as UpdateCurrentState(), UpdateTargetState() is a placeholder that should be overridden by your own logic.

Next is a collection of functions to set inputs for turning left and right or moving forwards and backward:

```
public virtual void TurnLeft ()
{
        horz= -1;
}
```

```
        public virtual void TurnRight ()
        {
                horz= 1;
        }


        public virtual void MoveForward ()
        {
                vert= 1;
        }


        public virtual void MoveBack ()
        {
                vert= -1;
        }

public virtual void NoMove ()
        {
                vert= 0;
        }
```

Each function above is there to make it easier to interface with other types of control systems. You can override them in a derived class or call them from another.

Next up is the LookAroundFor() function. This will be called when we need a bot to chase a target. For an example of using it, check out the AIBotController.cs script.

```
        public virtual void LookAroundFor()
        {
                if (_followTarget != null)
                {
                        float theDist = Vector3.Distance
(_TR.position, _followTarget.position);
                        bool canSee = CanSee(_followTarget);
                        if (theDist < maxChaseDistance)
                        {
                                if (canSee == true)
                                        SetAIState(AIState.
chasing_target);
                        }
                }
                else
                {
                        GameObject potential =
GameObject.FindGameObjectWithTag(potentialTargetTag);
                        _followTarget = potential.transform;
                }
        }
```

The LookAroundFor() function, above, starts by making sure we have something in the _followTarget variable. The target may be set by this script or another outside script. If we have a target to follow already, we can go ahead and do a distance check using Unity's built in function Vector3.Distance() – the result of which we put into a local variable named theDist. We also do a test to see if our target is visible to the AI by calling CanSee() and storing the result in the local variable canSee. The CanSee() function is further down in the script. It will return true if the AI has a clear line between it and the target.

If the distance to the target falls within our maxChaseDistance, we make sure that the result back from CanSee() was true (canSee==true). At this stage, we now know several things about the target:

1. We have a target.

2. The target is within maxChaseDistance away.

3. There is a clear view of the target from the AI.

If the above conditions are met, SetAIState() is called to change the target state to AIState.chasing_target – making our AI turn and move toward it.

Without a Transform in _followTarget, we have nothing to follow and the function drops through to the else statement. Here, we will instead try to find a suitable target using GameObject.FindGameObjectWithTag(). The new target object will be the first object (if any object is returned) from that search.

Coming up next is one of the core Components of the AI controller – the IsObstacleAhead() function. In this part, Physics.Raycast is used to raycast out ahead (and slightly to the left or right) to check for obstacles. It returns an integer, expressing its findings with the following values:

0 – No obstacles were found

1 – An obstacle was detected front, left side only

2 – An obstacle was detected front, right side only

3 – Obstacle or obstacles detected on both sides

The IsObstacleAhead() function is used to detect other Colliders, though in its current state it can be a little unpredictable and it could do with some more iteration to make it work nicer. It works, but it could work better, and I have to leave that up to you, dear reader!

```
private int obstacleFinding;

public virtual int IsObstacleAhead()
{
        obstacleHitType=0;

        if (_TR == null)
        {
                return 0;
        }
}
```

The return result for the function is stored in a variable named obstacle-HitType, which starts out getting set to a default value of 0 at the top of the function.

The beginning of the function above checks to make sure that we have an actual Transform in _TR. If not, we know that either this GameObject's Transform has been destroyed, or something has gone wrong, so we return a result of 0.

```
        // draw this raycast so we can see what it is doing
        Debug.DrawRay(_TR.position, ((_TR.forward +
(_TR.right * 0.5f)) * obstacleAvoidDistance));
```

```
        Debug.DrawRay(_TR.position, ((_TR.forward +
(_TR.right * -0.5f)) * obstacleAvoidDistance));
```

To make it easier to visualize what is happening with the AI, this function includes Debug.DrawRay calls which will make lines appear in the editor where the rays are being cast. This will only happen in the editor when Gizmos are set to true – use the Gizmos icon above the Scene or Game panels to set this.

Above, the position and direction data used to draw the debug rays match with the ones we use to do the actual ray casting, below:

```
        RaycastHit hit;
        // cast a ray out forward from our AI and put the
'result' into the variable named hit
        if (Physics.Raycast(_TR.position, _TR.forward +
(_TR.TransformDirection(Vector3.right) * 0.5f), out hit,
obstacleAvoidDistance, obstacleAvoidLayers))
```

The raycasting uses the AI bot's forward vector (_TR.forward) with an offset to the side. _TR.right is also multiplied by half and added to the forward vector, so that the angle goes diagonally out from the bot – with the ray starting at _TR.position.

What we consider to be obstacles are defined as anything which is set to use one of the collision layers defined in the obstacleAvoidLayers LayerMask. You can set one or multiple collision layers as obstacle layers in the Unity editors Inspector on this GameObject.

The variable obstacleAvoidDistance is used as the distance parameter for ray casting, which can be set in the Unity editor Inspector window.

If a call to Physics.Raycast finds something, it returns true, and that is exactly what the line above is looking for. If something is found we will react to that, next:

```
            // obstacle
            // it's a left hit, so it's a type 1 right
now (thought it could change when we check on the other side)
            obstacleHitType=1;
        }
```

obstacleHitType will form the return value for the function. Above, when the ray cast finds an obstacle, the variable obstacleHitType is set to 1. This represents an obstacle on the left side (remember the list of return results from earlier in this section?). Now a ray is cast out from the other side of the bot:

```
        if (Physics.Raycast(_TR.position, _TR.forward + (_TR.right
* -0.5f), out hit, obstacleAvoidDistance, obstacleAvoidLayers))
        {
```

Above, the only difference to this ray cast and the one previous is that we now reverse that right vector by multiplying it by –0.5 instead of 0.5, casting a ray out in the opposite direction.

```
        // obstacle
        if( obstacleHitType==0 )
        {
            // if we haven't hit anything yet, this is
type 2
            obstacleHitType=2;
```

If obstacleHitType has was not set by the first ray cast, its value will still be at its default of 0; this tells us that this ray is the first one to get a hit and that the function has only found an obstacle on this side – obstacleHitType gets set to 2.

```
                } else {               // if we have hits on both left and
right raycasts, it's a type 3
                        obstacleHitType=3;
                }
        }
```

Next, we deal with the situation where obstacleHitType is not at its default 0. If it is not 0, we know that both this ray cast and the previous one has found obstacles. To represent obstacles found on both sides, obstacleHitType gets set to 3.

All that is left to do now is to return the findings of our ray casting:

```
        return obstacleHitType;
}
```

The next part of BaseAIController.cs is TurnTowardTarget(). This function will turn the bot (more specifically, the Transform set in the variable rotateTransform) toward the Transform passed to it as a parameter:

```
    public void TurnTowardTarget( Transform aTarget )
    {
            if(aTarget==null)
                return;
```

If we are going to be doing anything with a target, the first step is making sure we have a target to turn toward (above) in the variable aTarget.

```
        relativeTarget = _ rotateTransform.InverseTransformPoint
( aTarget.position );
```

Above, we calculate a Vector3 that will represent the target position relative to the AI so that we can look at this vector's values and establish the direction toward the target. e.g. a positive x value means the target is to the right of the car, negative to the left, and a positive z means the target is in front of the car and negative z behind.

```
        // Calculate the target angle
        targetAngle = Mathf.Atan2 ( relativeTarget.x,
relativeTarget.z );
        // Atan returns the angle in radians, convert to
degrees
        targetAngle *= Mathf.Rad2Deg;
```

The newly calculated relativeTarget is then used above with Unity's Mathf. Atan2 function to find an angle of rotation from the vector. Atan returns the angle in radians, whereas radians are preferable for this, so we use Mathf. Rad2Deg to convert targetAngle from radians to degrees.

```
        targetAngle = Mathf.Clamp(targetAngle, - _
followTargetMaxTurnAngle - targetAngle, _ followTargetMaxTurnAngle);
```

Above, to enforce limits on the amount of rotation to apply in one step, Mathf.Clamp is used to keep the angle between the positive and negative versions of the value in the float followTargetMaxAngle. The maximum amount of turn can, as a public variable of course, be changed in the Inspector on this Component.

```
                rotateTransform.Rotate( 0, targetAngle *
modelRotateSpeed * Time.deltaTime, 0 );
        }
```

The last line of TurnTowardTarget() above, uses Transform.Rotate to turn the Transform. targetAngle is multiplied by modelRotateSpeed and multiplied by Time.deltaTime to make the rotation amount time based.

Next up, CanSee() does a simple line of sight check to see if anything is between the bot and its target. This is useful for cutting off chases when the target goes behind a wall or somewhere unreachable by the AI:

```
    public bool CanSee(Transform aTarget)
            {
                // first, let's get a vector to use for
raycasting by subtracting the target position from our AI position
                tempDirVec = Vector3.Normalize(aTarget.
position - _TR.position);
```

It creates a normalized vector from the two positions, then uses the new vector to cast a ray out from the bot at the length by maxChaseDistance.

```
                // let's have a debug line to check the distance
between the two manually, in case you run into trouble!
                Debug.DrawLine(_TR.position + (visionHeightOffset *
_TR.up), aTarget.position, Color.red);
```

Above, just before the actual ray cast, there is a debug line to represent what is going on in this function so that it is easy to see what the AI is supposed to be doing when you are in the Unity editor.

```
                if (Physics.Raycast( _ TR.position +
(visionHeightOffset * _ TR.up), tempDirVec, out hit, Mathf.Infinity))
                {
                    if (IsInLayerMask(hit.transform.gameObject.
layer, playerLayer))
                    {
                        return true;
                    }
                }
                // nothing found, so return false
                return false;
```

Above, the ray cast starts from our Transform (_TR) position along with a height offset. Sometimes you may not want the ray to be cast from the point of origin on the AI – one reason for this could be that the point of origin is at the bottom of the GameObject and may just hit the ground, so you can adjust the height offset in the Inspector on this Component to make this happen.

tempDirVec (that vector we calculated earlier between the AI and its target) is passed into Physics.Raycast() too, as the direction vector. Mathf.Inifinity is the limit of the ray cast, since we do not need to limit it. When a hit occurs in the ray cast, the next line of code checks to see if the hit object's layer is in the LayerMask playerLayer. If the target is on the correct layer, we know that there is nothing blocking the way so we can return true, otherwise execution falls through to return false at the end of the function.

The AI controller incorporates waypoint control into the mix, using the WaypointsController class to manage them:

```
public void SetWayController( WaypointsController aControl )
{
        _waypointsController=aControl;
        aControl=null;
```

Since the AI bot does not know which waypoints to use, another script (such as the game controller) will call SetWayController and pass in a WaypointsController object.

```
        // grab total waypoints
        totalWaypoints = _waypointsController.GetTotal();
```

Above, totalWaypoints contains a cached value of the total number of waypoints from the waypoints controller, to save having to look it up every time it is needed.

```
        if( shouldReversePathFollowing )
        {
                currentWaypointNum = totalWaypoints - 1;
        } else {
                currentWaypointNum = 0;
        }
```

If shouldReversePathFollowing is true, the starting waypoint will be the last one found in the list of waypoints made by the Waypoint_Controller script.

```
        Init();

        // get the first waypoint from the waypoint controller
        _currentWaypointTransform=
myWayControl.GetWaypoint(currentWaypointNum);
        if(startAtFirstWaypoint)
        {
                _TR.position=
_currentWaypointTransform.position;
```

Among other things, the Init() function in this class caches a reference to the AI bot's Transform in the variable _TR. The SetWayController() function calls Init() to make sure that the reference is set up and ready for it to use, as it repositions _TR at the first waypoint (when the Boolean variable startAtFirstWaypoint is set to true).

The next two functions in the class are interface functions for other scripts to change values, if needed:

```
public void SetReversePath( bool shouldRev )
{
        shouldReversePathFollowing= shouldRev;
}
public void SetRotateSpeed( float aRate )
{
        modelRotateSpeed= aRate;
}
```

UpdateWaypoints() takes care of keeping the current target waypoint up to date and carries out self-destruction, if required, when the AI reaches the end of the path:

```
        void UpdateWaypoints()
        {
                // If we don't have a waypoint controller, we safely
drop out
                If(_waypointsController==null )
                        return;
```

Above, UpdateWaypoints() starts with a check to make sure that _waypoints-Controller (a reference to an instance of the WaypointsController class) is not null, which should mean SetWayController() has been called and set up successfully.

The AI controller script has the option to automatically destroy itself when the last waypoint is reached. When destroyAtEndOfWaypoints is set to true, the GameObject is destroyed, and this code drops out of the UpdateWaypoints() script immediately.

```
        if( reachedLastWaypoint && destroyAtEndOfWaypoints )
        {
                // destroy myself(!)
                Destroy( gameObject );
                return;
        } else if( reachedLastWaypoint )
        {

                currentWaypointNum= 0;
                reachedLastWaypoint= false;

        }
```

When destroyAtEndOfWaypoints is false, the assumption is that waypoint following should go back to the beginning; currentWaypointNum is set to zero, reachedLastWaypoint is reset, and the AI is free to start over again.

```
        if( totalWaypoints==0 )
        {
                // grab total waypoints
                totalWaypoints= _waypointsController.
GetTotal();
                return;
        }
```

To keep this function safe (in case it is somehow called before the waypoints have been correctly set up in the WaypointsController class) there is a check to make sure that more than one waypoint was found. If totalWaypoints is zero, another attempt is made to get the total from _waypointsController before it drops out of the UpdateWaypoints() function.

```
        if( _currentWaypointTransform==null )
        {
                // grab our transform reference from the
waypoint controller
                _currentWaypointTransform= _
waypointsController.GetWaypoint( currentWaypointNum );
        }
```

If no currentWaypointTransform object has been set up at this point, _waypointsController is called upon to provide one with the index number held in the variable _currentWaypointNum.

Calculating distance between two Transforms will consider x, y, and z coordinates. In most cases, waypoint following need only work on a two dimensional plane and the y axis may be done away with completely. Doing so can solve

---

problems where the height combined with the x and y axis differences ends up not advancing the current waypoint at the right time. Particularly for steering or character led AI there is little need for the y axis at all in waypoint distance checking.

```
        // now we check to see if we are close enough to the
current waypoint
                // to advance on to the next one

            myPosition= _TR.position;
            myPosition.y= 0;

            // get waypoint position and 'flatten' it
            nodePosition= _currentWaypointTransform.position;
            nodePosition.y= 0;
```

Both myPosition, a cached Vector3 of the bot's position, and nodePosition, the cached waypoint position, are stripped of the y axis in the code above.

```
            currentWayDist= Vector3.Distance(
nodePosition,myPosition );

            if ( currentWayDist < waypointDistance ) {
                    // we are close to the current node, so let's
move on to the next one!
```

The distance between the AI bot and next waypoint is calculated using the two cached position variables, below. When the resulting currentWayDist value is less than the value of waypointDistance, it means that the bot is close enough to the current waypoint to advance to the next one.

```
            if( shouldReversePathFollowing )
            {
                    currentWaypointNum--;
```

Before advancing to the next waypoint, shouldReversePathFollowing is checked to see which direction along the path the AI needs to go. If the path is reversed, the value of currentWaypointNum is decremented rather than incremented.

```
            // now check to see if we have been all the way
around
            if( currentWaypointNum<0 ){
                    // just in case it gets referenced before we
are destroyed, let's keep it to a safe index number
                        currentWaypointNum= 0;
                        // completed the route!
                        reachedLastWaypoint= true;
                        // if we are set to loop, reset the
currentWaypointNum to 0
                        if(loopPath)
                        {
                                currentWaypointNum= totalWaypoints;
                                reachedLastWaypoint= false;
                        }
                        return;
            }
```

In the code block above, if the path is reversed, when currentWaypointNum drops below zero it needs to get reset to the waypoint at the other end of the path (only when loopPath is set). To make this happen, currentWaypointNum will be set to the value of the variable totalWaypoints.

Something else that happens in this chunk of code, when we know that the end of the path has been reached, is that the value of reachedLastWaypoint is set to true. This will be checked on the next UpdateWaypoints() call, to carry out any actions that need to be done at the end of the path (such as destroying the GameObject when destroyAtEndOfWaypoints is set to true.

```
        } else {
                currentWaypointNum++;
                // now check to see if we have been all the way
around
                if ( currentWaypointNum>=totalWaypoints ){
                        // completed the route!
                        reachedLastWaypoint= true;
                        // if we are set to loop, reset the
currentWaypointNum to 0
                        if(loopPath)
                        {
                                currentWaypointNum= 0;

                                // the route keeps going in a loop,
so we don't want reachedLastWaypoint to ever become true
                                reachedLastWaypoint= false;
                        }
                        // drop out of this function before we grab
another waypoint into currentWaypointTransform, as
                        // we don't need one and the index may be
invalid
                        return;
                }
        }
```

The shouldReversePathFollowing Boolean must have been set to false for the following code to be executed, meaning that the currentWaypointNum has gone past the final waypoint in the list held by the waypoints controller and that currentWaypointNum needs to be reset to zero, if the variable loopPath is set to true.

```
                // grab our transform reference from the
waypoint controller
                _currentWaypointTransform= _
currentWaypointTransform.GetWaypoint( currentWaypointNum );
        }
}
```

With the manipulations to currentWaypointNum complete, we can use its value as an index number to ask the waypoint controller myWayControl, to provide the Transform for the next waypoint. currentWaypointTransform is set to the result of a call to the Waypoint_Controller.cs function GetWaypoint().

```
        public float GetHorizontal()
        {
                return horz;
        }
        public float GetVertical()
        {
                return vert;
        }
}
}
```

Above, helper functions above provide access to the horizontal and vertical input variables.

10.3 Enemy Stats

The BaseEnemyStatsController class can be used to add stats to an enemy in a similar way to how we deal with players. The way we use it in this book, we have it derive from BaseAIController so that it can be layered – the Blaster game example from Chapter 15 has a blaster enemy class that derives from BaseEnemyStatsController. This way, we get all of the AI and stats merged together so we do not have to have any references to other script Components to deal with things like enemy health and so on.

If you wanted to use this script as a standalone in your own game, you can just change the class declaration to derive from MonoBehaviour rather than BaseAIController. You also need to remove the base.Init() from the Init() function and remove override from the Init() function declaration. Do these things and this class will work independently of the AI system and/or framework.

```
using UnityEngine;

namespace GPC
{
        [AddComponentMenu("CSharpBookCode/Base/Enemy Controller")]

        public class BaseEnemyStatsController : BaseAIController
        {
                [Header("Enemy stats")]
                public int myID;
                private static int enemyUniqueID;

                public int defaultHealthAmount = 1;

                public int enemyHealth;
                public int enemyScore;
                public string enemyName;

                public override void Init()
                {
                        base.Init();
                        myID = enemyUniqueID;
                        enemyUniqueID++;

                        enemyScore = 0;
                        enemyHealth = defaultHealthAmount;
                }

                public virtual void AddScore(int anAmount)
                {
                        enemyScore += anAmount;
                }

                public virtual void AddHealth(int anAmount)
                {
                        enemyHealth += anAmount;
                }

                public virtual void LoseScore(int anAmount)
                {
                        enemyScore -= anAmount;
                }
```

```
public virtual void ReduceHealth(int anAmount)
{
        enemyHealth -= anAmount;
}

public virtual void SetScore(int anAmount)
{
        enemyScore = anAmount;
}

public virtual void SetHealth(int anAmount)
{
        enemyHealth = anAmount;
}

public int GetHealth()
{
        return enemyHealth;
}

public int GetScore()
{
        return enemyScore;
}

public void SetName(string aName)
{
        enemyName = aName;
}
    }
}
```

Above, the script is self-explanatory. The Init() function sets default values for our enemy stats and each function provides a way to change or enemy stat set values.

■ 10.4 The AIBotController Class – Making an Enemy Bot Controller

Let's talk a little about how this AI is supposed to work. Its behavior is rather basic, but it should be a good start for your own bots. What happens is that the AI bot will patrol around randomly, avoiding walls, until a player comes into range. At that point, our bot will turn to face the player and then go into chase mode, trying to head directly for the player whenever it is in sight. Our AI will also fire its weapon at random intervals by using the weapon control outlined in Section 10.6 of this chapter.

The AIBotController class uses BaseAIController to move a bot around and derives from BaseEnemyStatsController from the previous Section 10.3 to deal with enemy health.

```
using UnityEngine;
using AIStates;

namespace GPC
{
        public class AIBotController : BaseEnemyStatsController
        {
                private Vector3 moveVec;
                private Vector3 targetMoveVec;
                private float distanceToChaseTarget;
```

```
[Header("Movement")]
public bool isStationary;
public float moveSpeed = 30f;
public bool faceWaypoints;
```

Skipping through the variables, the only thing to note above is the class declaration deriving from BaseEnemyStatsController as mentioned at the start of
the section.

```
public override void Update()
{
        UpdateCurrentState();
        DoMovement();
}
```

Update() is called by the engine automatically and it is where we call for
main AI updates to happen. We call out to UpdateCurrentState() and
DoMovement().

```
public override void UpdateCurrentState()
{
        // reset our inputs
        horz = 0;
        vert = 0;

        obstacleFinderResult = IsObstacleAhead();
```

UpdateCurrentState() is at the core of our state machine. The BaseAIController
had a placeholder function, but here we override it and put it to some real use. We
start by resetting the horz and vert inputs so that they start out at zero each pass. We
then call out to IsObstacleAhead() to check the path, with its return value going into
the variable obstacleFinderResult. This variable will be used by one or more of the
functions we call from the oncoming case statement that will react to the current
state, so we populate it here to avoid having to repeat calls to it each time further on.

```
switch (currentAIState)
{
        // ----------------------------
        case AIState.move_looking_for_target:
                LookForTarget();
                break;
        case AIState.chasing_target:
                ChasingTarget();
                break;
        // ----------------------------
```

This function is called every frame, which means the logic we place in this
case statement will be called each frame too. This is, essentially, the main loop for
our AI states.

The code above is relatively straightforward – in each case, we check to see if
currentAIState matches our case and, if it does, call a function to perform everything we want to do every frame in that state. For example, we call LookForTarget()
when the currentAIState is AIState.move_looking_for_target. When the state is
AIState.chasing_target, we call ChasingTarget().

The code for each state has been split out into an individual function, which
makes it easier to debug later. Having big chunks of code inside a massive case statement is a recipe for disaster, so it is better to split them out like this to save headaches!

```
                               case AIState.
backing_up_looking_for_target:
                                     BackUpLookingForTarget();
                                     break;
                         case AIState.stopped_turning_left:
                                     StoppedTurnLeft();
                                     break;
                         case AIState.stopped_turning_right:
                                     StoppedTurnRight();
                                     break;

                         case AIState.
paused_looking_for_target:
                                     Paused(true);
                                     break;
                         case AIState.
move_along_waypoint_path:
                                     MoveAlongWaypointPath();
                                     break;

                         case AIState.paused_no_target:
                                     break;

                         default:
                                     // idle (do nothing)
                                     break;
                   }
             }
```

Above, we go through all the AIStates we want the bot to react to and call functions to deal with each one. We only use the states chasing_target, move_looking_for_target, stopped_turning_right, stopped_turning_left and backing_up_looking_for_target.

When we have a target, the state is chasing_target unless an obstacle is found – if there is an obstacle, we change to either stopped_turning_left, stopped_turning_right or backing_up_looking_for_target to avoid it. Otherwise, chasing_target aims for the target and moves forward constantly.

If we are in any of the turning or backing up states, we remain in those until the obstacleFinderResult – populated by a call to IsObstacleAhead() – reports that the path forward is clear. When there are no obstacles in the backing_up_looking_for_target state, we choose a random direction to turn in, to reduce the risk of getting stuck whenever the path directly in front is blocked.

Next, the functions themselves:

```
             public virtual void DoMovement()
             {
                         // move forward
                         _TR.Translate(0, 0, vert * moveSpeed *
Time.deltaTime);
                         _TR.Rotate(0, horz * modelRotateSpeed *
Time.deltaTime, 0);
             }
```

Above, the DoMovement() function uses Transform.Translate to move the bot around and Transform.Rotate to handle turning. We take the vert value and multiply it by our moveSpeed and Time.deltaTime. Transform.Rotate() takes three parameters for x, y, and z. We only need to rotate the y axis to turn our bot, so our rotation goes in the second parameter. The actual rotation amount comes from the variable horz, holding our horizontal input value, which is multiplied by modelRotateSpeed and Time.deltaTime. Time.deltaTime is used here to make sure that the rotations and movements will be the same regardless of frame rate or frame glitches, basing the movement amounts on time rather than relying on each frame happening at the exact same time.

```
void LookForTarget()
{
    // look for chase target
    LookAroundFor();

    // if there are obstacles, this is where
we'll switch to a state that can avoid hitting them
    switch(obstacleFinderResult)
    {
        case 1: // go right
        SetAIState(AIState.
stopped_turning_right);
            break;

        case 2: // go left
        SetAIState(AIState.
stopped_turning_left);
            break;

        case 3: // back up!
        SetAIState(AIState.backing_up_looking_for_target);
            break;

        default: // default is just keep
moving forward
        MoveForward();
            break;
    }
}
```

The LookForTarget() function calls to LookAroundFor(), which will ensure that we have a suitable target and change the AI state to chase it if we do. LookAroundFor() is in the BaseAIController class, explained back in Section 10.2. of this book.

From there on, we take a look at what obstacleFinderResult is currently set to (you may remember this was set near the start of the UpdateCurrentState() function by calling the IsObstacleAhead() function). Depending on what obstacle-FinderResult returns, we react to potential obstacles by either turning left, right, or backing up when obstacles are found on both left and right sides. If no obstacles are found, our switch statement will drop through to the default case, which calls MoveForward() to continuously move the bot forward until either it gets a suitable target to chase or happens upon an obstacle.

```
void ChasingTarget()
{
    // chasing
    if (_followTarget == null)
    {
        SetAIState(AIState.move_looking_for_target);
        return;
    }
}
```

The ChasingTarget() function above is called by UpdateCurrentState() when the AI state is AIState.chasing_target. The first thing to check is that we have a valid target in _followTarget. If we do not, SetAIState() is called on to change the state to move_looking_for_target, instead, then we drop out of the function with a return.

```
TurnTowardTarget( _ followTarget);
distanceToChaseTarget =
Vector3.Distance(_TR.position, _followTarget.position);

// check the range
if (distanceToChaseTarget > minChaseDistance)
    MoveForward();
```

When the bot is chasing, the code above calls TurnTowardTarget() to turn the bot toward _followTarget. TurnTowardTarget() is in BaseAIController.

The next step is to find the distance between our bot (_TR.position) and the target (_followTarget.position) to go into the variable distanceToChaseTarget. We then compare distanceToChaseTarget to our minChaseDistance to make sure that we are not too close to the target. If the distance is higher than minChaseDistance, we continue to call MoveForward() which will set the vert input variable to continue to move the bot forward toward the target.

```
bool canSeePlayer = CanSee( _ followTarget);
if (distanceToChaseTarget > maxChaseDistance
|| !canSeePlayer)
        SetAIState(AIState.
move_looking_for_target)
}
```

Next, above, we declare a Boolean variable named canSeePlayer to store the result of a call to the CanSee() function. CanSee() will use Physics.Raycast to cast a ray between the bot and the player to tell if there is anything between them. CanSee() relies on collision layers to identify the player, referring to layers in the variable targetLayer (declared in BaseAIController) to ensure that the path to the player is clear. CanSee() returns true if the line is clear, false when there is an obstacle.

Above, we then check the distance to see if the target is too far away from the bot – further than maxChaseDistance. If distanceToChaseTarget is greater than maxChaseDistance, or CanSee() returned false, we call on SetAIState() to change the state back to look for a new suitable target in AIState. move_looking_for_target.

```
void BackUpLookingForTarget()
{
        LookAroundFor();
        MoveBack();

        if (obstacleFinderResult == 0)
        {
                if (Random.Range(0, 100) > 50)
                        SetAIState(AIState.
stopped_turning_left);
                else
                SetAIState(AIState.
stopped_turning_right);
        }
}
```

BackUpLookingForTarget() is called each frame from the UpdateCurrentState() function. It moves the bot backward when obstacles are found on both left and right sides, in front of it, blocking the path forward. We start the function by calling LookAroundFor(), which tries to find a suitable target to chase. MoveBack() sets the input variable vert to –1, to move backward. Then, we look at obstacle-FinderResult to see if any obstacles were found in front of the bot. If none were found, we now know that we have backed up enough to avoid whatever it was that was blocking the path prior to the state going into AIState.backing_up_looking_for_target. To help avoid the bot moving forward and moving right back into the obstacle that got it here, we generate a random number to decide which way to turn. If the number is above 50, the bot turns left. If less, it turns right. It will only turn a small amount, but it should be enough to avoid getting stuck.

```
void StoppedTurnLeft()
{
        // look for chase target
        LookAroundFor();

        // stopped, turning left
        TurnLeft();

        if (obstacleFinderResult == 0)
SetAIState(AIState.move_looking_for_target);
}
void StoppedTurnRight()
{
        // look for chase target
        LookAroundFor();

        // stopped, turning right
        TurnRight();

        // check results from looking, to see if path
ahead is clear
        if (obstacleFinderResult == 0)
        SetAIState(AIState.move_looking_for_target);
}
```

StoppedTurnRight() and StoppedTurnLeft() are identical except for a single line which calls out to either TurnLeft() or TurnRight() respectively. Both functions start with a call to LookAroundFor() to try to find a suitable target, and both functions will change the AI state to AIState.move_looking_for_target whenever no obstacles are found in front of the bot (via the obstacleFinderResult variable we set back in UpdateCurrentState().

```
void MoveAlongWaypointPath()
{
        // make sure we have been initialized before
trying to access waypoints
        if (!didInit && !reachedLastWaypoint)
                return;

        UpdateWaypoints();

        if (!isStationary)
        {
                targetMoveVec =
Vector3.Normalize(_currentWaypointTransform.position - _TR.position);
                moveVec =
Vector3.Lerp(moveVec, targetMoveVec, Time.deltaTime * pathSmoothing);
                _TR.Translate(moveVec * moveSpeed *
Time.deltaTime);
```

```
                    if (faceWaypoints)
TurnTowardTarget(_currentWaypointTransform);
                        }
            }
```

Although none of the examples in this book use it, the function MoveAlongWaypointPath() is provided here should you need it. It uses the waypoints system from Chapter 8 to move the bot along a path set by waypoints. The bool isStationary can be used to start or stop the bot along its path. You can also set the bool faceWaypoints to decide whether or not to have the bot face the waypoint it is moving toward, or to just move, and keep its rotation.

```
        public void SetMoveSpeed(float aNum)
        {
                moveSpeed = aNum;
        }
    }
}
```

Finally, in this class, we have the SetMoveSpeed() function which can be used by other scripts to change the movement speed of our bot.

■ 10.5   The AISteeringController Class – An AI Steering Controller

AISteeringController uses the waypoints system from Chapter 8 to provide inputs suitable for feeding into a vehicle script such as the BaseWheeledVehicle class from Chapter 6. This class will provide the variable horz (short for horizontal) with values between –1 and 1 suitable for steering toward waypoints and it will detect the angle to establish acceleration amounts. This script also ensures that the vehicle remains below a maximum speed.

```
using UnityEngine;
using AIStates;
namespace GPC
{
        public class AISteeringController : BaseAIController
        {
```

This class is derived from BaseAIController to use its state machine system.

```
                public Vector3 relativeWaypointPosition;
                public float turnMultiplier = 3f;
                public float maxSpeed = 10f;
                public BaseInputController _inputController;
```

Above, the few variables will become clearer as we go through the script. The _inputController should reference a BaseInsputController or class deriving from BaseInputController that this AI is using for its inputs to drive the vehicle.

```
                public override void Start()
                {
                        base.Start();
                        SetAIState(AIState.move_along_waypoint_path);
                }
```

Start() calls Start() on the class we derive from (BaseAIController) and starts things off with our AI state set to AIState.move_along_waypoint_path, which will serve as the main state for our steering behavior to work in when driving the vehicle.

```
public override void UpdateCurrentState()
{
        // reset our inputs
        horz = 0;
        vert = 0;

        // look for obstacles
        obstacleFinderResult = IsObstacleAhead();

        switch (currentAIState)
        {
                case AIState.
move_along_waypoint_path:
                        SteerToWaypoint();
                        break;

                case AIState.chasing_target:
                        SteerToTarget();
                        break;

                case AIState.paused_no_target:
                        // do nothing
                        break;

                default:
                        // idle (do nothing)
                        break;
        }
}
```

Above, just like the placeholder version of UpdateCurrentState in the BaseAIController class, we check each state, and call functions to run relevant code for each one. For the steering system, we only use three states: move_along_ waypoint_path, chasing_target and paused_no_target.

```
void SteerToWaypoint()
{
        if (!didInit)
                return;
        UpdateWaypoints();
        if (_currentWaypointTransform == null)
                return;
```

Above, we check that the class has initialized (didInit is true) then make a call to UpdateWaypoints() which is an inherited function from the BaseAIController class. We then check that __currentWaypointTransform has a Transform in it. The UpdateWaypoints() function takes care of updating our current waypoint, checking the distances and so on, including setting _currentWaypointTransform to provide us with a target to steer toward.

```
                relativeWaypointPosition = _
TR.InverseTransformPoint(_currentWaypointTransform.position);
                // by dividing the horz position by the
magnitude, we get a decimal percentage of the turn angle that we
can use to drive the wheels
                horz = (relativeWaypointPosition.x /
relativeWaypointPosition.magnitude);
```

The next step is to find out the relative position of the waypoint from the (_TR) Transform. Transform.InverseTransformPoint converts a position from world space into local space. In this case, we take the position of the waypoint and convert it into the local space of our Transform, _TR.

The result of the Transform.InverseTransformPoint space conversion is stored in a Vector3 type variable called relativeWaypointPosition. This vector now represents the direction that the AI would need to travel to reach the next waypoint.

By dividing the x value of relativeWaypointPosition by its magnitude, we end up with a number that says how much we would need to turn left or right to be facing the waypoint; the code places the calculated steer value into the variable horz (the variable name used for horizontal input throughout this book).

```
if (Mathf.Abs(horz) < 0.5f)
        vert = relativeWaypointPosition.z /
relativeWaypointPosition.magnitude - Mathf.Abs(horz);
```

Now that horz contains the amount required to turn toward the next waypoint, this value may be used to slow down the bot if it is moving too fast.

The absolute (never negative) value of horz is checked against 0.5 to decide whether acceleration should be used. If the turn is more than 0.5, vert is unmodified at this stage, leaving it at its default value of 0. If the turn is less than 0.5, the acceleration put into the variable vert is calculated by taking the relativeWaypointPosition z value divided by its magnitude, with the horizontal turn amount subtracted from it.

The idea is, the more the turn the less the acceleration. In many cases, this should help the AI to get around corners without crashing.

```
if (obstacleFinderResult == 1)
        TurnRight();
if (obstacleFinderResult == 2)
        TurnLeft();
```

Above, we check the result of obstacleFinderResult and turn to avoid them, if needed. I would recommend not using the obstacle avoidance system to avoid other vehicles by not adding the vehicle layer to the Inspectors Obstacle Avoid Layers field. If you are using this with a racing game, trying to avoid other vehicles as obstacles this way tends to force the AI to drive off the track. Not ideal behavior!

```
horz *= turnMultiplier;

if (_RB.velocity.magnitude >= maxSpeed)
        vert = 0;
}
```

Next, we multiply horz by a variable named turnMultiplier. Different vehicles and different physics systems may require different values of input to make them turn in a reliable manner that gets your vehicles around the world. To compensate for this, you can adjust the turnMultiplier field via the Inspector on your AI vehicle to scale the turn amount as needed.

The last part of this function checks the magnitude of our vehicle's Rigidbody against a maxSpeed value. If we are going faster than the allowed maxSpeed, the vertical input is set to 0 to avoid any further acceleration and slow the vehicle.

```
void SteerToTarget()
{
```

```
                    if (!didInit)
                        return;
                    if (_followTarget == null)
                        return;
```

SteerToTarget() is not used by any of the game examples in this book, but it is provided for you to have the functionality of steering at a target rather than waypoints. This may be useful in a game where you want vehicles to follow other vehicles.

We start the function by checking for initialization (didInit is true) and then we make sure that there is a target Transform to follow held in the _followTarget variable.

```
                    Vector3 relativeTargetPosition = transform.
InverseTransformPoint( _ followTarget.position);
                    horz = (relativeTargetPosition.x /
relativeTargetPosition.magnitude);
```

AIState.steer_to_target works in the exact same way as the waypoint steering code from SteerToWaypoint() above, except that it uses _followTarget to aim for instead of the waypoint in the _currentWaypointTransform variable. That is, we calculate a relative vector to the target from the vehicle then use it to calculate a steering amount.

```
                    if (Vector3.Distance( _ followTarget.position,
_ TR.position) > minChaseDistance)
                            MoveForward();
                    else
                            NoMove();
```

Above, a quick test to check our distance to the target and stop moving if we are too close or keep going – calling MoveForward() – if we are further than minChaseDistance.

```
            LookAroundFor();

            if (obstacleFinderResult == 1)
                    TurnRight();
            if (obstacleFinderResult == 2)
                    TurnLeft();
            if (obstacleFinderResult == 3)
                    MoveBack();
    }
```

We call LookAroundFor() to keep an eye on the distance between this vehicle and the target (looking for a new suitable target if this one is too far away) and then we run some obstacle avoidance checking to force the vehicle to turn if obstacles are found to the left or right, and to slow down, or potentially reverse when obstacles are found on both sides.

```
        public override void Update()
        {
            base.Update();
            if (_inputController == null)
                    _inputController = GetComponent<
BaseInputController>();

            // check that input is not enabled and drop
out if it is
```

```
                    if (_inputController.inputType !=
RaceInputController.InputTypes.noInput)
                            return;
```

The last function of the AISteeringController class is Update() – called by
Unity every frame. Here, we call out to run Update() on the code in our inherited
class BaseAIController, before checking that we have a reference to a
BaseInputController Component in the variable _inputController. If not, we use
GetComponent() to try to find it. We need this Component to be talk to, so that
we can pass on the steering and acceleration values we have calculated here.

We check the inputType of the _inputController instance, to make sure that
it is set to noInput and drop out if the input is set to anything else. We do this
because it is expected that all of the vehicles will have the exact same Components
attached to them (as they do in the racing game example in Chapter 14 of this
book) and we do not want the AI script to try to drive the players vehicle for them.

The last couple of lines set the vert and horz values of the BaseInputController
class:

```
                _inputController.vert = vert;
                _inputController.horz = horz;
            }
        }
}
```

■ 10.6 Adding Weapon Control to the AI Controller

The BaseEnemyWeaponController.cs script is intended to be added to a player to
take control of the weapons system and deal with firing. It does not specifically
reference or require the AI controller and it works independently, relying only on
the Standard_SlotWeaponController.cs script to operate the weapon and a separate class named AIAttackStates.

10.6.1 Attack States

The AIAttackStates.cs script stores an enumerated list of the possible states for
the armed enemy to take:

```
namespace AIAttackStates
{
        public enum AIAttackState
        {
                random_fire,
                look_and_destroy,
                no_attack,
        }
}
```

10.6.2 BaseEnemyWeaponController

BaseEnemyWeaponController will call a StandardSlotWeaponController Component
attached to the same GameObject. More specifically, it will call the Fire() function randomly so that the enemy fires at random times.

```
    using UnityEngine;
    using AIAttackStates;
```

In Section 10.3., we made a set of states for the AI to use when it comes to dealing with weapons. We wrapped the states into a namespace named AIAttackStates. Here, to tell Unity that we want to refer to the AIAttackStates namespace, this script starts out with the using keyword and the namespace we want to use.

```
public class BaseEnemyWeaponController :
ExtendedCustomMonoBehaviour
        {
                public bool doFire;
                public bool onlyFireWhenOnscreen;
                public int pointsValue = 50;
                public int thisEnemyStrength = 1;
                public bool thisGameObjectShouldFire;
                public Renderer _rendererToTestAgainst;
                public StandardSlotWeaponController
_slotWeaponController;
                private bool canFire;
                public float fireDelayTime = 1f;

                // default action is to attack nothing
                public AIAttackState currentState = AIAttackState.
random_fire;
                public string tagOfTargetsToShootAt;
```

Above, the BaseEnemyWeaponController class is derived from ExtendedCustomMonoBehaviour.

```
public void Init()
        {
                // cache our transform
                _TR = transform;
                _GO = GameObject;
```

As with most of the Init() functions in this book, the code above kicks off the function above, by caching references to the GameObject and Transform that this script Component is applied to.

```
if ( _slotWeaponController == null)
        {
                _slotWeaponController =
_GO.GetComponent<StandardSlotWeaponController>();
        }
```

The prime objective of this class is to manage the weapons system for the AI players, which means it is going to need a reference to the weapon controller script. If one has not been set in the Unity editor Inspector window on this scripts GameObject, the code above finds out and try to find it with a call to GameObject. GetComponent():

```
if ( _rendererToTestAgainst == null)
        {
                _rendererToTestAgainst =
_GO.GetComponentInChildren<Renderer>();
        }
```

The option is provided with this class to only fire the weapon when a specified Renderer is on screen by setting the Boolean variable onlyFireWhenOnScreen to true in the Inspector. The intention is that the main enemy mesh Renderer is used for this, so that weapon firing only happens when the enemy is on screen. If the variable (of type Renderer) renderToTestAgainst has not been set in the Unity editor Inspector window, the code above uses GameObject. GetComponentInChildren() to try and find a Renderer to use instead.

```
            canFire = true;
            didInit = true;
    }
```

Finally, in Init() above, we set didInit to true and canFire to true, too. canFire is used to stop firing when we want to have the firing pause between shots. canFire is used by this script to help control the delay between shots, but if you ever need to stop the AI from firing you can set canControl to false at any time.

```
    private RaycastHit rayHit;
    public void Update()
    {
            if (!didInit)
                    Init();

            if (!canControl)
                    return;

            Firing();
    }
```

Most of the core logic takes place in the Update() function, which is automatically called by the Unity engine each frame. It is declared here as a virtual function so that it can be overridden should you choose to inherit another class from this one.

Above, if canControl is false, no weapon control is allowed so this function drops out early before calling the Firing() function.

```
            void Firing()
            {
                    if (!didInit)
                            Init();
                    if(thisGameObjectShouldFire)
                    {
```

Above, the Firing() function first makes sure that thisGameObjectShould-Fire is set to true.

```
                    // we use doFire to determine whether or not
to fire right now
                    doFire=false;
```

Depending on the AIAttackState this enemy is currently set to use, it may be required to be able to have line of sight to a potential target before firing. doFire is a Boolean variable used to tell whether or not the conditions to fire (such as line of sight) have been satisfied and firing is allowed. Before fire condition checking starts, the assumption is made that firing will not be allowed and doFire is set to false.

```
                    if( canFire )
                    {
```

There will always be a pause in-between firing. As mentioned earlier in this section, the Boolean variable canFire is used manage the state of whether the script should be allowed to fire at this time. It will be set to false after a specified amount of time has passed further in the script.

```
if( currentState==AIAttackState.random_fire )
{
        // if the random number is over x, fire
        if( Random.Range(0,100)>98 )
        {
                doFire=true;
        }
}
```

AIAttackState.random_fire means just that – there is no checking other than to generate a random number and see if it turns out to be over a set number (98, in this case). When the randomly generated number is high enough, doFire is set to true so that firing occurs.

```
else if ( currentState == AIAttackState.look_and_
destroy )
        {
                if (Physics.Raycast(_TR.position, _
TR.forward, out rayHit))
                {
                        // is it an opponent to be shot at
                        if( rayHit.transform.CompareTag
( tagOfTargetsToShootAt ) )
                        {
```

AIAttackState.look_and_destroy will use raycasting to look out forward from this enemy's Transform to see if a potential target is in front. tagOfTargets-ToShootAt is set to hold a tag applied to enemies and Transform.CompareTag() is used to make sure that an object hit by a raycast has the correct tag in place.

```
                                doFire=true;
                        }
                }
        } else {
```

When an object is found in front of this Transform with the correct tag applied, doFire is set to true and firing can happen later in the function.

```
                // if we're not set to random fire or look
and destroy, just fire whenever we can
                doFire=true;
        }
}
```

The else condition is provided as a catchall. If in doubt, fire it out! If AIAttackState makes no sense, the function will just keep firing.

```
if (doFire)
{
                // we only want to fire if we are on-screen,
visible on the main camera
```

```
                if (onlyFireWhenOnscreen
&& !_rendererToTestAgainst.IsVisibleFrom(Camera.main))
                    {
                            doFire = false;
                            return;
                    }
```

Above, the state of doFire is a condition for executing the next chunk of code. The Boolean variable onlyFireWhenOnScreen states whether this enemy should be allowed to fire when not being drawn by the Camera. The Renderer Component referenced by rendererToTestAgainst is checked, using the Renderer.IsVisibleFrom() function provided by Unity. IsVisibleFrom() takes a Camera as a parameter and will return true if the Renderer is visible from that Camera (and, of course, false when it is not). Above, we use Camera.main to find the Camera with. For Camera.main to work, a Camera in the Scene must have the MainCamera tag applied to it in the Inspector. This is the easiest way to find the Camera in a Scene, but if for whatever reason this does not work for you, add a new Camera typed variable to the variable declarations and use that variable here, instead of Camera.main.

The code sets doFire to false when onlyFireWhenOnScreen is true and the Renderer is not visible on screen. If firing is cancelled in this way, it also drops out with a return statement since there is no value left in executing the script further on this pass.

```
                    // tell weapon control to fire, if we have a
weapon controller
                    if(_slotWeaponController!=null)
                    {
                            // tell weapon to fire
                            _slotWeaponController.Fire();
                    }
```

If _slotWeaponController is not null (suggesting that a WeaponController instance exists and we have a usable reference to it), the script now goes ahead and makes the call to _slotWeaponController.Fire().

```
                    // set a flag to disable firing temporarily
(providing a delay between firing)
                            canFire= false;
                            CancelInvoke("ResetFire");
                            Invoke ( "ResetFire", fireDelayTime );
                }
            }
```

After the call to fire the weapon has been made, canFire is set to false to delay firing until the function ResetFire() is called to set it back to true again. An Invoke call sets up the call to ResetFire() at a time set by fireDelayTime and the CancelInvoke just before that line ensures that any existing call to ResetFire() is wiped out before we add this new one.

```
        public void ResetFire ()
        {
                canFire=true;
        }
```

Above, the variable canFire is reset in the function ResetFire(). This function is called by the Invoke statement at the end of the Firing() function, which passed the variable fireDelayTime as the delay before invoking the call. This means that after the delay set by fireDelayTime, this enemy will be allowed to fire its weapon again. This pause exists so that we do not end up with a steady stream of projectiles coming out of the enemy blaster every frame it can fire. This way; we just get pulses of fire instead.

11 Menus and User Interface

In this chapter, first up is a full breakdown of the main menu used for all of the example games. The main menu structure should provide a perfect starting place for any main menu system.

The second part of this chapter will look at in-game UI.

11.1 CanvasManager Class/Canvas Management

CanvasManager is a class devoted to switching between user interface Canvases, for example when you want to move from a main menu to a sub menu such as an options menu. It relies on a Component called CanvasGroup, which is provided by Unity as part of the engine. CanvasGroup lets us set an alpha transparency level of an entire Canvas as well as providing methods to enable or disable inter-activity or enable or disable blocking of raycasts by a Canvas.

CanvasManager holds an array of Canvas GameObjects in _UICanvasGroups and you can then use the functions ShowCanvas(index), HideCanvas(index) and HideAll() to switch them around as needed. The CanvasManager class can also deal with fading in and out, if you provide a Canvas for it to use in its FadeCanvasGroup variable. For example, you can stretch out a simple UI Panel GameObject to fill a Canvas and then have the Canvas stretch to fill the screen. This Canvas makes up your FadeCanvasGroup and you can use CanvasManager's FadeOn(), FadeOff(), FadeIn() and FadeOut() functions to have it cover the game view.

CanvasManager.cs:

```
using System.Collections;
using UnityEngine;
namespace GPC
{
        public class CanvasManager : MonoBehaviour
        {
                public CanvasGroup[] _UICanvasGroups;
                public float fadeDuration = 0.25f;
                public float waitBetweenFadeTime = 0.1f;

                [Space]
                public CanvasGroup _FadeCanvasGroup;

                private int currentGroup;
                private int lastGroup;
```

CanvasManager derives from MonoBehaviour to use Unity's built-in functions.

```
                void Awake()
                {
                        HideAll();
                }
```

The first thing we want CanvasManager to do is to hide all the Canvases stored in the _UICanvasGroups list, so that we do not start the Scene with all the user interfaces Canvases on top of one another.

Next up, the HideAll() function loops through to hide all Canvases:

```
                public void HideAll()
                {
                        currentGroup = 0;
                        lastGroup = 0;

                        for (int i = 0; i < _UICanvasGroups.Length; i++)
                        {
                                _UICanvasGroups[i].alpha = 0;
                                _UICanvasGroups[i].interactable =
false;
                                _UICanvasGroups[i].blocksRaycasts =
false;
                        }
                }
```

As you can see above, we also set the alpha of each Canvas to 0 as well as setting the CanvasGroup's interactable and blocksRaycasts properties to false. This is so that the Canvases will not just be hidden, but they will also not interfere with other UI in the Scene.

We can also hide an individual Canvas with the HideCanvas() function, next:

```
                public void HideCanvas(int indexNum)
                {

        StartCoroutine(FadeCanvasOut(_UICanvasGroups[indexNum],
fadeDuration));
                }
```

The fading of our Canvases relies heavily on coroutines. There are three different coroutines in this class: FadeCanvasOut, FadeCanvasIn and

StartFadeCanvasSwitch. Above, the code to hide a Canvas uses FadeCanvasOut and passes in a reference to the CanvasGroup Component we want it to affect, followed by the time we want it to take to fade in seconds.

This class also offers up an alternative way of using HideCanvas. You can either just pass in the index number of the CanvasGroup you want to hide, or you can pass in the index number followed by a Boolean true or false to say whether the Canvas should be faded out with a fade or if it should just disappear instantly. The alternative HideCanvas function is up next and it looks like this:

```
public void HideCanvas(int indexNum, bool doFade)
{
    if (doFade)
    {
        StartCoroutine(FadeCanvasOut(_UICanvasGroups[indexNum],
fadeDuration));
    }
    else
    {
        _UICanvasGroups[indexNum].alpha = 0;
        _UICanvasGroups[indexNum].
interactable = false;
        _UICanvasGroups[indexNum].
blocksRaycasts = false;
    }
}
```

Above, if doFade is true we use the coroutine but if it is false then the alpha, interactable and blocksRaycasts properties of the Canvas are set directly from the reference held in the _UICanvasGroups array.

Now that we can hide Canvases, we get to showing them:

```
public void ShowCanvas(int indexNum)
{

    lastGroup = currentGroup;
    currentGroup = indexNum;

    StartCoroutine(FadeCanvasIn(_UICanvasGroups[indexNum],
fadeDuration));
}

public void ShowCanvas(int indexNum, bool doFade)
{
    lastGroup = currentGroup;
    currentGroup = indexNum;

    if (doFade)
    {
        StartCoroutine(FadeCanvasIn(_UICanvasGroups[indexNum],
fadeDuration));
    }
    else
    {
        _UICanvasGroups[indexNum].alpha = 1;
        _UICanvasGroups[indexNum].
interactable = true;
        _UICanvasGroups[indexNum].
blocksRaycasts = true;
    }
}
```

Again, you can see above that there are two versions of the same function – one that only takes the index of the Canvas and the other taking the index and an additional Boolean to specify fade mode, in the same way that HideCanvas() did.

The only differences between HideCanvas() and ShowCanvas() are that, above, we call the coroutine FadeCanvasIn() rather than FadeCanvasOut() from the HideCanvas() function – and the alpha gets set to 1 instead of 0 when we are dealing with the no fade code.

Next up, LastCanvas():

```
public void LastCanvas()
{
        TimedSwitchCanvas(currentGroup, lastGroup);
}
```

Often you need to provide a method to get from a sub-menu back to the main menu, or back to the previous screen. To speed up the process of developing menus with this behavior, we have the LastCanvas() function, which changes the Canvas currently being displayed to the last one. It uses the variable lastGroup to keep tabs on what was previously open. As this is only a single level system, if you need to get back from multiple levels of menu you will need to extend this further or manually set which menu should display next.

In LastCanvas(), notice that it is not using a coroutine this time, but instead a function named TimedSwitchCanvas() that will coordinate the timing to switch Canvases. TimedSwitchCanvas() takes two array index values – the first, the Canvas to hide and the second value is the Canvas to show. TimedSwitchCanvas() will carry out a fade out, a pause (specified by WaitBetweenFadeTime variable, accessible via the Inspector) and then fade in the new Canvas. This means to fade out a UI Canvas and to fade in another one, we can use TimedSwitchCanvas() without having to deal with the timing between fades.

The FadeIn() and FadeOut() functions are next:

```
public void FadeOut(float timeVal)
{
        StartCoroutine(FadeCanvasIn(FadeCanvasGroup,
timeVal));
}

public void FadeIn(float timeVal)
{
        StartCoroutine(FadeCanvasOut
(FadeCanvasGroup, timeVal));
}
```

FadeIn() and FadeOut() use the FadeCanvasIn and FadeCanvasOut coroutines to fade in or out a specific Canvas – the reference to which is held in the variable FadeCanvasGroup. As mentioned earlier in this section, CanvasManager provides a method for easily fading a Scene in or out using the above code.

When a Scene first loads, the fade Canvas needs to cover the screen for a fade out effect to work, so we also need functions to snap the fade Canvas on or off as needed:

```
public void FaderOn()
{
        FadeCanvasGroup.alpha = 1;
}
```

```
public void FaderOff()
{
        FadeCanvasGroup.alpha = 0;
}
```

Above, the fade Canvas can be hidden or displayed instantly by setting its alpha value to 0 or 1 depending on whether it's on or off.

The last function of CanvasManager is the TimedSwitchCanvas() function mentioned above:

```
public void TimedSwitchCanvas(int indexFrom, int
indexTo)
{
        lastGroup = indexFrom;
        currentGroup = indexTo;

    StartCoroutine(StartFadeCanvasSwitch(_UICanvasGroups[indexFrom],
_UICanvasGroups[indexTo], fadeDuration, waitBetweenFadeTime));
}
```

TimedSwitchCanvas uses the StartFadeCanvasSwitch coroutine, which you will find further on in the script below.

Below, we move on to the coroutines used for fading the Canvases:

```
public static IEnumerator FadeCanvasIn(CanvasGroup
theGroup, float fadeDuration)
{
        float currentTime = 0;
        float currentAlpha = theGroup.alpha;
```

The FadeCanvasIn coroutine starts by declaring a locally scoped current-Time variable, which will be used to track timing during the fade.

Next, as we should never assume what alpha level the Canvas might be set at, we get the start alpha value from the Canvas itself – theGroup.alpha – and store it in another locally scoped variable named currentAlpha.

The function is fading in a Canvas, so we go ahead next and enable interactions with it as soon as the fade starts. You could move this to the end, if you wanted to lock the interaction until after the fade ends, but I like to give users access to the Canvas as soon as possible to avoid any frustration from impatient clickers!

```
        theGroup.interactable = true;
        theGroup.blocksRaycasts = true;
```

Now we have everything set, the next chunk of code deals with the fade:

```
        while (currentTime < fadeDuration)
        {
                currentTime += Time.deltaTime;
```

The great thing about coroutines, in my opinion, is how self-contained they are and the linear way that the code runs. The coroutine does not stop until the while condition is met, above, that is, when currentTime is not less than fadeDuration.

Each time the while loop above runs, we add Time.deltaTime to the current-Time variable – which is increasing currentTime by the amount of time since the last engine update so we know exactly how long this coroutine has been running.

currentTime can be compared with fadeDuration to end the coroutine once the full fadeDuration has elapsed.

```
float newAlpha = Mathf.Lerp(currentAlpha, 1,
currentTime / fadeDuration);
        theGroup.alpha = newAlpha;
```

Above, Unity's Mathf.Lerp function takes the current alpha value as a start value, 1 as a destination and we calculate how much of a portion of that to put into newAlpha by using currentTime divided by fadeDuration – this calculation gives us a time value between 0 and 1, which in turn means Math.Lerp will return a value between currentAlpha and 1 at the percentage represented by that value.

The alpha property of the Canvas gets set next (to newAlpha) and the coroutine ends with:

```
        yield return null;
    }
}
```

Essentially, yield return null says to Unity that we are done running code here, for now, so wait for the next frame update and continue execution from this line after that. The next line is the curly bracket wrapping our while loop, so when the next frame starts, we go back to the top of the loop and go again until currentTime is more than fadeDuration. Once the while loop is done, the coroutine finishes.

Next, the FadeCanvasOut coroutine works the same as the coroutine we just discussed, except we set interactable and blocksRaycasts to false and the target value for the Mathf.Lerp is 0 instead of 1:

```
    public static IEnumerator FadeCanvasOut(CanvasGroup
theGroup, float fadeDuration)
    {
        float currentTime = 0;
        float currentAlpha = theGroup.alpha;

        theGroup.interactable = false;
        theGroup.blocksRaycasts = false;

        while (currentTime < fadeDuration)
        {
            currentTime += Time.deltaTime;
            float newAlpha =
Mathf.Lerp(currentAlpha, 0, currentTime / fadeDuration);
            theGroup.alpha = newAlpha;
            yield return null;
        }
    }
```

For the StartFadeCanvasSwitch coroutine, we are essentially molding together both the FadeCanvasOut followed by the FadeCanvasIn coroutines into one, neat coroutine of its own:

```
    public static IEnumerator StartFadeCanvasSwitch(Canva
sGroup startGroup, CanvasGroup endGroup, float fadeDuration, float
waitTime)
    {
        // fade out old UI
        float currentTime = 0;
        float currentAlpha = startGroup.alpha;
```

```
                startGroup.interactable = false;
                startGroup.blocksRaycasts = false;

                while (currentTime < fadeDuration)
                {
                        currentTime += Time.deltaTime;
                        float newAlpha =
Mathf.Lerp(currentAlpha, 0, currentTime / fadeDuration);
                        startGroup.alpha = newAlpha;
                        yield return null;
            }
```

Above, that's the fading out dealt with for the first Canvas. Between fades, we now need a delay – the timing for which is passed in by the function calling for this coroutine to start (in this script, this coroutine is called by StartFadeCanvasSwitch and this delay time is set in the Wait Between Fade Time field on the Component, in the Inspector):

```
            yield return new WaitForSeconds(waitTime);
```

As I mentioned earlier in this script breakdown, coroutines are linear chunks of code. They operate outside of regular script execution and we can do some cool things very easily, like pausing the script until a condition is met. Above, WaitForSeconds() is used to pause the scripts execution until the amount of time in waitTime has passed. When enough time has passed, script execution will continue, and we can get to the fading in of the new Canvas:

```
            // now fade in new UI
            currentTime = 0;
            currentAlpha = endGroup.alpha;

            endGroup.interactable = true;
            endGroup.blocksRaycasts = true;

            while (currentTime < fadeDuration)
            {
                    currentTime += Time.deltaTime;
                    float newAlpha =
Mathf.Lerp(currentAlpha, 1, currentTime / fadeDuration);
                    endGroup.alpha = newAlpha;
                    yield return null;
            }
        }
    }
}
```

CanvasManager is a useful script for lots of different situations. I use it to fade in-game user interface elements like get ready messages, count ins or game over messages, as well as to switch between menu Canvases. Just remember to drop a CanvasGroup Component onto the Canvas you want to fade, add it to the UI Canvas Groups array (via the Inspector in the editor).

▌ 11.2 The Main Menu

The menu system we will be building in this chapter will not be winning any awards, or enticing players in to play, but it will serve as a structural beginning and as a functional method for configuring the example games to get them started. The great thing about this menu is that it's completely open to interpretation. It could be built out to work for just about any kind of game with the addition of some graphics and sounds. As you develop your games and develop your style, having an operational menu will help during testing.

The main menu system is used by all the example games in this book. It is easy to port between games and have sub-menus for audio and graphics options.

Unity GUI is a flexible system that caters to interfaces that can act as overlays to a regular Camera as well as 3D interfaces presented as a part of a 3D environment. In this chapter, we will look at interfaces as an overlay to the main Camera in the Scene.

11.2.1 Designing the Main Menu

The overall design is very basic – the title of the game and three buttons beneath it. One to start the game, one to show the options menu and a button to exit. When you click on exit, a confirmation message appears to ask if you want to leave or not. The options menu contains music and sound volume sliders, and the volume settings will be saved out and remembered for next time.

As well as an interface, this menu utilizes the CanvasManager class (explained in detail back in Chapter 5, Section 5.9.1) to show and hide interfaces. Another important note is that the volume sliders use Unity's AudioMixers to control the volume levels. For more information on using AudioMixers, refer to Chapter 9, Section 9.4.

Each button has a script attached to it by default, added by Unity when you add a button to a Canvas. That script is used in this example to call functions on another GameObject's Script Component – the BaseMainMenuManager Component. BaseMainMenuManager handles all the logic for the menu, the scripts on the UI elements simply call them.

In the Scene, an empty GameObject named UI contains one Canvas for each menu. The hierarchy for that looks like this:

UI

    Menu_Canvas – the main menu

    Options_Canvas – the options menu

    Loading_Canvas – a screen to overlay that tells users loading is happening

    Exit_Confirm_Canvas – yes/no to exit

The main menu script in this example uses a script Component named MenuWithProfiles, which uses another Component named Base Profile Manager for the saving and loading of music volumes. An empty GameObject named MenuManager holds the menu script along with CanvasManager and the Component Base Profile Manager. The CanvasManager contains a list of all the canvases so that we can easily call on it to show or hide them as we need to.

To kick off this chapter, we take a look at the code behind the BaseMainMenuManager script and then how it is overridden to make a menu with profiles.

11.2.2 The BaseMainMenuManager Script

BaseMainMenuManager provides basic functionality for dealing with a main menu. The BaseMainMenuManager class requires a few extra namespaces than usual. Those are:

```
using UnityEngine;
using UnityEngine.Audio;
using UnityEngine.SceneManagement;
using UnityEngine.UI;
```

The volume sliders will need to access an AudioMixer object, so we need UnityEngine.Audio to be available to us. To load different Scenes in Unity, we use UnityEngine.SceneManagement to be able to access the SceneManager class. Finally, above, user interface Components are only accessible when we use the UnityEngine.UI namespace.

The class itself derives from MonoBehaviour:

```
namespace GPC
{
    public class BaseMainMenuManager : MonoBehaviour
    {
```

Variable declarations next:

```
        public CanvasManager _canvasManager;
        public AudioMixer _theAudioMixer;

        public Slider _sfxSlider;

        public Slider _musicSlider;
        public string gameSceneName;
```

Above, we start with a reference to CanvasManager, to use to show and hide canvases. The AudioMixer needs to be referenced in this script, too, so that we can access and set its volume properties via the sliders. Those sliders are referenced next. The sliders themselves use the Unity event On Value Changed() to call functions on this class that will change volume levels on the AudioMixer. The event and its corresponding reference to this scripts function must be set up in the Inspector on the slider's Slider Component.

```
        void Start()
        {
            Init();
        }

        public virtual void Init()
        {
            if (_canvasManager == null)
                Debug.LogError("You need to add a
reference to a _canvasManager Component on your main menu Component!");

            // set the values of the UI (visible) sliders
to those of the audio mixers
            SetupSliders();

            Invoke("ShowMainMenu", 0.5f);
        }
```

Above, Start() calls Init(). Init() checks that we have a reference in _canvas-Manager, then calls SetupSliders() to set slider values from the current volume levels. Finally, there is a call to show the main menu in an arbitrary amount of time. We use a delayed call so that the menu is not transitioning as soon as the Scene loads – it just looks a little more tidy when we are able to see what is happening before the transition starts.

```
void SetupSliders()
{
        // now set the UI sliders to match the values
in the mixer
        float value;
        _theAudioMixer.GetFloat("SoundVol", out
value);
```

SetUpSliders() is called by the Init() function above, and it starts by getting the current volume level of the group named SoundVol from the AudioMixer referenced in _theAudioMixer. By default, AudioMixers do not have any of their properties exposed to scripts and it is something you need to set up in the editor. For instructions on how to do this, see the earlier Chapter 9.

AudioMixers store levels in decibels, a range between a minimum of –80 up to 20db maximum, whereas sliders use arbitrary values we can set in the Inspector. In the example for this book, we use values between 0 and 1 representing a percentage amount. Our volume system, however, is complicated by the fact that not only does the AudioMixer run from –80 to 20 but decibel amounts are not linear, but instead logarithmic – essentially what this means is that we cannot rely on the midpoint between minimum and maximum decibels actually being a midpoint between silent and loud. If we were to use the sliders to set the decibel values, the relationship between slider and actual volume would be off. Certainly, it would not make a very intuitive interface. The user expects the slider to act as a linear scale between 0 and 100% volume levels, so we need to do a little work to make that happen. The AudioMixer value needs to be converted to something we can use.

Above, we grabbed the volume from the AudioMixer and put it in to the variable named value, so the next step is to convert value to a percentage:

```
        _sfxSlider.value = DecibelToLinear(value);
```

The next part of the code handles music volume in a similar way, except of course it uses a different slider and a different exposed property on the AudioMixer (MusicVol):

```
        _theAudioMixer.GetFloat("MusicVol", out value);
        _musicSlider.value = DecibelToLinear(value);
}
```

Next, two functions used to set the volume from values in our sliders:

```
public virtual void SetSFXVolumeLevel(float aValue)
{
        float dbVol = Mathf.Log10(aValue) * 20f;
```

Above, SetSFXVolumeLevel takes the percentage amount coming in via aValue and converts it to decibels.

```
        _theAudioMixer.SetFloat("SoundVol", dbVol);
}
```

AudioMixer.SetFloat() is used to set the volume level of our AudioMixer to the decibel value in dbVol. Next, we do the same for the music volume:

```
public virtual void SetMusicVolumeLevel(float aValue)
{
        float dbVol = Mathf.Log10(aValue) * 20f;
        _theAudioMixer.SetFloat("MusicVol", dbVol);
}
```

Above, the music volume is set the same way we did the sounds volume above.

```
private float DecibelToLinear(float dB)
{
        float linear = Mathf.Pow(10.0f, dB / 20.0f);
        return linear;
}
```

As mentioned earlier in this section, the user interface sliders work at a value between 0 and 1 in this example. The utility function DecibelToLinear above will take a value in decibels and return a number from 0 to 1 depending on how loud or quiet the volume should be – between the range of –80 to 20db.

```
void ShowMainMenu()
{
        _canvasManager.TimedSwitchCanvas(2,0);
}

public virtual void StartGame()
{
        _canvasManager.HideCanvas(0, false);
        _canvasManager.ShowCanvas(2, false);

        Invoke("LoadGameScene", 1f);
}
```

ShowMainMenu() calls on the CanvasManager Component to switch the active canvas from the loading screen (index of 2 in this example) to the main menu which has an index of 0. The index numbers refer to the Canvases position in the UI Canvas Groups list on the Canvas Manager Component on the MenuManager GameObject.

StartGame() starts by hiding the main menu Canvas and then goes on to show the loading screen. We use an Invoke() call to schedule the game to load after 1 second, which gives the CanvasManager enough time to fade out the menu and fade in the loading screen before we jump to the next Scene.

```
public virtual void LoadGameScene()
{
        // load your game here!
        SceneManager.LoadScene(gameSceneName);
}
```

LoadGameScene() does just that, utilizing SceneManager.LoadScene() to do it. The name of the Scene to load is stored in gameSceneName – this is a string you can set in the Inspector, which makes it easier to use the menu for different games without having to modify any code.

```
public virtual void ShowOptions()
{
        // switch to options menu
```

```
                _canvasManager.TimedSwitchCanvas(0, 1);
        }

        public virtual void ShowExitConfirm()
        {
                _canvasManager.TimedSwitchCanvas(0, 3);
        }

        public virtual void CloseExitConfirm()
        {
                _canvasManager.TimedSwitchCanvas(3, 0);
        }
```

Above, the three functions ShowOptions(), ShowExitConfirm() and CloseExitConfirm() all use CanvasManager.TimedSwitchCanvas() to switch from one Canvas to another. ShowOptions() and ShowExitConfirm() switch from the main menu to their respective Canvas whereas CloseExitConfirm() switches from the exit confirm canvas (3) back to the main menu.

```
        public virtual void ExitGame()
        {
                // close the app down
                Application.Quit();
        }
```

ExitGame() uses Application.Quit() to close the game, which will only happen in a standalone build. It will do nothing in the editor.

```
        public virtual void OptionsBackToMainMenu()
        {
                // return to main menu from options
                _canvasManager.LastCanvas();
        }

        public virtual void BackToMainMenu()
        {
                // return to main menu from options
                _canvasManager.LastCanvas();
        }
    }
}
```

The last two functions above deal with going back to the main menu, using the CanvasManager.LastCanvas() function which hides the current Canvas and shows the previous one.

11.2.3 Combining BaseMainMenuManager to Use the ProfileManager Script for Saving and Loading Audio Settings

The BaseMainMenuManager.cs script takes care of the menu functions, but it has no built-in method for saving or loading audio settings. The framework in this book includes a ProfileManager designed to deal with user profiles and the saving and loading of game data. The class we build out in this section, MenuWithProfiles, uses ProfileManager to save the volume amounts out as part of the user data and derives from BaseMainMenuManager.

MenusWithProfiles begins with:

```
using UnityEngine;
using GPC;

[RequireComponent(typeof(BaseProfileManager))]
```

The only things of note in the code above is that we use the GPC framework namespace and Unity's RequireComponent() is used to make sure that we have a BaseProfileManager Component attached to the same GameObject.

```
public class MenuWithProfiles : BaseMainMenuManager
{
        public BaseProfileManager _profileManager;
        public override void Init()
    {
                _profileManager = GetComponent<BaseProfileManager>();
```

Above, as mentioned earlier the class derives from BaseMainMenuManager to provide its menu functionality. Next up is a variable _profileManager to store a reference to the BaseProfileManager Component, which is set up in the Init() function using GetComponent() to find it.

```
                // init the profile manager to get preferences from
                _profileManager.Init();
```

ProfileManager needs to be initialized, since it stores and accesses profile data and if we will not be able to access data before it has either been loaded or set up for the first time.

```
                // need to grab profile volumes before base.Init sets
up the UI sliders
                LoadProfileVolumes();
```

In this function, we call the function LoadProfileVolumes() to grab volume information from the ProfileManager and set volumes on the AudioMixer.

```
                // now we can run the base init - we've set up the
profile info
                base.Init();
        }
```

As this class derives from BaseMainMenuManager, once it has done its own additional initialization in the Init() function we need to call Init() on the base class so that the main menu runs through its initialization for the main menu too.

```
        void LoadProfileVolumes()
        {
                // get volume values from profile manager
                _theAudioMixer.SetFloat("SoundVol",
_profileManager.GetSFXVolume());
```

Above, the LoadProfileVolumes() function uses SetFloat on the AudioMixer to set its SoundVol property. The volume level comes in from a call to the GetSFXVolume() function of the ProfileManager, which will either be at a level set on a previous run and saved to the save profile or its default value of 0. This value is in decibels, so 0 is not silent but instead Unity's default audible volume for an AudioMixer.

```
                _ theAudioMixer.SetFloat("MusicVol",
_ profileManager.GetMusicVolume());
```

Above, the process for setting the music volume is the same as we set the sound effects only the volume comes in from GetMusicVolume() and we set the MusicVol property on the AudioMixer this time to affect the music levels.

```
public override void SetSFXVolumeLevel(float aValue)
{
        float dbVol = Mathf.Log10(aValue) * 20f;
        _theAudioMixer.SetFloat("SoundVol", dbVol);

        // write the volume change to the profile
        _profileManager.SetSFXVolume(dbVol);
}
public override void SetMusicVolumeLevel(float aValue)
{
        float dbVol = Mathf.Log10(aValue) * 20f;
        _theAudioMixer.SetFloat("MusicVol", dbVol);

        // write the volume change to the profile
        _profileManager.SetMusicVolume(dbVol);
}
```

The SetSFXVolumeLevel() and SetMusicVolumeLevel() functions are declared in the BaseMainMenuManager class this derives from. Here, we override the base class version of them to add in calls to SetSFXVolume() and SetMusicVolume() on the _profileManager object. This will save out the volume levels along with the save profile whenever the save profile is saved.

```
public override void OptionsBackToMainMenu()
{
        // save updated settings
        _profileManager.SaveProfiles();

        // return to main menu from options
        _canvasManager.LastCanvas();}
}
```

Finally, for the MenuWithProfiles class, we override OptionsBackToMainMenu() from the base class to add saving of the profiles whenever the user exits the options menu to go back to the main. Calling SaveProfiles() will save out all of the profiles ProfileManager is storing data for (default is 3 profiles).

▌ 11.3 In-Game User Interface

The way the example games in this book deal with user interfaces is to have a dedicated script for UI actions (like updating the text of the score display and so on) that the Game Manager calls to keep user interface away from other game logic.

The main game interface is on its own Canvas and when we need to do things like display a message (for example, a get ready message before gameplay starts) the message is on its own Canvas so that we can fade out the main game Canvas first. The CanvasManager is used to switch between them and it also provides a nice bit of polish by fading in the main UI when the game first starts.

12 Saving and Loading Profiles

Saving and loading user data can be handled in many ways. For example, you might just store everything in a static class and dump it out to a .JSON file whenever you need to. Perhaps you want to use .xml format files, or even a database? In this chapter, we will look at a method for saving and loading user data that uses a ScriptableObject combined with .JSON for its format. The ScriptableObject contains an array of instances of a data class named ProfileData. The ProfileData class holds everything we want to save and load to Profiles. By using an array of ProfileData in the ScriptableObject, we can easily load, and save to more than one save profile.

The system in this chapter works with save slots, although there is no example user interface to choose a different slot. The example games simply use the first profile, but if you decide to take this further and build out an interface for multiple slots, you can call ChooseProfile(<slot number>) to select whichever slot ties up with your user interface.

12.1 The Save Profile ScriptableObject

We use a ScriptableObject for two reasons. One is so that the data is easily accessible from anywhere in our games – a reference to the ScriptableObject gives you a reference to the data. You can modify data on the ScriptableObject instance and wherever it is accessed from, the data will be up-to-date with the latest modifications. The second reason for a ScriptableObject is that we can instantly see it update inside the Unity editor, making it easier to debug storage. The ScriptableObject is an excellent way to store data and access it from anywhere.

You can find this ProfileScriptableObject.cs file in the folder Assets/GPC_ Framework/Scripts/COMMON/SCRIPTABLEOBJECTS.

The namespaces this script refers to are UnityEngine and System:

```
using UnityEngine;
using System;
namespace GPC
{
```

The class exists within the GPC namespace, which is used by this book for its framework. You could just as easily change or remove the namespace the scripts in this chapter reside in, but I find it helps to keep everything in a namespace like this so that you a) know where the script came from originally and b) scripts don't overlap each other with variable names or function names and so forth.

```
[CreateAssetMenu(fileName = "ProfileData", menuName =
"CSharpFramework/ProfileScriptableObject")]
```

Above, this is something those of you familiar with ScriptableObjects will recognize, though it may not mean much to anyone new to using them. When we declare a ScriptableObject, we do not actually use an instance of this class in the same way we might normally. What happens is that we instead create an object in the Unity editor that will become our ScriptableObject to use in the game(s). The object made in Unity will hold and display the data we outlined in the script file.

In order to make the ScriptableObject accessible to Unity editor users like us, we need to use CreateAssetMenu() to add a new menu option to Unity's menus. In the case above, we pass in two parameters to CreateAssetMenu(). Those are:

Filename – This will be used as the default name for a ScriptableObject when you use the menu to add it to the project.

Menu name – This defines how the item should appear in Unity's menus and where it should be located. By default, the item will appear in the Assets/Create menu. You can then specify sub-folders within that folder to categorize and organize your menu assets. In the example code above, the asset will appear in Assets/Create/CSharpFramework/ProfileScriptableObject.

```
[Serializable]
public class ProfileScriptableObject : ScriptableObject
{
        public Profiles theProfileData;
}
```

Above, the chunk of code starts out with [Serializable]. This is very important, particularly as we are saving and loading data. Serialization, put simply, is the act of taking a class like this and being able to read or write it as a sequence of data suitable for transport such as saving and loading to or from disk. If we do not tell Unity what we want to serialize, our profile save, and load code will not work.

The class declaration makes sure we derive from ScriptableObject, then inside the class there is a single variable declaration for the ProfileData. The ProfileScriptableObject ScriptableObject only needs this single variable named theProfileData. Its type, Profiles, refers to a class named Profiles declared next, in the same C# file:

```
[Serializable]
public class Profiles
```

```
        {
            public ProfileData[] profiles;
        }
```

The variable Profiles, above, can contain multiple instances of the ProfileData class so that we can store more than one user profile in the same system/file. The ProfileData class is next in the script and it contains everything we want to store from the game:

```
[Serializable]
    public class ProfileData
    {
            [SerializeField]
            public int myID;
            [SerializeField]
            public bool inUse;

            [SerializeField]
            public string profileName = "EMPTY";
            [SerializeField]
            public string playerName = "Anonymous";

            [SerializeField]
            public int highScore;
            [SerializeField]
            public float sfxVolume;
            [SerializeField]
            public float musicVolume;
    }
    }
```

Above, first note that [Serializable] is used on the class whereas [SerializeField] is used on each variable. Having these tags for your user data variables is important, again, for saving, and loading to work correctly.

ProfileData in its current state offers the most basic of settings and game information a game might need. When you develop your own games, should you use this system, you will need to add in more variables for whatever you need to store. Keep in mind that certain types like Vector3 are not directly serializable and you may have to do some work to store them in imaginative ways. For example, whenever I store a Vector3 for saving and loading I store them as an instance of my own 'clone' of the Vector3 type containing three separate variables for the x, y, and z coordinates.

I do not know if there is an easy way to tell which types are serializable, or if there is a list anywhere you can refer to, so Google search is going to be your best option for this.

12.2 The BaseProfileManager Class

For saving and loading profile data, the example in this book uses the .JSON data format and utilizes Unity's built-in JsonUtility for encoding and decoding the .JSON strings. We then use the System.IO.File class to save and load the strings formatted by JsonUtility. It is important to note that these files are not secure. You may want to look at an encryption library if you need to secure the user Profiles or you are concerned with cheaters changing the data, but we will not be covering that here.

As well as providing the functionality for saving and loading the data, BaseProfileManager.cs has functions for getting and setting the data out of the

Profiles, too. This is to make accessing the data easier, as the path to the data can sometimes be a little long to be repeatedly typing out in other functions. We save a bunch of repetition by providing the functions to return data right from inside the BaseProfileManager class. As you grow and expand your own save Profiles, you should bear that in mind and consider adding functions to this class to make it easy to get or set save profile data from your other scripts.

```
using UnityEngine;
using System;
namespace GPC
{
    public class BaseProfileManager : MonoBehaviour
    {
        [System.NonSerialized]
        public bool didInit;
        public ProfileScriptableObject profileObject;
        public static ProfileData loadedProfile;
        public string profileSaveName = "Game_ProfileData";

        private int numberOfProfileSlots = 3; // you can
change this to whatever you want, but for this example we'll only
need 3 slots
```

BaseProfileManager derives from MonoBehaviour, so that we can easily change and set values in the Inspector as needed.

We use the regular didInit, just as a safeguard we can look to whenever we need to make sure that the script has run its Init() function.

Next above, we declare the variable profileObject – this is typed as a ProfileScriptableObject (yes, the same one we made in Section 12.1 earlier!) and it will hold a reference to the ScriptableObject we use for storing user Profiles in. Below that, you can see the variable loadedProfile, a ProfileData typed variable that will be used to store the currently loaded profile data whenever we need it. Note that the actual profile data is still stored in the ScriptableObject but we use this to hold the individual profile we are accessing (during the game or whenever we need to get data from a profile).

Whenever we save and load data, it needs a filename. We hold a filename in profileSaveName and it is publicly declared so it can be edited in the Inspector. Just be sure that the filename is the name if you use BaseProfileManager in multiple Scenes.

The last variable above is numberOfProfileSlots. In effect, this just defines the length of the array used to store data in the ScriptableObject (then, in turn, the save files). You can have as many Profiles as you like, but it will be up to you to provide an easy way to display them to the user.

Note that this book does not include an interface for selecting a save profile. We just save to the first profile – if you need to add additional save profile functionality, that is left up to you.

The Init() function is up next:

```
    public void Init()
    {
        // grab the ScriptableObject from Resources/
ScriptableObjects folder
        if(profileObject==null)
            profileObject = Resources.Load
("ScriptableObjects/ProfileData") as ProfileScriptableObject;
```

The variable profileObject should contain a reference to the ScriptableObject used for profile data storage. When profileObject is null, we know that it has not been populated in the editor's Inspector on this Component. If we know profileObject has not yet been populated, Init() begins by trying to automatically grab a reference to it by looking in Resources. If you are unfamiliar with Resources, this is Unity's system for including files that may not always need to be loaded in memory and can be loaded at runtime. You do this by simply naming a folder Resources in your project. Anything in the folder will need to be loaded through code or referenced in variables via the Inspector. By putting a ScriptableObject in Resources, we can find it easily through code.

Resources.Load takes a file path and file name as a string, for a parameter, which in the case above is ScriptableObjects/ProfileData. Note that the file path and file name here points to the ScriptableObject – not the .JSON file. Also notice that we do not need to include the Resources folder as a part of the file path – Unity will always assume a Resources.Load() function refers to files inside a Resources folder and we do not have to be explicit about it. As well as the file path and file name, it is important to state the type of object you are loading from Resources by using the as keyword at the end of the statement. Above, we are loading a ProfileScriptableObject.

```
                    string theFileName =
Application.persistentDataPath + "/" + profileSaveName + ".JSON";
```

Above, theFileName is a string that makes up the file path and file name of our save profile .JSON file. Using Application.persistentDataPath gives you a safe place to store profile data. Although it can still be deleted by the user, you can be confident that your game will have access to this location and that it will not be wiped out by updates to the main game files. Added to this is the string held in profileSaveName and we add the file extension .JSON to the end. You could change the file type to whatever you wanted, by the way. It will not make any difference to the loading or saving of the file – it is just there to tell other users what type of file this is. If this was used in my game, I would probably save it as a .jef file!

```
                    // if we already have saved profiles on disk,
load them.. otherwise, we create them!
                    if (System.IO.File.Exists(theFileName))
                    {
                            LoadAllProfiles();
                    }
                    else
                    {
                            CreateEmptyProfiles();
                    }
```

Before we can do anything with Profiles, we either load them, or create new ones. The code above uses System.IO.File.Exists() to see if our file exists before trying to access it (you should always do this!). If the file exists, we know we can load it so the LoadAllProfiles() function is called. If not, we call CreateEmptyProfiles() to make new ones.

```
                    // by default, we'll choose the first profile
(we can load another after this, but for now this will be the place
to save settings etc.)
                    ChooseProfile(0);

                    didInit = true;
            }
```

At the end of the Init() function, ChooseProfile() sets the default profile to 0. This is used simply as an index later in the script when we access the array containing Profiles. As Init() is done, the didInit variable is set to true.

```
public string GetProfileName(int whichSlot)
{
        return
profileObject.theProfileData.profiles[whichSlot].profileName;
}
```

GetProfileName() is used to get the name of the save profile. In many games, this would be something like the name of the user followed by the data and time that the profile was last accessed. Making the profile names easy to identify like that will help your players to figure out which profile to load.

The profile name is stored as a variable in the profile data, but unfortunately this means that the path to get to it is a little long-winded: profileObject (the ScriptableObject) .theProfileData (the data) .profiles[whichSlot] (item whichslot in the array of profile data) .profileName – finally, the profile name!

```
public void ResetProfile(int whichSlot)
{
        // here, we reset all of the variables in our
profile to their default values

    profileObject.theProfileData.profiles[whichSlot].inUse = false;

    profileObject.theProfileData.profiles[whichSlot].musicVolume =
0; // default music and sound to full volume (NOTE: In decibels!)

    profileObject.theProfileData.profiles[whichSlot].sfxVolume = 0;

    profileObject.theProfileData.profiles[whichSlot].profileName =
"EMPTY PROFILE";

    profileObject.theProfileData.profiles[whichSlot].highScore = 0;
}
```

Most profile systems include a method for players to delete old Profiles or overwrite them with new ones. Above, the ResetProfile() script takes the profile index number as a parameter and will set up the default values for that particular profile. If you extend the profile system to include additional data, you will need to add additional default states to this function.

The first thing we set is the .inUse Boolean. This is used by the profile manager to tell which Profiles are active and which are not. One example use for the inUse flag might be, since we are using multiple Profiles in a single file, display code checking inUse to know whether to show details of the save profile or whether to show a 'create new profile' button instead.

The rest of the default values are: musicVolume, sfxVolume, profileName, and highScore. Above, they are set to whatever values I think make good defaults.

```
public void CreateEmptyProfiles()
{
        // create an array in the profileObject
ScriptableObject, consisting of numberOfProfileSlots x ProfileData
objects
        profileObject.theProfileData.profiles = new
ProfileData[numberOfProfileSlots];

        // make empty profiles
```

```
                            for (int i = 0; i < numberOfProfileSlots;
i++)
                            {
                                    profileObject.theProfileData.
profiles[i] = new ProfileData();
                            }

                            // save the new empty profile file to disk
                            SaveProfiles();
                }
```

Back in the Init() function, when a profile save file was not found by System.
IO.File.Exists(), we called the CreateEmptyProfiles() function above. At this
point, we can assume that the ScriptableObject used for holding profile data is
empty. This function will set up a new array to go into the ScriptableObject's
array, and then new ProfileData instances to populate the array with.

After the array is populated, a call to SaveProfiles() goes out to save the file to
disk. Next time Init() runs, rather than calling this function it should find the
new file and load it, instead.

```
                public void ChooseProfile(int whichSlot)
                {
                            // we need to see if this profile is in use
yet or not, if not we set it to used and name it

                            if (profileObject.theProfileData.
profiles[whichSlot].inUse == false)
                            {
```

Above, ChooseProfile is used to select a profile. If you build out an interface
to choose save Profiles, this is the function you would call when the user clicks on
a particular profile slot.

```
        profileObject.theProfileData.profiles[whichSlot].profileName =
DateTime.Now.ToString();

        profileObject.theProfileData.profiles[whichSlot].inUse = true;
```

The profileName is set above to a string containing the date and time, courtesy of C Sharp's DateTime class. This will make it easy to identify the latest saved
game when there are multiple Profiles in play.

Next, the inUse flag is set to true for this profile so that we can easily tell it is
active.

```
        profileObject.theProfileData.profiles[whichSlot].playerName =
"Anonymous";

        profileObject.theProfileData.profiles[whichSlot].musicVolume =
0; // default music and sound to full volume (NOTE: In decibels!)

        profileObject.theProfileData.profiles[whichSlot].sfxVolume = 0;

        profileObject.theProfileData.profiles[whichSlot].highScore = 0;
                            }
```

The code above sets up default values for the player name, audio volumes,
and high score.

```
                            // set the loaded profile and put it into a
var for easy access
```

```
                    loadedProfile =
profileObject.theProfileData.profiles[whichSlot];

                    Debug.Log("CHOSEN PROFILE " + whichSlot);
        }
```

The variable loadedProfile is set to the chosen profile above, with a quick debug log message sent out so that we can easily see which profile is active from inside the Unity editor.

```
        public void LoadAllProfiles()
        {
                    Debug.Log("LOAD PROFILES!!!!");

                    string theFileName =
Application.persistentDataPath + "/" + profileSaveName + ".JSON";
```

Remember that the save game profile system is essentially an array of objects. As long as those objects are serializable, we can use save time by using built-in functions for saving and loading. And this is exactly what we are doing in this next section of code. Above, we set the file path and file name. This is made up of Application.persistentDataPath followed by a forward slash (very important) and them the profileSaveName variable and our file extension. If you change any of the code in this class you will need to be absolutely sure that whenever file names are used, they match exactly. For example, if you changed the file extension earlier to .jef you would need to do so here, too.

```
                    string jsonString =
System.IO.File.ReadAllText(theFileName);
```

The file already on disk should be formatted in JSON, since it was created by our BaseProfileManager class. To load it back in, we use System.IO.File. ReadAllText() to load the entire file into one big string. Now that we have our JSON formatted data in a string, it can be parsed in using the JsonUtility class:

```
                    Profiles tempProfiles =
JsonUtility.FromJson<Profiles>(jsonString);
                    profileObject.theProfileData = tempProfiles;
        }
```

You may recall from Section 12.1 inside the ScriptableObject we declared only one variable named theProfileData. It was typed Profiles, which is a small class holding an array of profile data. Above, we use JsonUtility.FromJson to translate the data inside the string we just loaded, back to a Profiles object like the one it started out as, when the file was last saved. tempProfiles holds the loaded data, so on the next line it is just a case of setting our profileObject's variable theProfileData to tempProfiles. In summary, what we did in those two lines above was to parse the data out from the string into a local (temporary) variable, then copy the data inside that local variable into our ScriptableObject profileObject.

```
        public void SaveProfiles()
        {
                    // we never actually just save one profile,
we save them all!
                    Debug.Log("SAVE PROFILES!!!!");
```

The first thing SaveProfiles() does is put out a quick message to the debug log. Feel free to remove this, but I find it helpful to see certain messages like this in the logs if anything ever goes wrong.

```
string jsonString =
JsonUtility.ToJson(profileObject.theProfileData);
```

We use Unity's JsonUtility class and its ToJson() function to convert our profile data into a JSON formatted string. Wait, what? This requires a little more explanation. Right now, all the profile data is held in the ScriptableObject profileObject. All we do to get this converted into JSON is to pass in the instance of the class containing the data. Just as long as the data is serializable, JsonUtility. ToJson() will iterate through the class and all of its variables and format it into a string for us. Pretty neat, right?

```
// now write out the file
string theFileName =
Application.persistentDataPath + "/" + profileSaveName + ".json";
System.IO.File.WriteAllText(theFileName,
jsonString);
}
```

Above, we set up the file path and filename for saving the file to (again, making sure that this exactly matches the file path and filenames used elsewhere in the class).

The profile data is now JSON formatted in the local string variable named jsonString, so we can just dump it all out as a text file using System.IO.File. WriteAllText(), which takes two parameters – the file name and the string data.

The remaining functions in this class are used to get and set individual variables on the profile data, such as setting audio volumes or getting the high score:

```
public void SetSFXVolume(float aVal)
{
        loadedProfile.sfxVolume = aVal;
}

public void SetMusicVolume(float aVal)
{
        loadedProfile.musicVolume = aVal;
}

public float GetSFXVolume()
{
        return loadedProfile.sfxVolume;
}

public float GetMusicVolume()
{
        return loadedProfile.musicVolume;
}

public bool SetHighScore(int score)
{
        // if we have a high score, this function
returns true.

        // if the incoming score is higher, set the
high score
```

```
                         if (loadedProfile.highScore < score)
                         {
                                 loadedProfile.highScore = score;
                                 SaveProfiles();
                                 return true;
                         }

                         return false;
                 }

        public int GetHighScore()
        {
                 if (!didInit)
                         Init();
                 return loadedProfile.highScore;
        }
   }


}
```

13 Loading Level Scenes

Loading and saving Scenes in Unity is done with the built in SceneManager class. SceneManager offers a range of utilities for Scenes – everything from straight loading to combining and manipulating multiple Scenes at the same time.

The RunMan game example from Chapter 2 used SceneManager to load the game from the main menu using SceneManager.LoadScene(). It is a function that will load a new Scene and unload the current one without you having to do anything further. Later in this book, the Blaster and Racing Game examples both use an alternative method that loads two Scenes, combines them together into one and then manually unloads the current Scene. This is useful in cases where the game logic remains the same throughout, but you want to load in different environments and/or enemies and so forth. Rather than copying the game logic to every Scene, you can make a core Scene and separate individual level Scenes which are combined at runtime into one. Traditionally, in Unity, this has been achieved by using a single GameObject containing the game logic and making it persist across Scenes with the DoNotDestroyOnLoad tag. Having to maintain that object and make sure that all references are correctly disposed of, states reset, and new objects created each time, can be messy, and difficult to manage.

When you just use SceneManager's LoadScene() function in Unity, loading locks everything up until the new Scene has finished loading. This may be fine if the delay is less than a few seconds, perhaps loading a simple Scene like the RunMan game from Chapter 2. On the other hand, long delays or lockups negatively impact the perceived polish level of your game and it can look as though something has gone wrong as the user waits for the Scene to update. The LevelLoader class from this chapter loads levels asynchronously, meaning we can do cool things as the loading takes place such as showing a percentage complete amount, a progress bar, or a spinning image. It is, after all, the small touches like these that help your game appear more polished to its players.

In the Unity editor, you can work on multiple Scenes at the same time by dragging Scenes from the Project browser directly into the Hierarchy panel. Check out the example Blaster and Racing games in this book for more on setting up and editing separated core and level Scenes like this.

All of the scripts for this chapter can be found in the folder Assets/GPC_ Framework/Scripts/COMMON/LEVEL LOADING.

▌ 13.1   A Script for Loading Levels: LevelLoader.cs

LevelLoader.cs starts with:

```
using System.Collections;
using UnityEngine;
using UnityEngine.SceneManagement;

namespace GPC
{
        [AddComponentMenu("CSharpBookCode/Utility/Level Loader")]

        public class LevelLoader : MonoBehaviour
        {
```

Above, something to note is that we need to access the namespace System. Collections. Without the using statement giving us access to those types, we would not be able to use the IEnumerator type we need to be able to run co-routines during loading.

We also need to use UnityEngine.SceneManagement to be able to access the SceneManager class for loading.

LevelLoader derives from MonoBehaviour – at some point, if you are using co-routines you will need to derive from MonoBehaviour (even if it is further down in the Hierarchy of inheritance!) for them to work correctly.

```
        public bool loadOnSceneStart;
        public string coreSceneName;
        public string levelSceneToLoad;
```

Variable declarations are basic for this script. If you want to start the loading process automatically when the Scene that this script runs in, check the loadOn-SceneStart checkbox in the Inspector on this Component and set our first declared variable, a Boolean, to true.

Next above, there are two strings. One for the coreSceneName and one for the levelSceneToLoad. Remember when we said that we use two independent Scenes? You need to populate these strings with the names of your core and level Scenes if you want to start the loading process automatically. Of course, if your players are going to be moving from level to level, the level name will need to be changed and updated as they progress through the game.

```
        public virtual void Start()
        {
            if (loadOnSceneStart)
                LoadLevel();
        }
```

The Start() function is there to see if we are automatically starting the loading process. When loadOnSceneStart is true, we call LoadLevel().

```
public void LoadLevel()
{
        LoadLevel(levelSceneToLoad);
}
```

The LoadLevel() function comes in two flavors. The first, which takes no parameters, will use the string in the variable levelSceneToLoad as the Scene to load, and load it. This is provided mostly so that we can automatically initiate a load in the Start() function, but you may find other uses for it. The first LoadLevel() calls the second LoadLevel() function in our script below, requiring a Scene name string as a parameter:

```
void LoadLevel(string levelSceneName)
{
        StartCoroutine(LoadAsyncLevels(levelSceneName));
}
```

The second LoadLevel above calls StartCoroutine() to start the loading process, starting the co-routine named LoadAsyncLevels.

```
IEnumerator LoadAsyncLevels(string whichLevel)
{
        Scene loaderScene = SceneManager.GetActiveScene();
```

Above, we get to the start of the LoadAsyncLevels() co-routine. Loading is handled by a co-routine named LoadAsyncLevels and it takes the Scene name to load as a parameter. The name we pass into LoadAsyncLevels will be used to load the level, not the core Scene. We assume that the core Scene will remain the same throughout the game and so we get its Scene name from the variable coreScene-Name rather than passing it in each time.

The first thing we do inside the co-routine is to get a reference to the currently active Scene. We do this so that we know which Scene to unload once the load process is done.

```
        AsyncOperation asyncLoad =
SceneManager.LoadSceneAsync(whichLevel, LoadSceneMode.Additive);
```

Step 1 of our loading process is to use LoadSceneAsync to grab the level Scene. We do this with the LoadSceneMode set to additive, meaning the Scene will be loaded without encroaching on the currently loaded Scene. Whenever you call SceneManager to load a Scene asynchronously, it will return an AsyncOperation – an object we can use to check on load progress and can access to see if the loading sequence has finished.

```
        // Wait until the asynchronous scene fully loads
        while (!asyncLoad.isDone)
        {
                yield return null;
        }
```

The variable asyncLoad (typed as an AsyncOperation) is used to find out when the load sequence has finished. We do this by polling its isDone property in

---

a while loop so that it will continue to execute the code between the curly brackets right up until the Scene has finished loading. Inside the brackets, the line yield return null. Whenever you do not use a yield, the co-routine will run the loop until it is done. The yield tells our code to wait until the next frame before continuing to run. The code above checks isDone every frame so that the load process can continue and asyncLoad can be updated. Without continuing Unity's regular operations, asyncLoad would never update, and the loading would never complete.

```
AsyncOperation asyncLoad2 =
SceneManager.LoadSceneAsync(coreSceneName, LoadSceneMode.Additive);
```

Now that the level Scene has finished loading, above we start the next load with another call to SceneManager.LoadSceneAsync. This time, we pass in the coreSceneName to tell it to load the core Scene. Again, the LoadSceneMode is additive so that it will not interfere with the level already in memory.

```
// Wait until the asynchronous scene fully loads
while (!asyncLoad2.isDone)
{
        yield return null;
}
```

Above, the same procedure as for level loading in that we poll isDone and yield each frame until the Scene is ready to go. Now that our two Scenes are loaded, we can move on to getting them set up and running:

```
// disable the camera before the scene starts to
avoid Unity getting stuck in some sort of complaining loop
// about more than one camera in the scene :(
Camera.main.gameObject.SetActive(false);
```

A little diversion above, as we need to deal with a little problem that occurs when Unity detects more than one Camera in a Scene – it reports an error to the debug log console. At the time of writing, a bug in the engine causes the error to continue being reported even after any additional Cameras have been removed. Although it may be possible there is a way to rearrange this sequence of events so that Unity does not do this, the only solution I could find was to set the current main Camera's active state to false – effectively disabling the Camera before Scene activation happens.

```
SceneManager.MergeScenes(SceneManager.
GetSceneByName(whichLevel),
SceneManager.GetSceneByName(coreSceneName));
        SceneManager.SetActiveScene(SceneManager.
GetSceneByName(coreSceneName));
```

The next part of the co-routine uses SceneManager's MergeScenes() function to take the two Scenes loaded earlier in the code and merge them into a single, new Scene in memory. Note that the merged Scene does not exist on disk, only in memory. To merge the two Scenes, SceneManager.MergeScenes takes two Scene references as parameters – which we get by using SceneManager.GetSceneByName(). Using GetSceneByName() means we can get references to the correct Scenes by using the string passed into the co-routine (the level Scene name string) and the string in the variable coreSceneName. When you use

MergeScenes(), the order of the parameters also affects how the Scenes are merged, in that the first Scene is a Scene to merge and the second is the Scene to merge the first into. That is, the new merged Scene will be referred to in memory as the second Scene you passed in as a parameter to SceneManager.MergeScenes().

SceneManager.SetActiveScene() tells Unity that we now want to use the core Scene already loaded into memory with the level merged into it (above, we refer to the coreSceneName in SetActiveScene() to get to our new, merged Scene).

```
            AsyncOperation asyncLoad3 =
SceneManager.UnloadSceneAsync(loaderScene);
```

With the current Scene set to our new, merged Scene, the SceneManager. UnloadSceneAsync() function is used to unload the Scene we were in whenever the loading started.

```
            // Wait until the asynchronous scene fully unloads
            while (!asyncLoad3.isDone)
            {
                    yield return null;
            }
```

Before we reach the end of the co-routine, the code chunk above checks isDone to monitor the unloading process. Once the previous Scene has been fully unloaded, its AsyncOperation.isDone Boolean will be true and we can move on to the end of the co-routine:

```
            yield return new WaitForSeconds(1);


        }
    }
}
```

The last piece of the puzzle is to wait for one second before the co-routine shuts down.

■ 13.2 Multiple Level Loading

When you have a game that has multiple levels, you need a method for using the LevelLoader class to load levels but how can we set the filename if the Scene loading Scene is a different one to the main game? The answer lies in a LevelVars class that will hold a few static variables for the Scene loading code to pick up on and use for loading our levels during gameplay.

To hold information about which Scenes to load, we have LevelVars.cs:

```
using UnityEngine;
namespace GPC
{
            [AddComponentMenu("CSharpBookCode/Utility/Level Vars")]

        public class LevelVars : MonoBehaviour
        {
                public static int currentLevel;
                public static string levelNamePrefix =
"game_level_";
                public static string coreSceneName = "game_core";
        }
}
```

Now, from anywhere in our game we can access LevelVars.currentLevel – an index number used to form a part of the filename for levels – as well as set the level name and core Scene name prefixes for our level loader Scene to use.

Rather than changing LevelLoader to include this functionality, it is better to make a new script that derives from it so that the LevelLoader class's functionality remains intact. Here, we build a LevelLoader derivative called MultiLevel Loader.cs:

```
namespace GPC
{
        public class MultiLevelLoader : LevelLoader
        {
```

Above, our script starts with the usual namespaces and a class declaration that states our new class derives from LevelLoader.

```
        public override void Start()
        {
            // construct a level name from the values held in
LevelVars static vars (hopefully set by the main menu at game
start)
            levelSceneToLoad = LevelVars.levelNamePrefix +
LevelVars.currentLevel.ToString();
            coreSceneName = LevelVars.coreSceneName;
            LoadLevel();
        }
    }
}
```

This is a relatively straightforward script. The Start() function overrides Start() from the base class. We first construct a filename for the levelSceneToload variable, using the levelNamePrefix and currentLevel strings out of the LevelVars class we made earlier in this section. The assumption here is that your level Scenes will be named with a prefix followed by a number (for example, racing_track_1 or blaster_level_2 and so on).

With the level string set up, we go on to copy over the coreSceneName string from LevelVars and put it into the variable coreSceneName.

You may recall from the script breakdown of LevelLoader earlier in this chapter in Section 13.1, that the LoadLevel() function will use these two string variables to know which Scenes to load and that parameters for the LoadLevel() function are optional. Above, we call LoadLevel() and it should then go ahead and use the variables we just populated at the top of the script to load and merge our game Scenes into one, before activating them ready to play.

▌ 13.3 Building a Multi-Scene Level Loader in Unity

Here, we start by creating a new Scene in Unity.

Click the plus sign at the top of the Project panel. Choose Scene, to create a new Scene. Name the new Scene sceneLoader and double click to open it.

At the top of the Hierarchy, click the plus sign to add a new GameObject. Choose Create Empty from the list and rename the new GameObject to SceneLoader.

Click on your new SceneLoader GameObject in the Hierarchy to highlight it and show its properties in the Inspector. In the Inspector, click Add Component, and start typing Multi Level Loader until you can see it in the list, then choose Multi Level Loader from the menu to add it to the GameObject.

In the newly added Component, you can set the Core Scene Name and Level Scene to Load, but for now leave them at their default values. We will have the code update these fields, instead. Remember, in the last Section 13.2. we built out the MultiLevelLoader.cs script to override the original LevelLoader. The fields we see in the Inspector are from the base class and our derived class will not even use Load On Scene Start, it will just go ahead and start loading from its Start() function.

You may wish to build out some user interface in this Scene, too, such as a loading message and perhaps a spinner (automatically spinning image) to keep things moving as it loads.

Save the Scene.

To use the principles outlined in this chapter, your main menu should load another Scene to deal with the loading of the game Scenes.

Load your menu Scene or the Scene that loads just before the game starts. Wherever you would normally load a Scene to start the game, we need to load our scene loader Scene instead. To do this:

1. Make sure that you have using UnityEngine.SceneManagement at the top of the script.

2. Where you want to start the game, add the following code:

```
// set up LevelVars static vars so that the sceneloader knows
what it's supposed to be loading
LevelVars.coreSceneName = "core_game";
LevelVars.currentLevel = 1;
LevelVars.levelNamePrefix = "level_";

// start the game
SceneManager.LoadScene("SceneLoader");
```

3. Make sure that the core Scene name above matches with whatever you name your core Scene and the same with the levelNamePrefix variable – make sure it matches exactly (including case) with how you name your level Scenes.

4. If you need to change the current level, set LevelVars.currentLevel so that your scene loader Scene will form a filename with the correct level number at the end of it.

14 Racing Game

In this chapter, we will be building out a racing game (Figure 14.1) and it will have almost everything a no-nonsense racer might need – AI opponents, a respawning system, wrong way detection, and modern video game car physics using Unity's Wheel Colliders for suspension and car control.

The focus for this chapter is on the scripts, which means it will not be the same step by step tutorial format used in Chapter 2 for the RunMan example. There may be some work on the Unity side that will not be covered. You are expected to open up the example project and use this chapter as a guide to find out how it all works, but there will be full script breakdowns and enough information for you to be able to make your own game – this is just a heads up that in this chapter we focus on the programming a lot more than steps on how to use Unity.

The overall structure of our racing game is shown in Figure 14.2. At its core is a Game Manager to deal with overall game states, which will be talking to a Global Race Controller script. The Global Race Controller acts to wrangle all the player information into coherent racing info such as current lap, who has finished the race and so on. The structure for vehicles (Figure 14.3) uses a Race Player Controller Component to provide information to, and communicate with, the Global Race Controller. The scripts used to calculate and monitor race information (current lap, race position and so on) work independently, meaning it does not matter what type of vehicle or avatar the player is – it could be a vehicle, a humanoid running, a space ship, or a rolling ball – as long as Race Player Controller is provided with what it needs, the racing specific logic will work.

This game may be found in the example games project. The files for this game can be found in the Assets/Games/Racing Game folder. If you want to play

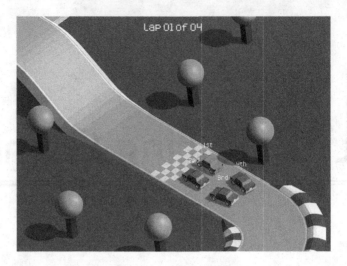

Figure 14.1 The Racing Game example.

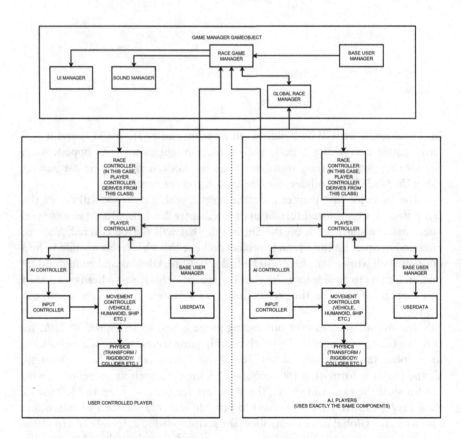

Figure 14.2 Racing game structure.

the game, the controls are the arrows – up and down to accelerate or brake, with left and right to turn left or right respectively.

The game works over six Scenes: a main menu, a level select, a Scene loader, a core Scene containing the Game Manager and GameObjects shared across levels and then two further track Scenes.

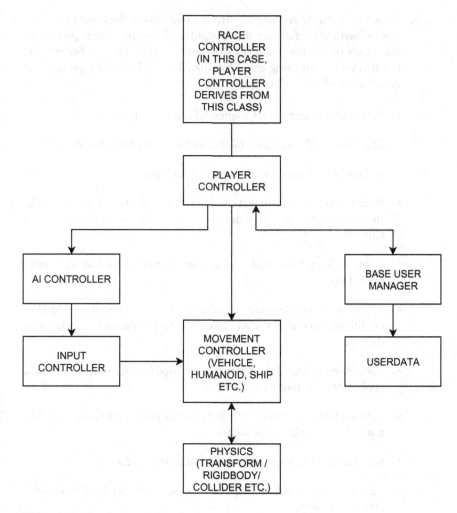

Figure 14.3 The player structure for the racing game example.

▌ 14.1 Ingredients

The racing game example uses these ingredients:

1. Main menu – The menu code is based on MenuWithProfiles.cs from Chapter 11.

2. Level select – The level select relies on a Scene loader using LevelVars.cs.

3. Scene loader – MultiLevelLoader.cs, derived from LevelLoader.cs (covered in Chapter 13) is used for Scene loading.

4. The Game Manager – RaceGameManager derives from BaseGameManager (from Chapter 3).

5. Race Management – Each player has a race controller script attached to it, which holds information relevant to its race stats (position/waypoints and so on). The race manager talks to all the player's race controllers and tracks global information on the state of the race, such as player race positions and whether the race is still in progress.

6. Vehicles – Both AI and user controlled vehicles use the exact same pre-fabs. When the prefabs are first instantiated into the Scene, properties are set on the prefab instances Components to make each behave differently, such as enabling and disabling AI control. The Components we need for the player prefabs are:

- BaseUserManager from Chapter 3, Section 3.2.1

- The WheeledVehicleController class from Chapter 6, Section 6.2

- A Race Input Controller Component for input

- Steering AI Glue to connect the AI system to the steering of a vehicle: the SteeringAIGlue class derives from AISteeringController from Chapter 10.

- Camera Target to make sure the Camera looks at the right GameObject

- A Texture Setter Component, to set the texture of the user vehicle to on different to that of the AI players so that players can easily tell who they are

- Race Player Controller – a Component used to communicate with the Global Race Manager Component

- Position Graphic Setter – which shows the players current position in a small display above the vehicle

- Car Audio – a Component for vehicle sounds and hits

- Fake Friction – a helper script to increase friction and make the vehicle easier to drive

7. User Interface – The user interface for in game will use a basic script to display the current lap and to show or hide other GameObjects and/or Canvas as needed.

8. Sound Controller – The BaseSoundController class from Chapter 9, Section 9.2

9. A RaceUIManager Component will be used to 'pass' information from other scripts into the user interface.

10. BaseUserManager is used by both the player and the RaceGameManager class to access player information. RaceGameManager uses BaseUserManager at the start of each level, to decide which types of players to spawn into the game (AI controller or user).

11. IsoCamController is a basic class for controlling a Camera suitable for isometric rendering. This is attached to a parent GameObject, with the Camera as a child object offset.

Scripts for this chapter can be found in the folder Assets/Games/Racing Game/Scripts.

■ 14.2 Main Menu Scene Overview

The main menu is made from the template main menu found in the GPC_Framework/TemplateScenes folder.

A RaceMainMenu.cs script, derived from the framework's MenuWithProfiles class from Chapter 12, loads the level select Scene and adds players to the game, when the start button is pressed. RaceMainMenu.cs:

```
using GPC;
public class RaceMainMenu : MenuWithProfiles
{
        public override void LoadGameScene()
        {
                AddPlayers();
                base.LoadGameScene();
        }

        void AddPlayers()
        {
                BaseUserManager _baseUserManager =
GetComponent<BaseUserManager>();
                _baseUserManager.ResetUsers();

                // there's no players set up so add default ones
here
                for (int i = 0; i < 4; i++)
                {
                        int playerID = _baseUserManager.
AddNewPlayer();
                        if (i == 0)
                                _baseUserManager.SetType(playerID,
0);
                        else
                                _baseUserManager.SetType(playerID,
2);
                }
        }
}
```

■ 14.3 Level Select Scene Overview

The level select screen has three buttons, one for each level, and a back button. Events on the buttons point to a script Component named RaceLevelSelect, which is attached to a GameObject named LevelMenu. RaceLevelSelect uses LevelVars (see Chapter 13, Section 13.2. for more on this) to set the filenames and current level number for our Scene loader to use. It can then either load the Scene loader Scene or go back to the main menu in its BackToMenu() function.

RaceLevelSelect.cs looks like this:

```
using UnityEngine;
using UnityEngine.SceneManagement;
using GPC;

public class RaceLevelSelect : MonoBehaviour
{
        public void LoadLevel(int whichLevel)
        {
                LevelVars.currentLevel = whichLevel;
                LevelVars.levelNamePrefix = "race_level_";
                LevelVars.coreSceneName = "race_core";
```

```
                    SceneManager.LoadScene("race_sceneLoader");
        }
        public void BackToMenu()
        {
                    SceneManager.LoadScene("race_mainMenu");
        }
}
```

▌ 14.4 The Core Scene Overview

The main parts of the game are split into two Scenes. The first contains the level –
that is, an environment (track) with waypoints, starting points, and so forth –
and the second core Scene contains just game logic.

When the game starts, the Game Manager in the core Scene looks to
BaseUserManager (the same one from Chapter 4, Section 4.3) to find out which
types of racers to add to the game. It adds the racers to the Scene, instantiating
their prefabs, and then we have a countdown before the race starts.

14.4.1 Game Manager – The RaceGameManager Class

The Game Manager starts:

```
using UnityEngine;
using System.Collections.Generic;
using UnityEngine.SceneManagement;
using GPC;

public class RaceGameManager : BaseGameManager
{
```

Above, we add the System.Collections.Generic namespace so that Lists can
be used. In the previous edition of this book, storage was mostly done in
ArrayLists. Since then, ArrayLists have fallen out of favor due to problems with
memory management. The problems may have been resolved, but generic Lists
are now more commonly used and regarded to be less cumbersome.

UnityEngine.SceneManagement is there so that we can access SceneManager
to load the main menu once the game has finished, and finally, the GPC
namespace you may remember from previous chapters is the namespace for the
framework in this book.

The RaceGameManager class derives from BaseGameManager (the same
one from Chapter 3, Section 3.2.1.), which means we get access to all its game
states and events right from the get-go. This will save a considerable amount of
development time in dealing with state transitions and triggering events for them.

```
[Header("Game Specific")]
        public string mainMenuSceneName = "mainMenu";
        public int totalLaps = 3;
        public Transform _playerParent;
        public IsoCamera _cameraScript;
        public GameObject _playerGO1;
        public GameObject[] _playerPrefabList;
        public RaceUIManager _uiManager;
        public BaseSoundManager _soundController;
        public WaypointsController _WaypointController;
        public bool didInit;
        // user / player data
        public BaseUserManager _baseUserManager;
        public List<UserData> _playerInfo;
```

```
private List<Transform> _startPoints;
private int focusPlayerID;
private List<RacePlayerController> _playerList;
private List<Transform> _playerTransforms;
private bool oldIsWrongWay;
private bool doneFinalMessage;
// position checking
private int theLap;
private int numberOfRacers;
```

We will skip past the variable declarations, as they should become clear as we make our way through the script. Instead, jump ahead to:

```
public static RaceGameManager instance { get; private set; }

    public RaceGameManager()
    {
            instance = this;
    }
```

Above, technically yes that is a variable declaration, so we did not skip them all. The variable instance is used to create a simple Singleton pattern. It is a static variable that will refer to this instance of the script. That is, the one instance in our Scene. By making this variable static, it is accessible from anywhere. Since it is a reference to an instance of this class, we can call functions on it like RaceGameManager.instance.SomeFunction().

The RaceGameManager() function above is known as a Constructor. It will be called when this class is instanced automatically, making it the ideal place to populate our static instance variable with a reference to 'this' instance.

Next, a call to Init() is made:

```
void Start ()
{
    Init();
}
```

Start() is called automatically by Unity whenever the Scene starts. As we need to do a little set up when the Scene starts this is the place to call our Init() function. That may seem obvious, but there will be things in Init() that need to be done after the Scene has initialized but before the game starts, which is why we call Init() from Start() rather than any other built in Unity functions such as Awake() or OnEnabled().

The Init() function is up next:

```
    void Init()
    {
            // tell race manager to prepare for the race
            GlobalRaceManager.instance.InitNewRace( totalLaps );
```

This game uses a global race manager script. As discussed at the beginning of this chapter, the race manager tracks state for the race overall. The game controller needs to tell the race manager that the race is starting, and a new race should be initialized. As GlobalRaceManager follows the Singleton pattern again, we can call functions on it using GlobalRaceManager.instance. GlobalRaceManager will also need to know the total laps for the race so that it can tell when players finish the race, so we pass that into its InitNewRace() function.

```
SetupPlayers();

// do initial lap counter display
UpdateLapCounter(1);

// start the game in 3 seconds from now
Invoke("StartRace", 4);
```

The code above first calls out to SetupPlayers() to get our player prefabs into the Scene, then sets the lap counter to 1 through the UpdateLapCounter() function.

The 3,2,1 count in is about to begin. It will take 4 seconds to go through it, so the Game Manager uses Unity's Invoke function to schedule a call to StartRace in 4 seconds' time.

```
InvokeRepeating( "UpdatePositions", 0.5f, 0.5f );
```

There is no need for the user interface to update every frame or every step. It would be unnecessary load on the CPU to update positions like that, so instead the Game Manager schedules a repeating call to the UI updating function UpdatePositions() every half second. The InvokeRepeating function takes three parameters; the name of the function to call, the time from the call to the first function call and the last one is the time between each function call after that and ongoing until either this script instance is destroyed or CancelInvoke is called to stop the continuing calls.

```
// hide our count in numbers
HideCount();
```

All three of the 3,2,1 count in numbers should be hidden at the start of the game (otherwise we'll just have a big blob of all three numbers on the screen at the same time!). A call to the game controller's HideCount() function takes care of that.

```
// schedule count in messages
Invoke( "ShowCount3", 1 );
Invoke( "ShowCount2", 2 );
Invoke( "ShowCount1", 3 );
Invoke( "HideCount", 4 );
```

The code to make the 3,2,1 count in happen is made simple by Unity's Invoke function. The functions our Game Manager uses to display each number will hide each previously displayed number, so all that needs to be done is some staggered calling to each one followed by a final call to HideCount() to hide the final number at the end of the count in sequence.

```
// hide final position text
_uiManager.HideFinalMessage();
```

When the race is over, a message tells the user what their final race position was. At the start of the race, this should be hidden. We call HideFinalMessage() on the _uiManager (an instance of RaceUIManager in the Scene) to hide it.

```
// start by hiding our wrong way message
wrongWaySign.SetActive( false );
```

The final in game message that needs to be hidden is the wrong way message. Its GameObject is referenced in the wrongWaySign variable and GameObject. SetActive() is used to hide it.

```
                didInit=true;

    }
```

The Init() function is done, so didInit gets set to true so that we can easily find out if the Game Manager has initialized.

Next in the class, the SetupPlayers() function:

```
    void SetupPlayers()
    {
            // if we can't find a ref to user manager, try to
find one instead..
            if (_baseUserManager == null)
                    _baseUserManager =
GetComponent<BaseUserManager>();
```

The BaseUserManager class holds information about our players. Before the game started, on the main menu, one or more players were added through BaseUserManager. Not physical players with vehicles and so on – just representations of them in data. Placeholders, if you like. What happens in SetupPlayers() is we go through the List of players in _baseUserManager and spawn vehicles for each one. Right now, the infrastructure for more than one human player is not in place – that would need two lap counter displays and a split screen camera system along with some code to set those up when the game starts – but this system would simplify the process of adding more players. The player List in BaseUserManager is made up of instances of the UserData class. UserData contains a type integer that could easily represent human players or AI players but for the purposes of this example game we do not go so far and we only allow one human player vs. AI.

In the code above, we grabbed a reference to BaseUserManager using Unity's built in function GetComponent(). _baseUserManager contains the reference we need to talk to it further in this function.

```
            // get player list from user manager
            _playerInfo = _baseUserManager.GetPlayerList();
```

_playerInfo will be populated with a List of UserData instances. We will look at them to decide which players to spawn.

```
            if (_playerInfo.Count < 1)
            {
                    Debug.Log("USING DEBUG PLAYERS..");

                    // there's no players set up so add default
ones here
                    for (int i = 0; i < 4; i++)
                    {
                            int playerID =
_baseUserManager.AddNewPlayer();
                            if (i == 0)
                            {
                                    // if this is the first
player, make it human
                                    _baseUserManager.
SetType(playerID, 0);
```

```
                        }
                    else
                    {
                        // all other players are AI
                        _baseUserManager.
    SetType(playerID, 2);
                    }
                }

                // now we can grab that player list from user
    manager
                _playerInfo = _baseUserManager.GetPlayerList();
            }
```

The code above is only there to make testing your racing game easier. It looks at the length of the _playerInfo List to see if there is anything in it. As an example, if you were running the game from the main menu our main menu code adds players to BaseUserManager before the game starts and so those players that were added there will appear in our _playerInfo List since we got it from a static List inside BaseUserManager. If you are running the game inside Unity and you just want to test out the game without going out to the menu and back in again, the List of players will be empty. So, we check to see if the List is empty and populate it with some default user data if we need to. This way, you can play the game from the core Scene and it will spawn players that otherwise would only appear if you had run the menu Scene first.

```
            // get number of racers to spawn from the player list
            numberOfRacers = _playerInfo.Count;
```

One way or another, we are now at a stage where there is data in our player List. The game does not know how many players there will be in the game yet and we get this number by looking at the count value of _playerInfo – giving us the length of the List.

```
            GetStartPoints();
            GetWaypointsController();
```

The level Scenes need to contain at least enough start points for the number of players in a race. A start point is just an empty GameObject placed in a safe position for one of the racers to spawn into when the race begins. In the example game, these points are near to the start line like a regular racing game.

GetWaypointsController() is called to find a reference to a waypoints controller. We will need to pass the waypoints controller into each player for the AI to be able to find their way around the track as well as for position calculation. The way we calculate race position relies on being able to compare how far around the track the different racers are, and for this we use the waypoints.

```
            _playerTransforms = new List<Transform>();
            _playerList = new List<RacePlayerController>();
```

Next, above, we create two new Lists. One to store all of the player Transforms in so that we can get direct access to their positions later on, and another List to store references to our racer's RacePlayerController Components. Having references to the RacePlayerControllers gives us access to their race positions and lap information.

Now, we can start spawning our player prefabs:

```
for (int i = 0; i < numberOfRacers; i++)
{
        Transform _newPlayer =
Spawn(_playerPrefabList[0].transform, _startPoints[i].position,
_startPoints[i].rotation);
```

This part of the code is going to spawn all the vehicles for the race. Most of what happens in this function takes place inside the loop above, which goes from 0 to however many players we need to spawn – representing by the variable numberOfRacers.

A function named Spawn() is used to deal with the instantiation of our prefabs, rather than calling out to Instantiate here. By splitting out spawning into its own function, we can easily replace out the spawning system with something more performance friendly should the game grow to a stage where it might need it or if the target platform is limited by performance. If you need to improve performance, I would recommend replacing the Instantiate call inside with Spawn() function with some kind of pool management, whereby objects are recycled rather than destroyed and replaced with new ones.

Our Spawn() function takes a prefab (Transform) followed by a Vector3 position and a Quaternion rotation value to apply immediately after spawn.

As we only ever use one prefab in this game, for both AI and users, the _playerPrefabList array only needs to point to one prefab. This will be the first item in the array (note that this array is set up via the Inspector on this Component in the editor) and we get the prefab with _playerPrefabList[0] since Lists always start at position 0. We pass in the prefab from _playerPrefabList followed by a startpoint position and rotation from the _startPoints List that was populated by a call to GetStartPoints() earlier in the code.

```
        RacePlayerController _ raceController =
_ newPlayer.GetComponent<RacePlayerController>();
```

Above, we grab a reference to the newly spawned object's RacePlayerController script and, for now, hold it in the locally scoped variable _raceController. This will be used throughout the SetupPlayers() function further along.

```
        _ newPlayer.parent = _ playerParent;
```

The line above is important. We need to tell Unity to parent these new GameObjects to something, otherwise they will be parented to nothing and disappear into the Unity void! I can only assume this is a bug that occurs when you load and merge Scenes together, so to work around it we just have to make sure anything made at Start() has a parent set.

```
        // assign the user's ID based on the list from
baseUserManager
        _raceController.userID = _playerInfo[i].id;
```

In order to tie the players in the Scene to the players in our player List together, we use an id system. Above, the RacePlayerController Component attached to the player we just spawned will have its id value set to the same id held by the player from BaseUserManager's player List that we are creating the vehicle for.

```
// store the race controller in our list so we can talk to
it as needed later on
        _playerList.Add(_raceController);
        _playerTransforms.Add(_newPlayer);
```

As mentioned earlier in the script, _playerList is a List of our player's RacePlayerController Components. Above, _playerList.Add() puts our newest RacePlayerController into the List. In a similar way, we add the new player's Transform to the _playerTransforms List above, too.

The BaseWheeledVehicle class is used to provide movement for our vehicle – this is the same movement script from Chapter 6, Section 6.2, earlier in this book.

```
// SET UP AI
        BaseAIController _tempAI =
_newPlayer.GetComponent<BaseAIController>();

        // tell each player where to find the waypoints
        _tempAI.SetWayController(_WaypointController);
```

As mentioned earlier in this section, every player vehicle is an instance of the same prefab – that is, both AI and user vehicles use the same prefab set up. The AI script will be used by the user's vehicle at the end of the race when the AI controller takes over driving the car.

Above, we grab a reference to the newly spawned player's BaseAIController. Quick note that the AI script can derive from BaseAIController and GetComponent() will still find it.

The AI script relies on the waypoints system, so we need to tell each player which WaypointsController Component to use. Above, we use SetWayController() to tell _tempAI (the BaseAIController) about the waypoint controller Component we found earlier and stored in the variable _WaypointController.

```
        if (_baseUserManager.GetType(_playerInfo[i].id) == 0 &&
_playerGO1==null)
        {
```

As this is a single player game, we need a player to observe during the game (for the camera to follow) and to use to populate the user interface's lap counter with. In this function, we assume that the first user-controller player we find will be the one to follow. Above, the If statement checks the type of our player to see if it is user controlled (its type will be 0) and then sees that we do not already have a player in the _playerGO1 variable – in effect, making sure we follow the first player found.

```
            // focus on the first vehicle
            _playerGO1 = _newPlayer.gameObject;
            _playerGO1.AddComponent<AudioListener>();
```

The _playerGO1 variable has two uses here. One is to hold which GameObject we will be following and the other is to add an AudioListener to. By default, Unity automatically adds an AudioListener to the Main Camera GameObject in a Scene but here we put the AudioListener on our vehicle instead.

Note: If you have more than one listener in a Scene, Unity will produce a warning in the console repeatedly.

```
            focusPlayerID = i;
        }
```

The focusPlayerID variable stores the ID of the player we need to be focused on throughout the game. It will be used to update the lap counter further on in the script.

With the players prefabs instantiated, we now need to set them up depending on their player types from BaseUserManager:

```
// SET INPUT TO PLAYER TYPE
//-----------------------------------------------------------------------

    if (_baseUserManager.GetType(_playerInfo[i].id) == 0) // <-
- get the type of this player from baseusermanager
    {
    _newPlayer.GetComponent<RaceInputController>().SetInputType
( RaceInputController.InputTypes.player1 );
```

Above, _baseUserManager.GetType is passed in the id of this player to find out what type of player it is we are spawning. If the type is 0, this is a user-controller player, and we need to set it up as such. The next line uses GetComponent() to find the RaceInputController Component attached to the vehicle prefab and then calls on its SetInputType() function to set how the player should be controlled. The input type is set to player1, which means it will use the arrow keys for input.

```
        // tell race controller that this is an AI vehicle
        _raceController.AIControlled = false;

        // set the skin
    _raceController.GetComponent<MaterialSetter>().SetMaterial(0);
```

There are just two more properties to affect the player above, when it is user controlled. The first is to set AIControlled on the RacePlayerController class to false so that the AI does not try to drive for us. We want the player to have full control at this point.

A Component named MaterialSetter is used to set the material of the car body. The MaterialSetter Component is attached to the Vehicle_Player prefab and it holds an array of materials that can be applied to the vehicle. Using SetMaterial, we pass in the array index of the material to set and it will take care of the rest. In this game, we have two materials – one for the user controlled player and the other for AI so that it will be easy for the user to determine which car they are controlling.

```
    }
    else if (_baseUserManager.GetType(_playerInfo[i].id) == 2)
    {
```

If the player type is not user controlled (0), in the line above we check to see if it is AI (2).

```
    _ newPlayer.GetComponent<RaceInputController>().SetInputType
( RaceInputController.InputTypes.noInput );

        // tell race controller that this is an AI vehicle
        _raceController.AIControlled = true;

        // let the AI controller know to control this vehicle
        _tempAI.AIControlled = true;
```

```
                // set the skin
                _raceController.GetComponent<MaterialSetter>().
SetMaterial(1);
        }
                            //-------------------------------------------
----------------------
}
```

The code above is very similar to how we set up the user controlled player, except instead of setting AIControlled to false we set it to true. Below that, _tempAI (a reference to this player's BaseAIController Component) gets its AIControlled variable set to true, too. Finally, we set the material to a material from the position 1 in MaterialSetter's array.

At this stage, I understand that having to set AIControlled on two separate Components is not ideal. The only alternative would be to have either one of the BaseAIController or the RacePlayerController Components look at the other one and copy its AIControlled value across. As the goal of this book is to make stand-alone scripts wherever we can, making one script reference another goes against this principle. You may not always decide to pair up the BaseAIController with RacePlayerController, perhaps replacing BaseAIController entirely with different AI code, so having to reference two scripts AIControlled variables here is a trade-off that ultimately gives us more freedom later on.

```
        // look at the main camera and see if it has an audio
listener attached
            AudioListener tempListener =
Camera.main.GetComponent<AudioListener>();

            // if we found a listener, let's destroy it
            if (tempListener != null)
                Destroy(tempListener);
```

Outside of the player spawning loop, we look to see if an AudioListener Component is attached to the Main Camera. We use Camera.main in the code above. This will only work with a camera that has its Tag set to MainCamera in the Inspector. If there is a reason not to set the Tag to MainCamera on your camera, you will need to replace Camera.main with a variable referencing it instead.

If tempListener is not null, we know that GetComponent() found a listener that needs to be destroyed, and the next line uses Unity's Destroy() function to do just that.

```
        // tell the camera script to target this new player
        _cameraScript.SetTarget(_playerGO1.
GetComponent<CameraTarget>().cameraTarget);

                // lock all the players until we're ready to go
                LockPlayers(true);
}
```

RaceGameManager requires a reference to a camera controller script. In this game, the camera script Component is named Iso Cam Controller and you can find it attached to the CameraParent GameObject in the core Scene. Here, we set the target for the camera to follow. We do not set the target to the player directly, however. The player prefab has a CameraTarget Component attached to it that will reference the exact Transform we want the camera to follow and so a call to GetComponent() above grabs that and passes its cameraTarget Transform to _cameraScript.SetTarget() instead.

The last line of this function calls LockPlayers() to hold all of the players in place at the start of the game – they will stay locked until the countdown introduction has finished, at which point code elsewhere in this class will call to unlock them all again.

```
void StartRace()
{
        // play start race sound
        _soundController.PlaySoundByIndex(1);

        // the SetPlayerLocks function tells all players to
unlock
        LockPlayers(false);

        // tell the global race manager that we are now
racing
        GlobalRaceManager.instance.StartRace();
}
```

StartRace() is called when the countdown finishes, and we are ready to actually get the race going.

Above, _soundController plays a nice sound effect to tell the player to go. The variable _soundController points to a BaseSoundController script attached to the GameManager in our core Scene, which is used to play incidental sounds. When we call it with PlaySoundByIndex(), the BaseSoundController script will play a sound at the world position 0,0,0 and with a very wide drop-off area so that our Audio Listener will 'hear' it.

We unlock all of the players next, passing false as a parameter into the function LockPlayers(). After that, we need to tell the GlobalRaceManager class that we are ready to race too – so that it will start tracking positions and so on – so there's a quick call to GlobalRaceManager's instance (reminder: GlobalRaceManager is a Singleton!) to StartRace().

Next up is the LockPlayers() function:

```
void LockPlayers(bool aState)
{
        // tell all the players to set their locks
        for (int i = 0; i < numberOfRacers; i++)
        {
                RacePlayerController aRaceCarController =
_playerList[i];
                aRaceCarController.SetLock(aState);
        }
}
```

Called a few times by this class already, the LockPlayers() function tells players whether or not they should be allowed to move. As discussed in Chapter 6 (Section 6.2), locking the vehicles will constrain them along their x and z axis but not on the y axis. This is so that the vehicle will still be affected by gravity. If the vehicle's y axis were locked too, it would sit exactly at its start position in the game world, possibly floating, and not in its natural rested suspension state.

The code to lock our vehicles in place is in the RacePlayerController class. What we do here is to iterate through all the RacePlayerController instances held in the List _playerList[] – which was populated back in the SetupPlayers() function – and we call SetLock() on each one. SetLock() takes a Boolean as its parameter, stating whether or not to lock the vehicle.

```
        void UpdatePositions()
        {
                // here we need to talk to the race controller to
get what we need to display on screen
                theLap =
GlobalRaceManager.instance.GetLapsDone(focusPlayerID) + 1;

                // update the display
                UpdateLapCounter(theLap);
        }
```

Above, UpdatePositions() gets the lap currently being run by the player we are focusing on, whose ID is in focusPlayerID. This was another variable set in the SetupPlayers() function when we first added all of the vehicles to the Scene. The GlobalRaceManager class takes care of tracking positions and laps, and to find out how many laps the player has completed we can call GlobalRaceManager.instance. GetLapsDone(). Passing the player ID as a parameter means that it will return the current lap count of that player as an integer. We store that into the variable theLap, which is used in the next line above to pass into the UpdateLapCounter() function as a parameter. This will update the user interface lap display.

To update the user interface's lap counter, we have the function UpdateLapCounter():

```
        void UpdateLapCounter(int theLap)
        {
                // if we've finished all the laps we need to finish,
let's cap the number so that we can
                // have the AI cars continue going around the track
without any negative implications
                if (theLap > totalLaps)
                        theLap = totalLaps;

                // now we set the text of our GUIText object lap
count display
                _uiManager.SetLaps(theLap, totalLaps);
        }
```

The current lap number is passed into UpdateLapCounter() as a parameter, then it gets checked to make sure that the lap number is within the total laps for the race. If it is too high, it will be capped at the value of totalLaps.

A class named RaceUIManager will deal with setting the Text object in the Scene – this is added as a Component to the GameManager GameObject in our core Scene.

We call out to _uiManager to SetLaps() above, passing in the current lap and total number of laps as parameters. This will be displayed as 'Lap x/x'.

When the race is over, RaceComplete() is called to start bringing everything to a halt:

```
        public void RaceComplete()
        {
                // set all players to AI so that they continue driving
                for (int i = 0; i < _playerList.Count; i++)
                {
                        // set to AI
                        _playerList[i].AIControlled = true;
                        // disable the keyboard input Component for
AI players..
                        _playerList[i].GetComponent<RaceInputController>().SetInput
Type(RaceInputController.InputTypes.noInput);
                }
```

We iterate through all the players in _playerList and do two things: The first is to set AIControlled to true so, if this was our player vehicle, it will now be taken over by the AI class. Next, we use GetComponent() to find the RaceInputController Component on this vehicle. This is all on one line, so we assume that all vehicles will have a RaceInputController and this line will produce an error if that is not the case. Once we've used GetComponent to find a RaceInputController, we call SetInputType() on it. SetInputType uses the enumerator RaceInputController.InputTypes (a List of what types of input the Component supports) and here we set the vehicles input type to RaceInputController.InputTypes.noInput so that a user will no longer be able to have any input into how the vehicle is driven.

```
        if (!doneFinalMessage)
        {
                doneFinalMessage = true;
                _soundController.PlaySoundByIndex(2);

                // show final text
                _uiManager.ShowFinalMessage();

                // drop out of the race scene completely in
10 seconds...
                Invoke("FinishRace", 10);
        }
}
```

Above, doneFinalMessage is a Boolean we check to ensure that this code can only ever run once in a race. A duplicate call should never happen, but just in case it does our doneFinalMessage will make sure that the code does not get stuck in a loop of calling and never completing.

We set doneFinalMessage to true inside the condition's curly brackets, then play a sound through _soundController to let the player know that the race is complete.

_uiManager.ShowFinalMessage() will display the 'race finished' message to the user, and finally we schedule a complete shutdown of the Scene – using Invoke() to make a call to FinishRace() in 10 seconds.

When called, FinishRace() will load the main menu, effectively ending the game altogether:

```
void FinishRace ()
{
    SceneManager.LoadScene(mainMenuSceneName);
}
```

The ShowCount1(), ShowCount2() and ShowCount3() functions switch the active states of the user interface objects used to display the numbers during the 3,2,1 count in, at the start of the race and a sound is played via the BaseSoundController Component for each one:

```
    void ShowCount1()
    {
            _uiManager.ShowCount(1);
            _soundController.PlaySoundByIndex(0);
    }
    void ShowCount2()
    {
            _uiManager.ShowCount(2);
            _soundController.PlaySoundByIndex(0);
    }
```

```
void ShowCount3()
{
        _uiManager.ShowCount(3);
        _soundController.PlaySoundByIndex(0);
}
```

HideCount() hides all of the 3,2,1 count images:

```
void HideCount()
{
        _uiManager.ShowCount(0);
}
```

The next part of the Race Game Manager class is a function to find the player starting points in the level Scene:

```
void GetStartPoints()
{
        _startPoints = new List<Transform>();
```

As you may recall, this game is split into two Scenes per level – the core Scene containing the game logic and the level Scene containing level specifics like the environment itself and start positions. As we load levels in at runtime, there is no way of setting start positions via the Inspector in the editor (as they will change from level to level) so an automated system is necessary.

Above, GetStartPoints() kicks off by making a new List in the variable _startPoints. This is a variable used by the SetupPlayers() function as it creates the players, adds them to the Scene and requires a start position for each one.

```
        GameObject _ startParent =
GameObject.Find("StartPoints");
```

The starting points for our players are parented to an object named StartPoints. It does not matter so much what the start point GameObjects themselves are called, just as long as they are parented to a GameObject named StartPoints. The reason being that we use GameObject.Find() to look for a GameObject named StartPoints in the Scene. Once we have that, we iterate through all of its child objects like this:

```
        foreach (Transform sp in _ startParent.transform)
        {
                _startPoints.Add(sp);
        }
}
```

The foreach loop above will go through all Transforms found under our StartPoints GameObject – but it is important to note that this method is not recursive and if any of the StartPoints are at a level below this (i.e. children of children of StartPoints) they will be left out.

As the loop goes through each child object, we use _startPoints.Add() to add them to our List of start points. At the end of this function, _startPoints should be a List populated with all the starting points from any open Scene.

```
        void GetWaypointsController()
        {
                _WaypointController =
FindObjectOfType<WaypointsController>();
        }
```

Above, we use Unity's built in function FindObjectOfType() to look for a GameObject that has a WaypointsController Component attached to it. FindObjectOfType() will return the first one it finds – thankfully, there should only ever be a single WaypointsController in any of the levels for this game. The first WaypointsController it finds will be the one we use.

To hide or show a message to the user that the main player is driving the wrong way on the track; the UpdateWrongWay() function:

```
public void UpdateWrongWay ( bool isWrongWay )
{
            if( isWrongWay==oldIsWrongWay)
                return;
```

To keep a track of changes, we have two variables: oldIsWrongWay and isWrongWay. We set oldIsWrongWay at the end of this function. This function is called repeatedly as the game progresses, so if isWrongWay is not equal to oldIsWrongWay we know that something has changed between the last time this was called and this time. When isWrongWay and oldIsWrongWay are the same, we know that the state of whether or not the player is going the wrong way has not changed since the last time we update the display. Above we can just drop out of this function when isWrongWay==oldIsWrongWay.

If isWrongWay is not equal to oldIsWrongWay, we know that isWrongWay has changed its state and we need to update the user interface display to reflect that.

If the script execution reaches this point, the value of wrong way must have changed so the script can go ahead and tell _uiManager what to display:

```
if (isWrongWay)
{
        _uiManager.ShowWrongWay();
}
else
{
        _uiManager.HideWrongWay();
}

oldIsWrongWay = isWrongWay;
}
```

Above, after dealing with the display state we set oldIsWrongWay to isWrong-Way so we can keep track of state changes. At the bottom of the RaceGameManager class, the Spawn() function:

```
Transform Spawn(Transform spawnObject, Vector3 spawnPosition,
Quaternion spawnRotation)
    {
            return Instantiate(spawnObject, spawnPosition,
spawnRotation);
    }
}
```

We talked a bit earlier about having our Spawn() function separated like this so that it would be easy to switch out the call to Instantiate() with something more performance-friendly such as an object pool manager. All that happens in this function is that we add a GameObject to the Scene based on the parameters passed into it and then return a reference to the new GameObject.

14.4.2 Race Control – The GlobalRaceManager Class

You can find GlobalRaceManager.cs in the folder GPC_Framework/Scripts/ COMMON/GAME MANAGEMENT.

The GlobalRaceManager relies on RacePlayerController Components being attached to each player. RacePlayerController Components register themselves with GlobalRaceManager as they initialize. Our GlobalRaceManager class then takes care of managing the bigger picture, dealing with comparing players positions to calculate race positions, to calculate the number of completed laps and to provide race state.

GlobalRaceManager exists within the GPC namespace and derives from MonoBehaviour so it can be attached to GameObjects and access some of Unity's built-in functions:

```
namespace GPC
{
        public class GlobalRaceManager : MonoBehaviour
        {
                public int totalLaps;
                public bool raceAllDone;
                public int racersFinished;
                private int currentID;
                private Hashtable raceControllers;
                private Hashtable racePositions;
                private Hashtable raceLaps;
                private Hashtable raceFinished;
                private int numberOfRacers;
                private int myPos;
                private bool isAhead;
                private RaceController _tempRC;

                public static GlobalRaceManager instance;
```

This class can be accessed via its static variable instance.

```
        public void Awake()
        {
                if (instance != null)
                        Destroy(instance);
```

Its Awake() function ensures that only one instance of the script exists at any time, by checking to see if its static variable named instance is null. If instance is null, we know that an instance of this script has not yet been made. If instance is not null and already has a reference to an existing Component, we destroy it here.

```
                instance = this;

                // we set this to -1 so that the first returned id
will be 0 (since it gets incremented on request)
                currentID = -1;
        }
```

Above, we set instance to reference this instance of GlobalRaceManager. Next, the variable currentID is set to –1.

currentID is an integer that will be used to generate unique IDs for each player in the game. Whenever an ID number is requested by the RacePlayerController, currentID is incremented so that players have ascending ID numbers in the order they are spawned in. As the numbers are incremented at the start of each call to GetUniqueID() further in the class, we start currentID at –1 so that the first ID issued to a player will be 0.

```
public void InitNewRace( int howManyLaps )
{
```

When a race is started, the Game Manager (RaceGameManager) calls this InitNewRace() function to get GlobalRaceManager ready for the race. The parameter for this function is an integer for how many laps the race should go on for.

```
// initialise our hashtables
racePositions= new Hashtable();
raceLaps= new Hashtable();
raceFinished= new Hashtable();
raceControllers= new Hashtable();
```

Above, several hashtables are used to store and access the data this script needs to use. Hashtables have a key and a value, which makes them ideal for storing player related info or objects. Instead of using an index number, as you do with an array, you can provide a key and get access to its associated value. In this case, each player's unique ID is used to store data about the state of each player, and we can use a player ID to quickly get data back out again.

In this class, we use hashtables for:

Race positions – Each player's race position is stored as an integer.

Race laps – Each player's current lap number is stored as an integer.

Race finished – When a player crosses the finish line after completing the set number of laps (held in the variable totalLaps), an entry into the raceFinished Hashtable will be set to true. Otherwise, it will be false.

Race controllers – Here, we store references to a RaceController Component attached to each player.

All the above hashtables use the player ID as a key.

```
raceAllDone = false;
totalLaps= howManyLaps;
}
```

The end of the InitNewRace() function sets a Boolean variable raceAllDone to false – which may come as no surprise tells the class when the race has finished – and sets our totalLaps integer variable to the amount of laps passed in as a parameter to this function via howManyLaps.

```
public int GetUniqueID(RaceController theRaceController)
{
```

GetUniqueID() does more than provide a unique ID for each player of the game. When the RaceController script (RaceController.cs – discussed earlier in this chapter) calls in, it passes in a reference to itself (its instance) as a parameter. This function then adds a reference to the new player's RaceController script Component to the raceControllers Hashtable, using the player's unique ID as a key.

```
currentID++;
```

Making each ID number unique is a case of incrementing an ID counter called currentID whenever an ID is called for.

```
// this player will be on its first lap
raceLaps.Add(currentID, 1);
```

At the start of the race, when the RaceController is first registered with GlobalRaceManager, the raceLaps Hashtable adds an entry for this player starting at 1 to indicate that this is the first lap.

```
// this player will be in last position
racePositions.Add(currentID, racePositions.Count + 1);
```

racePositions is a hashtable for storing the current race position of each player. There will need to be some ordering to find out who is winning the race, so at this stage we add an entry to the hashtable in a default position, which is calculated with by taking the current number of entries in the hashtable and adding one (racePositions.Count +1) to it. This will be updated later in the class when the race positions are calculated.

```
            // store a reference to the race controller, to talk
to later
            raceControllers.Add ( currentID, theRaceController );
```

Above, the RaceController script Component attached to the player requesting an ID gets added to the raceControllers Hashtable.

```
// default finished state
raceFinished[currentID]=false;
```

As the race is just beginning, not ending, the raceFinished state of this player is defaulted to false above.

```
            // increment our racer counter so that we don't have
to do any counting or lookup whenever we need it
            numberOfRacers++;
```

May as well keep a count of how many players there are here, since all new players will have to be fed through this function. It will save having to count anything later to find out how many players there are, as the integer numberOfRacers will hold the count for us.

```
            // pass this id back out for the race controller to
use
            return currentID;
        }
```

The currentID is finally returned to the RaceController calling this function at the end of the function above.

```
        public int GetRacePosition(int anID)
        {
            // just returns the entry for this ID in the
racePositions hashtable
            return (int)racePositions[anID];
        }
```

GetRacePosition() takes an ID as a parameter and returns the race position of that player, as stored in the racePositions Hashtable. Accessing data from the hashtable is a straightforward exercise of providing the key inside square brackets.

```
public int GetLapsDone(int anID)
{
        // just returns the entry for this ID in the
raceLaps hashtable
        return (int)raceLaps[anID];
}
```

Just as GetRacePosition(), the GetLapsDone() function takes an ID as a parameter and returns the current lap count of that player, as stored in the raceLaps Hashtable.

```
public void CompletedLap(int anID)
{
```

CompletedLap() is called by a RaceController when the player passes all of the waypoints and crosses the start/finish line. The parameter it takes is an integer; the player's unique ID.

```
        // if should already have an entry in race laps,
let's just increment it
        raceLaps[anID] = (int)raceLaps[anID] + 1;
```

The entry for anID in the raceLaps Hashtable is incremented by adding one to its current value. Note that we do not shortcut with something like raceLaps[anID]++ because this refers to a hashtable, at this stage, not a number to increment. Instead, the first part of the statement says we want to set the entry in the hashtable, and the second part of the statement gets a value out of the hashtable and increases it.

```
        if ((int)raceLaps[anID] == totalLaps &&
(bool)raceFinished[anID]!=true)
        {
                raceFinished[anID] = true;
racersFinished++;
```

Above, we check to see if this player has completed enough laps (by checking its entry in raceLaps against the variable totalLaps) and not yet finished the race (its entry in raceFinished should be false right now) then, if these conditions are met, this player's entry in the raceFinished Hashtable is updated to true.

```
        // tell the race controller for this ID that
it is finished racing
        _tempRC = (RaceController)raceControllers
[anID];
        _tempRC.RaceFinished();
}
```

Above, we retrieve this player's race controller from the raceControllers Hashtable, so that it can call on its RaceFinished() function to let the RaceController Component know that this player's race is over.

```
                    // check to see if the race is all done and everyone
has finished (all players)
                    if (racersFinished == raceFinished.Count)
                        raceAllDone = true;
        }
```

Closing up the CompletedLap() function now, we see how many racers have done their laps by comparing racersFinished to raceFinished.Count. If all the racers have finished, we set raceAllDone to true. This will be used by our player controllers as a way for them to know when the entire race is finished.

```
        public void ResetLapCount(int anID)
        {
                    // if there's ever a need to restart the race and
reset laps for this player, we reset its entry
                    // in the raceLaps hashtable here
                    raceLaps[anID]=0;
        }
```

If there is ever a need to restart the race for a specific player, ResetLapCount() takes a player ID number and resets its entry in the raceLaps Hashtable to zero.

Next, the GetPosition() function:

```
        public int GetPosition(RaceController focusPlayerScript)
        {
```

We calculate race positions on demand. Our player's race position is only updated when a position is requested. GetPosition() takes a reference to the RaceController instance calling the function. We can then use it to get information we need out of the RaceController to calculate the current race position.

```
                    // start with the assumption that the player is in
last place and work up
            myPos = numberOfRacers;
```

myPos is an integer which starts out set to the maximum value – last place in the race – then it will be decremented whenever we find out that the current player is in front of another.

```
                    // now we step through each racer and check their positions
to determine whether or not
                    // our focused player is in front of them or not
                    for ( int b = 0; b <= numberOfRacers; b++ )
                    {
                        // assume that we are behind this player
                        isAhead = false;
```

A loop (b) goes from 0 to the value of numberOfRacers. The value of b will be used to retrieve RaceController references from the raceController Hashtable. As we step through the loop, we grab one other player and compare properties to the player passed in as a parameter (such as current waypoint, current lap and so on) to see which one is in front. At the start of the position calculation, we assume that the player passed in will be behind the player being checked – isAhead is false. If we find otherwise, isAhead will be set to true and we will decrement this player's race position at the end of the loop – bringing one closer to 1st place.

```
                    // grab a temporary reference to the 'other' player we
want to check against
                    _tempRC = (RaceController) raceControllers [b];
```

Above, _tempRC is populated with a reference to a RaceController script from another player. We use the loop's variable (b) as the index number to access our raceControllers Hashtable.

```
                // if car 2 happens to be null (deleted for
example) here's a little safety to skip this iteration in the loop
                if(_tempRC==null)
                        continue;
```

To keep the function safe, _tempRC is null checked just in case one of the players has somehow been removed from the game. If it is null, the continue command will move the loop on to the next pass without continuing to execute the code in subsequent lines.

```
        if ( focusPlayerScript.GetID() != _tempRC )
        { // <-- make sure we're not trying to compare same objects!
```

focusPlayerScript is the main player we are interested in (passed in as a parameter). The race controller instance held by _tempRC is taken from the hashtable based on the value of b from the loop, which means eventually _tempRC will hit upon the same RaceController instance as the one held by focusPlayerScript. Before position or waypoint checking happens, we compare focusPlayerScript and _tempRC to make sure they are not the same.

```
        // is the focussed player a lap ahead?
        if ( focusPlayerScript.GetCurrentLap() >
_tempRC.GetCurrentLap() )
                isAhead = true;
```

There are several conditions we test against to find out whether the player within focusPlayerScript is ahead of the one that the loop is currently looking at. Above, the first condition is whether the current lap of the focused player is higher than the lap of the race controller in _tempRC – if it is, we know right away that focusPlayerScript is ahead of _tempRC and we can set isAhead to true.

```
    // is the focussed player on the same lap, but at a higher
waypoint number?
    if (focusPlayerScript.GetCurrentLap() ==
_tempRC.GetCurrentLap()
&& focusPlayerScript.GetCurrentWaypointNum() > _tempRC.
GetCurrentWaypointNum() && !_tempRC.IsLapDone())
            isAhead = true;
```

The above condition checks to see whether the current lap of the focused player is the same as the lap of the race controller in _tempRC. If they are both on the same lap, we look to the waypoints to see if the focusPlayerScript waypoint index number is greater than that of _tempRC. If it is, we know that focusPlayerScript is ahead of _tempRC because its waypoint is further along the track: in which case, isAhead gets set to true. There is also a check to make sure that the player in _tempRC has not yet finished its current lap.

```
    // is the focussed player on the same lap, same waypoint, but
closer to it?
    if (focusPlayerScript.GetCurrentLap() ==
_tempRC.GetCurrentLap() && focusPlayerScript.
GetCurrentWaypointNum() > _tempRC.GetCurrentWaypointNum()
&& focusPlayerScript.IsLapDone() && _tempRC.IsLapDone())
            isAhead = true;
```

The third condition, above, checks that focusPlayerScript and _tempRC are on the same lap as well as both aiming at the same waypoint. From there, it checks to see if the distance between focusPlayerScript and its target waypoint is less than _tempRC's distance to its waypoint. If focusPlayerScript is closer to its waypoint (which is the same waypoint as _tempRC) and _tempRC has not finished its lap, then we know that focusPlayerScript must be ahead and the script can go ahead and set isAhead to true.

Note that we check IsLapDone() on the _tempRC object to make sure that this player has not yet crossed the finish line.

```
    // has the player completed a lap and is getting ready to move
onto the next one?
    if (focusPlayerScript.GetCurrentLap() ==
_tempRC.GetCurrentLap() && focusPlayerScript.
GetCurrentWaypointNum() == _tempRC.GetCurrentWaypointNum() &&
focusPlayerScript.GetCurrentWaypointDist() <
_tempRC.GetCurrentWaypointDist())
            isAhead = true;
```

The fourth condition checks that both players are on the same lap and the same waypoint, but this time looks to see whether the focus player has registered a lap done before _tempRC has. If focusPlayerScript.IsLapDone() is true and _tempRC.IsLapDone() is false, we know the passed in player has completed its lap before the one we are checking against, and isAhead is set to true.

```
    if (focusPlayerScript.GetCurrentLap() ==
_ tempRC.GetCurrentLap() && focusPlayerScript.GetCurrentWaypointNum() ==
_ tempRC.GetCurrentWaypointNum() && (focusPlayerScript.IsLapDone()
== true && _ tempRC.IsLapDone() == false))
            isAhead = true;
```

Above, a fifth condition does a similar check to the last one, only this time omitting any waypoint distance checking. Here, the code focuses on whether the two players are on the same lap and, when they are on the same lap, whether the focusPlayerScript has finished its lap or not. When focusPlayerScript.IsLapDone() is true and tempRT.IsLapDone() is false, we know that the focused player is ahead and can go ahead and set isAhead to true.

```
    if (focusPlayerScript.GetCurrentLap() ==
_ tempRC.GetCurrentLap() && (focusPlayerScript.IsLapDone() ==
true && ! _ tempRC.IsLapDone()))
        isAhead = true;
```

The final condition (phew!) checks to see if both players are on the same lap and that our passed in player has finished a lap before the one in _tempRC.

```
    if ( isAhead )
    {
        myPos--;
    }
  }
}
```

At this point, isAhead tells us whether the player represented by focusPlayerScript is ahead of the current player represented by _tempRC. If isAhead is true, the code above reduces the value of myPos to move the player's race position up by one.

```
        return myPos;
    }
  }
}
```

By the time this loop has iterated all the way through the players, myPos shows exactly which race position the focused player is in. The function ends by using myPos as a return value.

14.4.3 Race Control – The RaceController Class

RacePlayerController is a class that works hand in hand with GlobalRaceManager. You can find RacePlayerController.cs in the games folder GPC_Framework/ COMMON/GAME CONTROL folder.

A RacePlayerController Component is attached to each player, which derives from this class. Some of its functions will be overridden in RacePlayerController.cs but we will cover that in Section 14.4.4 when we breakdown the RacePlayerController class in full.

RacePlayerController is going to be keeping track of everything we need for a race game (other than players). It derives from ExtendedMonoBehaviour:

```
using UnityEngine;
namespace GPC
{
    public class RaceController : ExtendedCustomMonoBehaviour
    {
        private bool isFinished;
        private bool isLapDone;
        public float currentWaypointDist;
        public int currentWaypointNum;
        public int lastWaypointNum;
        public float waypointDistance = 20f;
        public WaypointsController _waypointsController;
        public int lapsComplete;
        public bool goingWrongWay;
        public bool oldWrongWay;
        public float timeWrongWayStarted;
        // another script tries to GetID
        public int raceID = -1;
        private Transform _currentWaypointTransform;
        private Vector3 nodePosition;
        private float targetAngle;
        private Vector3 myPosition;
        private Vector3 diff;
        private int totalWaypoints;
        private bool doneInit;
```

We skip through down past the variable declarations to bring us to the first function, Awake():

```
        public void Awake()
        {
            raceID =
GlobalRaceManager.instance.GetUniqueID(this);
        }
```

Above, we start this class in the Awake() function, where the first task is to get a unique ID for this player from the GlobalRaceManager. The ID number will be returned as an integer that we store in the variable raceID.

```
public virtual void Init()
{
        _TR = transform;
        doneInit= true;
}
```

Init() grabs a cached reference to the Transform on this GameObject (to store in _TR) and sets its doneInit Boolean to true.

```
public int GetID ()
{
        return myID;
}
```

There may be occasions where other scripts need to get this player's unique ID number, which is why the GetID() function, above, returns the value of myID.

```
public bool IsLapDone ()
{
        return isLapDone;
}
```

When the player has passed by all the waypoints around the track, the variable isLapDone is set to true. This value can then be used when the player hits the trigger on the start/finish line to see whether the lap should be increased. Increasing laps in this way (rather than just incrementing the current lap counter at the start/finish line) ensures that the player has driven all the way around the track and crosses the finish line.

```
public void RaceFinished ()
{
        isFinished=true;
        PlayerFinishedRace();
}

public virtual void PlayerFinishedRace() {}
```

RaceFinished() will be called by the GlobalRaceManager class to tell this player when the race has ended. Above, we set isFinished to true so that we have something to check against if we need to elsewhere in the script, and then a call to PlayerFinishedRace() is made. Below that, we can see that PlayerFinishedRace() does not contain anything. The intention here is that you override PlayerFinishedRace() with whatever you want the player to do at the end of the race – perhaps that is bring the vehicle to a halt or perhaps to have it play an animation or something like that. The default behavior is that the players will just continue driving but in the RacePlayerController.cs overridden version for this game example, we tell the user's vehicle to be taken over by the AI so that it will drive itself when the race is done. We will cover that in Section 12.5.4 later in this chapter.

```
public void RaceStart ()
{
        isFinished=false;
}
```

At RaceStart(), our Boolean variable isFinished needs to be set to false, as the race has only just begun!

```
public bool IsFinished ()
{
        return isFinished;
}
```

Above, other scripts may need to know if this player has finished racing. When it is called, the IsFinished() function will return our isFinished state Boolean.

```
public int GetCurrentLap ()
{
    return GlobalRaceManager.Instance.GetLapsDone(myID) +1;
}
```

When other scripts need to find out what the player's current lap is, the GetCurrentLap() function gets the latest information to be calculated by the GlobalRaceManager instance. It passes in this player's ID as a parameter (so that the global race manager knows who is asking for their lap count) and adds one to the return value because the return value from GlobalRaceManager.Instance. GetLapsDone() will be how many laps have been completed rather than the value we want to return, which is the current lap number.

```
public void ResetLapCounter()
{
        GlobalRaceManager.Instance.ResetLapCount(myID);
}
```

The game could be reset by another script, calling for the lap counter for this player to be reset too. Remember that lap counting is handled entirely by the GlobalRaceManager class, so we need to ask GlobalRaceManager to reset our lap counter as we do not store the current lap here. GlobalRaceManager provides a ResetLapCount() function for this, with its parameter being the player's unique ID we kept in the variable myID.

```
public int GetCurrentWaypointNum ()
{
    return currentWaypointNum;
}
```

This class keeps a track of the where the player is on the track by monitoring its progress along a set of waypoints. In the example game here, those waypoints are the same ones used to drive the AI players around. The GlobalRaceManager class will need to know which is this player's current waypoint index number to compare it to other players and calculate race positions. Above, GetCurrentWaypointNum() returns the player's currentWaypointNum integer.

```
public float GetCurrentWaypointDist ()
{
    return currentWaypointDist;
}
```

currentWaypointDist is a floating point variable containing the current distance from the player to its current waypoint, in 3d units. GetCurrentWaypointDist() returns its value as a float. It is called by the GlobalRaceManager class when comparing two vehicles that are both focused on the same waypoint and we need to find out which one is closer to that waypoint to determine the closest to it.

```
public bool GetIsFinished ()
{
        return isFinished;
}

public bool GetIsLapDone ()
{
        return isLapDone;
}
```

Above, GetIsFinished() and GetIsLapDone() both return Boolean values.

```
public void SetWayController ( Waypoints_ Controller
aControl )
{
        _waypointsController= aControl;
}
```

As this script uses a waypoint controller to track the player's progress around the track, its _waypointsController variable (of type WaypointsController) needs to be set by another script. In the case of this game, it is set by the RaceGameManager when players are first spawned into the game Scene.

```
public Transform GetWaypointTransform()
{
        if (_currentWaypointTransform == null)
        {
                currentWaypointNum = 0;
                _currentWaypointTransform =
_waypointsController.GetWaypoint(currentWaypointNum);
        }
        return _currentWaypointTransform;
}
```

Above, the current waypoint can be retrieved as a Transform with a call to GetWaypointTransform(). We hold a reference to the current waypoint Transform in the variable _currentWaypointTransform. If this variable is null, this function will detect that and retrieve the Transform from the _waypointsController instance instead.

```
public Transform GetRespawnWaypointTransform()
{
        _currentWaypointTransform =
_waypointsController.GetWaypoint(currentWaypointNum);
        return _currentWaypointTransform;
}
```

GetRespawnWaypointTransform() is used to get to the Transform that our waypoint system is currently aiming for. One example of where this is used is the respawn function. Respawn() gets the current waypoint Transform and sets our players rotation and position to match those of the waypoint, so that the player is in a safe place on the track and facing in the correct direction.

```
public void UpdateWaypoints()
{
```

RaceController.cs keeps track of waypoints in UpdateWaypoints(). This function is not called from this class but will be called by the player control script.

```
                    if(!doneInit)
                            Init();

                    if (_waypointsController == null)
                            return;
```

Above, before any waypoint checking can happen, the class must have run its initialization Init() function and set doneInit to true. If doneInit is false, we call Init() above. Next, the variable _waypointsController is null checked, just in case this function is called before a reference to the WaypointsController instance has not yet been set.

```
                    if(totalWaypoints==0)
                    {
                            // grab total waypoints
                            totalWaypoints =
_waypointsController.GetTotal();
                            return;
                    }
```

It may be possible for this function to be called before the WaypointController class has finished setting up, but after it has been instanced. This means our null check will go through before the class has set up its waypoints. To catch that and stop trying to do anything with the waypoints too early, we check to see if total-Waypoints is at 0. If it is, we need to make a quick call out to WaypointsController. GetTotal() to get a new total and drop out of the function. This action will be repeated every time the UpdateWaypoints() function is called, until we know that WaypointController has its waypoints ready for us to access.

```
                    // here, we deal with making sure that we always have
a waypoint set up
                    if (_currentWaypointTransform == null)
                    {
                            currentWaypointNum = 0;
                            _currentWaypointTransform = _
waypointsController.GetWaypoint(currentWaypointNum);
                    }
```

Above, if there is no Transform referenced in the _currentWaypointTransform, this code assumes that we must be on the first run and sets currentWaypointNum to zero. It then makes a call to the waypointManager.GetWaypoint() function to return a usable Transform for _currentWaypointTransform.

```
                    // now we need to check to see if we are close
enough to the current waypoint
                    // to advance on to the next one
                    myPosition = _TR.position;
                    myPosition.y=0;

                    // get waypoint position and 'flatten' it
                    nodePosition = _currentWaypointTransform.position;
                    nodePosition.y=0;
```

Waypoint checking works by looking at the distance between the player and the waypoint and moving on to the next waypoint when that distance gets too low. For this type of waypoint following, the y axis may be discounted. It will serve only to make the distance checking more complicated since it would be on three axis instead of two. So, the first part of this code takes the positions of player and waypoint and copies them into variables. The copies have the y positions set to zero, removing the y axis from the equation.

```
// check distance from this car to the waypoint

currentWaypointDist = Vector3.Distance(nodePosition,
myPosition);

if (currentWaypointDist < waypointDistance) {
        // we are close to the current node, so let's
move on to the next one!
        currentWaypointNum++;
```

Above, the built in Unity function Vector3.Distance() takes two Vector3 positions and returns the distance between them. We put our distance into currentWaypointDist. When the distance in currentWaypointDist drops below waypointDistance, it increments currentWaypointNum; in effect, advancing to the next waypoint.

```
        // now check to see if we have been all the
way around the track and need to start again
        if (currentWaypointNum >= totalWaypoints)
        {
                // reset our current waypoint to the
first
                currentWaypointNum = 0;
                isLapDone = true;
        }
```

When currentWaypointNum is greater or equal to the number in totalWaypoints, we know that the player has been all the way around the track. This is not the place to increase the lap counter, however, as the player needs to cross the start/finish line before the lap counts. Instead, when the currentWaypointNum goes beyond the total number of waypoints, the variable isLapDone is set to true and the value of currentWaypointNum is set back to zero ready to aim for the next waypoint (which is now the first waypoint).

```
        // grab our transform reference from the
waypoint controller
_currentWaypointTransform=waypointManager.GetWaypoint(currentWaypointNum);
        }
```

The code above deals with the updating of the _currentWaypointTransform variable to reflect any changes to currentWaypointNum. We call on _waypointsController.GetWaypoint() and store the return value in the _currentWaypointTransform variable.

```
        // we finish by recalculating currentWaypointDist
        nodePosition = _currentWaypointTransform.position;
        nodePosition.y = 0;

        // check distance from this car to the waypoint
        currentWaypointDist = Vector3.Distance(nodePosition,
        myPosition);
    }
}
```

Above, at the end of the UpdateWaypoints() function, we remove the y axis from nodePosition (which could now hold the position of a different waypoint than the one we were aiming for at the start of the function) and then recalculate currentWaypointDist. The reason for this is that currentWaypointDist is used to calculate the race positions and if it is not up to date and the GlobalRaceManager class uses it between now and the next time this function is called, the race positions could be wrong. Since GlobalRaceManager only calculates race positions intermittently (not every frame), if currentWaypointDist is wrong the position display on screen could jitter between the right and wrong values.

```
public void CheckWrongWay()
{
        if(_currentWaypointTransform==null)
                return;

        Vector3 relativeTarget =
myTransform.InverseTransformPoint
(_currentWaypointTransform.position);
```

To ensure the player is heading in the right direction around the track, the CheckWrongWay() function uses the waypoints system to look ahead to the next waypoint and check the angle of the vehicle vs. the ideal angle to reach the waypoint. When the angle goes over a certain threshold (here, it is set to 90 degrees) then the wrong way message is displayed, and a timer will count. When the timer reaches a certain amount, we automatically respawn the player back on to the track.

First, the function checks that _currentWaypointTransform has something in it. If this reference was at null, it would break the code, so we drop out here, if we need to.

The script uses the waypoint from _currentWaypointTransform to check that the vehicle is traveling in the right direction. The first step in doing that is to calculate a vector, relative to the vehicle, with Transform.InverseTransformPoint(). Essentially, what happens here is that the world vector provided by _currentWaypointTransform.position is converted to the local space belonging to _TR (the vehicle), providing relativeTarget with a vector.

```
        targetAngle = Mathf.Atan2 (relativeTarget.x,
relativeTarget.z);
        targetAngle *= Mathf.Rad2Deg;
```

Mathf.Atan2 is used to convert the x and z values of the vector relativeTarget into an angle. The result of Mathf.Atan2 will be in radians, so a quick call to Mathf.Rad2Deg is required to convert it to degrees. As relativeTarget is a vector relative to the vehicle, when we convert that to an angle we know that 0 degrees will be forward along the vehicle's forward axis and that 90 degrees will be to the right and –90 degrees to the left. In effect, targetAngle now holds the result of how many degrees the vehicle (along its forward vector) is out from facing the waypoint.

```
        if(targetAngle<-90 || targetAngle>90){
                goingWrongWay=true;
        } else {
                goingWrongWay=false;
```

Above, we see if targetAngle is –90 or 90 degrees out (outside of our wrong way threshold angle) and will set the goingWrongWay Boolean variable accordingly.

```
                timeWrongWayStarted=-1;
        }
```

If a vehicle is going the wrong way for a set amount of time, it will be automatically respawned by the game code. The variable timeWrongWayStarted is, in effect, a timestamp, which is used to hold the time at which the wrong direction was first detected. When the code no longer detects the vehicle going in the wrong direction, timeWrongWayStarted is set to –1 which has the effect of cancelling a respawn and restarting the timer.

Next, we set timeWrongWayStarted when the wrong way first happens:

```
        if(oldWrongWay!=goingWrongWay)
        {
                // store the current time
                timeWrongWayStarted= Time.time;
        }
```

Above, we check to see if goingWrongWay has changed by comparing it to oldWrongWay. When the detection of a wrong way first happens, oldWrongWay will not be equal to goingWrongWay so it is safe to start the timestamp. timeWrongWayStarted is set to Time.time and it will be compared to the current value of Time.time to see how long has passed since the wrong way began.

```
        oldWrongWay=goingWrongWay;

    }
```

It's the end of the CheckWrongWay() function and oldWrongWay may now be set to the current value of goingWrongWay so that we can track it for changes the next time this function runs.

As discussed earlier in this section, the current lap will not be increased as soon as the player reaches the end of its waypoints. The player also needs to cross the start/finish line before the lap counter will be updated and a simple trigger Collider is used on an invisible box crossing the track. When the player hits the trigger, the OnTriggerEnter function is automatically called by the Unity engine:

```
public virtual void OnTriggerEnter(Collider other)
    {
                if (other.gameObject.layer == 12 && isLapDone ==
true)
            {
```

When OnTriggerEnter is called, the call contains information about the Collider that the Transform has hit. The variable other is of type Collider, which means it has all the properties of a Collider and may be accessed as one. The function starts out by looking at the layer of the Collider to see if it was the correct layer for the start/finish line trigger. If isLapDone is true and the start/finish line trigger was hit, the code continues by incrementing the lap counter in the variable lapsComplete:

```
                        // increase lap counter
                        lapsComplete++;

                        // reset our lapDone flag ready for when we
finish the next lap
                        isLapDone = false;
```

```
                            // tell race controller we just finished a
lap and which lap we are now on
                         GlobalRaceManager.instance.
CompletedLap(raceID);
                    }
              }
       }
}
```

As the lap is incremented, the end of this lap has been reached so we need to use the isLapDone variable to track the next lap. It is reset to false above, then we call GlobalRaceManager to let it know that a lap completed. We make a call out to the GlobalRaceManager's CompletedLap() function, passing in this vehicle's unique ID to identify itself.

14.4.4 Race Control – RacePlayerController Class

RacePlayerController is a class that is attached to the vehicle prefabs in our example racing game. It derives from the script from the previous section, the RaceController class, so that we get to build on top of the functionality of RaceController rather than building a completely new script for our racing game. This is how most of the framework is intended to work – you take a base class, inherit it, and override some of its functions to extend it for your game's specification.

RacePlayerController starts with the usual namespaces and a class declaration that tells Unity it derives from RaceController:

```
using UnityEngine;
using GPC;

public class RacePlayerController : RaceController
{       // this userID ID number ties up with the player data in
UserDataManager
       public int userID;

       public int myRacePosition;
       public float stuckResetTime = 3f;
       public float stuckTimer;
       public bool blockRespawn;
       [Space]
       public BaseWheeledVehicle _myController;
       public BaseAIController _AIController;
       public bool AIControlled;
       private float timedif;
       public LayerMask respawnerLayerMask;
```

We skip ahead, past the variable declarations, to the first function:

```
       void Start()
       {
              Init();
       }

       // Update is called once per frame
       public override void Init()
       {
              base.Init();

              ResetLapCounter();
              _myController = GetComponent<BaseWheeledVehicle>();

              didInit = true;
       }
```

Start() calls Init(). Init() calls to the base class (RaceController) to run its Init() first, and then we are into this script. A call to ResetLapCounter() is first up, to make sure that everything is reset and ready to start counting laps. We grab a reference to BaseWheeledVehicle next and store it in the variable _myController. This script is intended to work with BaseWheeledVehicle, so you will have to make some changes if you are copying this to use in your own racing game that uses a different vehicle type.

With Init() done, we set didInit to true at the end of the function.

```
void LateUpdate()
{
        // tell race control to see if we're going the wrong
way
        CheckWrongWay();
```

Above, LateUpdate() calls CheckWrongWay(). CheckWrongWay() was covered back when we looked at the RaceController class in Section 12.5.3.

```
if (goingWrongWay)
{
        if (!AIControlled)
                RaceGameManager.instance.
UpdateWrongWay(true);

        // if going the wrong way, compare time since wrong
way started to see if we need to respawn
        if (timeWrongWayStarted != -1)
                timedif = Time.time - timeWrongWayStarted;
```

If our vehicle is going in the wrong direction, we do want to show a wrong way message but only if the player is not AI controlled. As long as this is not an AI player, we make a call out to the RaceGameManager instance to UpdateWrongWay(). RaceGameManager will take care of showing the message to the user.

Something we also want to do if we are going the wrong way is to time how long the player has been going the wrong way ready to respawn them in case they are stuck. Above, as long as timeWrongWayStarting is not −1 (−1 is the default value we give this variable when we want to reset the spawn time) then we can go ahead and calculate how long the player has had its goingWrongWay variable set to true. We do that simply by taking Time.time and subtracting the value stored in timeWrongWayStarted. Remember that timeWrongWayStarted is a time-stamp that is set when goingWrongWay first becomes true, so by subtracting it from the current time we know how long it has been since the start.

```
                if (timedif > stuckResetTime)
                {
                        // it's been x resetTime seconds in
the wrong way, let's respawn this thing!
                        Respawn();
                }
```

When timedif (how long the player has been facing the wrong way) is greater that stuckResetTime, above, we call the Respawn() function.

```
        }
        else if (!AIControlled)
        {
```

```
                    RaceGameManager.instance.
UpdateWrongWay(false);
                }
```

Above, we deal with what happens when goingWrongWay is not set to true. If this is not an AI controlled vehicle, RaceGameManager gets another call to its UpdateWrongWay() function to tell it that we are no longer going the wrong way.

```
                // stuck timer
                if(_myController.mySpeed<0.1f &&
_myController.canControl)
                {
                    stuckTimer += Time.deltaTime;
```

Above, we check our vehicle controller _myController has a speed of less than 0.1f (an arbitrary low value I came up with through trial and error) and that it is actually being controlled. If the conditions are met, we can increase the value of stuckTimer with the amount of time since the last frame update.

```
                if (stuckTimer > stuckResetTime)
                {
                    // it's been x resetTime seconds in
the wrong way, let's respawn this thing!
                    Respawn();
                    stuckTimer = 0;
                }
```

When stuckTimer goes over the value of stuckResetTime, we know that the vehicle has been extremely slow or stopped for that amount of time and now it is time to call Respawn() in the hopes of getting the player moving again. Above, we call Respawn() and reset the stuckTimer to zero.

```
            } else
            {
                stuckTimer = 0;
            }
```

On the other hand, if the vehicle speed is above our minimum 0.1f amount, we just set stuckTimer to 0 so that the code above does not respawn the vehicle.

```
            UpdateWaypoints();
```

As mentioned in Section 12.5.3, the RaceController class contains the function UpdateWaypoints() that has to be called manually each frame – hence why it is here in the LateUpdate() function.

```
                // check to see if this is the last player and the
race is now complete (and tell game manager if it is!)
                if (GlobalRaceManager.instance.raceAllDone)
                {
                    RaceGameManager.instance.RaceComplete();
```

If the race finishes, above we tell the RaceGameManager about it. I chose to put this call here (rather than in the GlobalRaceManager class) because GlobalRaceManager is intended to be a generic script that can be used anywhere without ties to any other non-Unity class than RaceController. This means that RaceComplete() will likely be called more than once, but the way

RaceGameManager updates its game states means this will have no effect other than ending the game.

```
        } else
        {
                // we only update the position during the
game. once the race is done, we stop calculating it
                UpdateRacePosition();
        }
    }
```

Above, since we now know that the race is not finished (this is the else that comes after checking if GlobalRaceManager.raceAllDone is true) we can do whatever needs to be done during the race. Above, this means we call out to UpdateRacePosition() to keep the race position indicator up to date. Which leads us to the UpdateRacePosition() function, next:

```
    public void UpdateRacePosition()
    {
            // grab our race position from the global race manager
            myRacePosition =
GlobalRaceManager.instance.GetPosition(this);
    }
```

From the point of view of the RacePlayerController class, there is not much to do to update the race position. We just get the return value from an instance of GlobalRaceManager.GetPosition() and store it in myRacePosition. The RaceGameManager class deals with updating the user interface to show on screen.

```
    void Respawn()
    {
            if (blockRespawn)
                    return;
            // reset our velocities so that we don't reposition
a spinning vehicle
            _myController._RB.velocity = Vector3.zero;
            _myController._RB.angularVelocity = Vector3.zero;
```

The Respawn() function first checks that respawning is not currently blocked. We set blockRespawn to true just after a respawn, then it gets reset after a set amount of time. This is to prevent multiple respawns within a short amount of time – usually one respawn within a few seconds should be enough.

As long as we are good to respawn, the code above then goes on to zero out the velocity and angular velocities of the RigidBody on our player. This stops the vehicle moving and rotating after the respawn.

```
            // get the waypoint to respawn at from the race controller
            Transform _tempTR = GetRespawnWaypointTransform();
            Vector3 tempVEC = _tempTR.position;
```

The function GetRespawnWaypointTransform(), found in the RaceController class, deals with finding the waypoint that we are going to be respawning at and returns its Transform so that we can use it to get position and rotation information from. We put the waypoint Transform into a locally scoped variable named _tempTR then on the next line, take the position of the Transform and put it into a locally scored tempVEC variable.

```
            // cast a ray down from the waypoint to try to find
the ground
            RaycastHit hit;
            if (Physics.Raycast(tempVEC + (Vector3.up * 10), -
Vector3.up, out hit))
            {
                tempVEC.y = hit.point.y + 2.5f;
            }
```

As it is quite common for the waypoints to be either off the ground or too close to the ground for our respawn to work correctly, the code above deals with ray casting down to find the ground Collider. We project a ray from tempVEC (the waypoint's position) add 10 units upward. The ray goes straight down at -Vector3. up and we put raycast hit information into the locally scoped variable, hit.

If the raycast was successful, it will return true, and we run the code between the graphics. What happens there is that tempVEC has its y position set to the ground position we just found through the raycast (hit.point) add 2.5 units. This number (2.5f) may be adjusted to respawn the vehicle closer or further from the ground as required. By the way, tempVEC will be used as the final position for the vehicle during repositioning:

```
        _myController._TR.rotation = _tempTR.rotation;
        _myController._TR.position = tempVEC;

        blockRespawn = true;
        Invoke("ResetRespawnBlock", 5f);
    }
```

Above, Respawn() ends by setting our vehicles rotation to that of the way-point Transform in _tempTR. Then on the next line, its position is set to the Vector3 in tempVEC. We then set blockRespawn to true and in the last line of the function, a call to ResetRespawnBlock() is scheduled for 5 seconds' time. This means that the respawn function will be disabled for 5 seconds after a respawn.

```
    void ResetRespawnBlock()
    {
        blockRespawn = false;
    }
```

ResetRespawnBlock sets blockRespawn to false, allowing respawns again after a delay.

```
    public override void PlayerFinishedRace()
    {
```

When a player has completed all of the laps in the race, GlobalRaceManager calls the PlayerFinishedRace() function in the RaceController class. Above, we override RaceController's version of PlayerFinishedRace() to do something specific to this game. When our player has finished all of their race laps, we have the AI take control of the vehicle and drive it around until the entire race finishes when all players have completed their laps, too.

```
    if (!AIControlled)
        {
            // make sure we give control over to AI if
it's not already
            AIControlled = true;
```

```
            GetComponent<RaceInputController>().SetInputType(RaceInputCo
ntroller.InputTypes.noInput);
                        GetComponent<AISteeringController>().
AIControlled = true;
                    _AIController.canControl = true;
                }
            }
```

We begin by making sure that the player is not already being controlled by
AI with a check on the AIControlled Boolean variable. If we are not yet AI, the
code inside the curly brackets for this condition will change that.

AIControlled gets set to true, so that we now know our player is AI controlled. Next, it is a rather long line that uses Unity's GetComponent() function
to find our RaceInputController Component, then it calls SetInputType on it
and sets the input type for the player to be RaceInputController.InputTypes.
noInput, to disable user input. Next, GetComponent goes off to find an
AISteeringController Component (or, remember this could be a class that
derives from AISteeringController and it would still find it) and then tells the
steering controller that we are now AI controlled by setting its AIControlled
variable to true.

To complete the AI takeover, we tell _AIController that it can control this
player by setting its canControl variable to true.

At the end of the race, if you ever wanted to do something different like have
the cars keep going, the PlayerFinishedRace() function would be the place to
start.

```
        public void SetLock(bool state)
        {
            if (!didInit)
                Init();
            _myController.canControl = !state;
        }
```

Above, SetLock is used to tell our vehicle that it cannot be controlled. First,
we make sure that Init() has completed (as this will be called when the player first
spawns to hold them in place and it may be that this script has not yet initialized)
but if has not, we call to Init() from here so that _myController will be populated
and we can access it in the next line.

_myController.canControl is a Boolean we can set to decide whether the
vehicle will be allowed to receive input and act on it. Above, this is not an ideal
situation. We actually set canControl to the opposite of the state being passed in
because of the fact that the function is named SetLock (i.e. set whether a lock
should be in place) whereas canControl is whether the vehicle can be controlled.
They are opposites. SetLock() is named so for the sake of continuity elsewhere in
the framework, but it is always better to avoid any naming contradiction like this,
if you can.

```
        public override void OnTriggerEnter(Collider other)
        {
            base.OnTriggerEnter(other);
            if (IsInLayerMask(other.gameObject.layer,
respawnerLayerMask))
            {
                Respawn();
            }
        }
    }
```

The last part of the RacePlayerController class overrides what happens when the vehicle hits a trigger, to add the extra functionality of respawn zones. A respawn zone is a trigger that will force an instant respawn of the player. For this to work, there needs to be a specific collision layer set up in Unity and respawner-LayerMask should be set to it in the Inspector on this Component (on the prefab).

OnTriggerEnter() is a built-in Unity function, called by the engine for us and passing in the Collider this object hit as a parameter. Here, we named the Collider other.

To run the code from the original RaceController class that this one derives from, we then call base.OnTriggerEnter() and pass other as a parameter – effectively taking what got passed into this function and passing it on to the base class version.

The ExtendedCustomMonoBehaviour class provides a function named IsInLayerMask(), which can be used to find out if a layer falls within a LayerMask. To use it, you pass in the layer you want to check as the first parameter and the LayerMask as the second. Above, we pass in the Collider's GameObject's layer to look for and the respawnerLayerMask LayerMask as the LayerMask to look at.

When we know that the layer is the right one for a respawner, the code within the conditions curly brackets calls Respawn() to take care of respawning the vehicle.

14.4.5 Audio

For the vehicle audio in this game, we use a set of GameObjects with AudioSource Components attached to them. These GameObjects are child objects of the vehicle, moving around with the vehicle wherever it goes and activated to play by other scripts. For incidental sounds, a BaseSoundController Component holds an array of sounds such as bleeps during the countdown that can be played from other scripts.

14.4.5.1 Vehicle Audio

Vehicle audio is controlled by the following classes:

WheeledVehicleController – The engine audio has its pitch controlled by this class. The engine audio is made up of a single sound loop which is played by an AudioSource Component attached to a GameObject named Engine, a child of the Vehicle_Player prefab.

CrashSound – This Component takes an AudioSource (attached to a CrashSound GameObject on the player prefab in this game) and plays it at different volumes depending on the severity of impact, whenever the impact magnitude is greater than a value set in the Inspector. The magnitudeToPlay variable decides the minimum magnitude for an impact sound. The pitch is also randomized slightly to make the impact sounds more varied.

How the WheeledVehicleController deals with sound was outlined in Chapter 6, Section 6.2, during the breakdown of this script.

14.4.5.2 Incidental Sounds

Incidental sounds are controlled by a single BaseSoundController Component attached to the GameManager GameObject in the core Scene. You can find a full breakdown of the BaseSoundController in Chapter 9, Section 9.2.

14.4.6 User Interface

In the Hierarchy of the core Scene, the user interface is all under the GameObject named UI_Canvas. There are two Canvases:

In-Game UI – The user interface contains a Text object to show the current lap number, a Text object to show the wrong way message and a third Text object to show when the race is over.

Intro_UI – The intro Canvas contains three Text objects for the three numbers we show during the countdown at the start of the race.

All the game's user interface is managed from a single class named RaceUIManager. It is added as a script Component to the GameManager GameObject in the Scene.

The RaceUIManager class derives from MonoBehaviour so that it can be added to a GameObject as a Component:

```
using UnityEngine;
using UnityEngine.UI;

public class RaceUIManager : MonoBehaviour
{
        public Text _lapText;

        public GameObject _count3;
        public GameObject _count2;
        public GameObject _count1;

        public GameObject _finalText;
        public GameObject _wrongWaySign;
```

Above, the variable declarations reference the individual GameObjects that make up the user interface. These need to be set up in the Unity editor, via the Inspector.

```
        public void SetLaps(int aLap, int totalLaps)
        {
                _lapText.text = "Lap " + aLap.ToString("D2") + " of "
+ totalLaps.ToString("D2");
        }
```

Above, the SetLaps() function takes the current lap, followed by the total race laps as its parameters. The Text Component references in _lapText has its text set to the word Lap and then we do something very cool with the lap number. Instead of simply converting it into a string with the ToString() function, we add "D2" inside the brackets. What this does is tell ToString() how to format the number when it converts it. D2 will format the lap string to have two numbers. For example; if the current lap is less than 10, it will be displayed with a zero in front of it.

We add the word "of" to the string next, then at the end of the line we take totalLaps and convert it to a string in the same way we did the current lap. That is, we use D2 to format the conversion. Note that there is no technical reason to do this – I think it just looks nicer to have the extra number in the user interface.

```
        public void HideFinalMessage()
        {
                _finalText.SetActive(false);
        }
```

To hide the final message (it will need to be hidden at the start of the game) we call the above HideFinalMessage() function. All it does it to call SetActive() on the GameObject referenced in the _finalText variable. Passing in false as a parameter will cause the SetActive() function to render our GameObject inactive in the Scene.

```
public void ShowFinalMessage()
{
        _finalText.SetActive(true);
}
```

In ShowFinalMessage() we do pass true into SetActive() on the _finalText GameObject, to make it active in the Scene.

```
public void HideWrongWay()
{
        _wrongWaySign.SetActive(false);
}

public void ShowWrongWay()
{
        _wrongWaySign.SetActive(true);
}
```

Both HideWrongWay() and ShowWrongWay() use SetActive() to hide or show their GameObjects respectively.

```
public void ShowCount(int whichOne)
{
        switch(whichOne)
        {
                case 0:
                        _count1.SetActive(false);
                        _count2.SetActive(false);
                        _count3.SetActive(false);
                        break;
                case 1:
                        _count1.SetActive(true);
                        _count2.SetActive(false);
                        _count3.SetActive(false);
                        break;
                case 2:
                        _count1.SetActive(false);
                        _count2.SetActive(true);
                        _count3.SetActive(false);
                        break;
                case 3:
                        _count1.SetActive(false);
                        _count2.SetActive(false);
                        _count3.SetActive(true);
                        break;
        }
}
```

ShowCount() takes an integer as a parameter, who represents which part of the countdown should be shown. We could just as easily write a function using a loop that would have avoided duplicating the SetActive statements in each case, but sometimes it can be just as easy (and quick) to write them out. Feel free to improve this function, if you so wish!

15 Blaster Game Example

In the late 1970s came a turn-based game called Robots for the Berkeley Software Distribution (BSD). In Robots, the player must escape from a swarm of enemies that move in closer toward the player each turn. In the original version of the game, the player moves around the arena to avoid contact between enemies and player, which would end the game.

Robots is often referred to as the beginning of the arena shooter – a term used to describe a top-down shoot 'em up game with the action locked into a limited area like an arena. The Blaster game example from this chapter is a basic template for an arena shooter, which borrows heavily from its predecessors; the action has a single player moving around an arena fighting off hordes of killer robots.

In this chapter, we look at the scripts used to build an arena shooter (Figure 15.1) where bots will spawn and the goal is to destroy them all to be able to progress to the next level. This chapter is less of a tutorial and more of a companion guide to the example project. It is expected that you will open the example project and dig around to see how it works, using this chapter as a guide to what everything does in the game and how it all fits together. This chapter is mostly focused on the C# scripts, what they do, and how they work.

Additions to the core framework are minimal and you can see the structure of the game in Figure 15.2.

You can find the Blaster game in the example project folder Assets/Games/Blaster. Scenes are in the Assets/Games/Blaster/Scenes folder.

Figure 15.1 The Blaster Game Example.

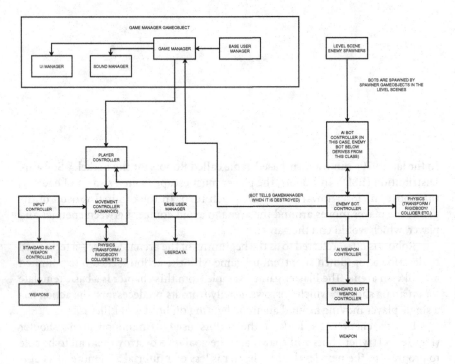

Figure 15.2 The game structure for the Blaster game.

▮ 15.1 Ingredients

The Blaster game uses the following ingredients:

1. Main menu – The menu code is based on MenuWithProfiles.cs from Chapter 11, Section 11.1.2. We are using the same template menu as we did in Chapter 2 for the RunMan game menu.

2. Scene loader – MultiLevelLoader.cs, derived from LevelLoader.cs (covered in Chapter 13, Section 13.2) is used for Scene loading. The LevelVars class is used to hold information about which level to load.

3. BlasterGameManager derives from BaseGameManager and uses BaseUserManager to decide what player to spawn when the game starts (and how many lives the player has etc.). It will also use the ScreenAndAudioFader class from GPC_Framework/COMMON/USER INTERFACE to fade the Scene in or out.

4. Sound Controller – The BaseSoundController class from Chapter 9, Section 9.1, is used to play game over and level complete sounds, with individual prefabs making their own sounds like firing noises or explosions.

5. User Interface – The user interface for in game will derive from the CanvasManager script from Chapter 11, Section 11.1, to fade UI elements in or out.

6. The BlasterPlayer class (the main class for the player) derives from BasePlayerStatsController, which also uses BaseUserManager to provide stats for the player for lives and score values.

7. CameraThirdPerson uses BaseCameraController.

Note that those Components already described in detail elsewhere in this book will not be repeated in this chapter, it is expected that you will find them in their respective chapters instead.

15.2 Main Menu Scene Overview

The main menu is made from the template main menu found in the GPC_Framework/TemplateScenes folder.

The main menu loads another Scene that acts as a game loader. The game loading Scene loads two addition Scenes – a core Scene, and an additional level Scene. The Scene loader merges the core and level Scenes together and starts the game.

15.3 The Core Scene Overview

The main parts of the game are split between two Scenes. One contains the level – that is, walls and enemy spawn positions (this could be expanded out to a full 3d environment if you wanted to) – and the second is a core Scene containing game logic and anything which is shared in every Scene during the game like the main outside walls of the arena and the Camera.

In most cases, you would put the full 3d level into the level Scenes, but in the case of this game we have the Arena and Lights in the core Scene. We do this just because the arena (the outside walls of the play area and a ground plane) are shared across all levels. If you use this as a template for your own games, you will most likely remove Arena and Lights from the core Scene and keep all level objects in the level Scenes.

15.3.1 The BlasterGameManager Class

The BlasterGameManager is a central communications hub for the game. It derives from BaseGameManager and overrides some of its base functions as well as adding some of its own.

BlasterGameManager derives from BaseGameController, which in turn derives from MonoBehaviour so that it can tap into some of Unity's built in calls to functions like Update(), Awake() and Start() etc.:

```
using System.Collections.Generic;
using UnityEngine;
using UnityEngine.SceneManagement;
using GPC;

public class BlasterGameManager : BaseGameManager
{       public Transform _playerPrefab;
        public Transform _playerSpawnpoint;
        public BaseCameraController _cameraManager;
        public Transform _thePlayer;
        public BlasterPlayer _thePlayerScript;
        public List<BlasterPlayer> _playerScripts;
        public BlasterUIManager _uiManager;
        public ScreenAndAudioFader _fader;
        public int enemyCounter;
        public BaseUserManager _baseUserManager;
        public BaseSoundManager _soundComponent;
```

Above, we require System.Collections.Generic for using Lists. UnityEngine. SceneManagement for returning to the main menu at the end of the game and GPC for the framework.

The class declaration above shows we derive from BaseGameManager. Next, we skip past all but one of the variable declarations and get to the constructor:

```
        public static BlasterGameManager instance { get; private
set; }

        public Awake()
        {
                instance = this;
        }
```

As with any other Singleton style classes we produce in this book, above we declare a variable named instance that gets set to this instance in its Awake() function.

```
        private void Start()
        {
                // start with audio muted and fade covering the
screen
                _fader.SetFadedOut();

                // schedule a fade in after a little time
                Invoke("StartFadeIn", 1f);

                SetTargetState(Game.State.loaded);
        }
```

When the Start() function runs, automatically called by Unity, the first thing we need to do is to make sure that the screen starts blacked out so that we can have a nice fade in. To pull this off, we call out to the ScreenAndAudioFader class reference in _fader and run its SetFadedOut() function. This will set the state of the fader to black right away.

The next line is an Invoke statement that will call the StartFadeIn() function in one second. We delay this to make it work nicely – it appears better to a user if the Scene loads and then we give the user a brief time to see the black screen before the fade starts than it does if the fade is already starting as soon as the Scene loads.

We then go on to call SetTargetState(), changing the game state, to Game. State.Loaded.

```
void StartFadeIn()
{
        _fader.FadeIn();
}
```

Above, the StartFadeIn() function called from Start() calls on _fader. FadeIn() to give a nice fade from black when the level starts.

```
void Init()
{
        // if we're running this in the editor, LevelVars.
currentLevel will not have been set to 1 (as it should be at the
start)
        // so we just do a little check here so that the
game will run OK from anywhere..
        if (LevelVars.currentLevel == 0)
        {
                LevelVars.coreSceneName = "blaster_core";
                LevelVars.levelNamePrefix = "blaster_level_";
                LevelVars.currentLevel = 1;
        }
```

There is a little set up required before the game can begin. Above, the first thing we do is make it easier to test the game in the editor by setting up some default values in LevelVars, if none have already been set up. To find out if LevelVars have already been set, we look to see if LevelVars.currentLevel is 0. We want the level numbering to start from 1, so if it sits at 0, we know that the default value of 1 has not yet been set up.

Normally, these variables would have been filled in by the main menu but if you are running in the editor it will need to know what values to use when you get to the end of the level and the game tries to load in the next one.

```
        CreatePlayers();
        _cameraManager.SetTarget(_thePlayer);

        // now we've done init, we can start the level..
        SetTargetState(Game.State.levelStarting);
}
```

The next task in Init() is to call CreatePlayers() to add the main player to the Scene. The current game is only single player, but creating players in this manner would make it easier to add multiple players in the future.

By the time we reach the next line of code, the players have been created so we can go ahead and tell the Camera script which player to follow around. A direct reference to the Camera script can be found in _cameraManager – this was set via the Inspector on the Component. The CreatePlayers() function set a variable named _thePlayer to the first player it created, and we can pass this over to the SetTarget() function of the Camera script for it to follow our user-controlled player.

At the end of Init(), the time has come again to update the game state. This time, we set it to Game.State.levelStarting.

```
void CreatePlayers()
{
        // refresh our player script list
        _playerScripts = new List<BlasterPlayer>();

        List<UserData> _playerInfo =
_baseUserManager.GetPlayerList();

        // for editor testing..
        if (_playerInfo.Count == 0)
            _baseUserManager.AddNewPlayer();
```

Above, we start CreatePlayers() by making a new List to store references to the players in. To figure out what players need to be created and to get their stats, we use the BaseUserManager class (as seen in Chapter 4, Section 4.3. of this book). BaseUserManager should contain a List of players for the game to create which we can get to via the BaseUserManager.GetPlayerList() function. GetPlayerList() will return a List of UserData objects (user stats – see Chapter 4, Section 4.4. for more information on this).

If we are testing the game in the editor and have not gone through the main menu, the player List in BaseUserManager will be empty. This will cause problems here, so rather than making it impossible to test I have added code above that looks to see if _playerInfo.Count is 0 (our player List is empty) and, when it is, to add a new player with BaseUserManager.AddNewPlayer().

```
        // iterate through the player list and add the
players to the scene ..
        for (int i = 0; i < _playerInfo.Count; i++)
        {
                // remember to name your spawnpoints
correctly! PlayerSpawnPoint_1, PlayerSpawnPoint_2 etc. depending on
how many players!
                string spawnPointString = "PlayerSpawnPoint_"
+ (i + 1).ToString();

                _playerSpawnpoint =
GameObject.Find(spawnPointString).transform;
```

The next step is to iterate through the player List we grabbed out of BaseUserManager and spawn a player for each one. Before we can spawn a player, though, we need to figure out where to place it. For that, the level Scene should contain at least one spawn point named PlayerSpawnPoint_ with a number after it. In the example Scene, the spawn point is named PlayerSpawnPoint_1.

Above, we construct a string named spawnPointString to find the spawn position with. Once we have the string, GameObject.Find is used to populate _playerSpawnpoint (a Transform type variable) with the Transform of the GameObject it finds.

```
        _thePlayer = Instantiate(_playerPrefab, _
playerSpawnpoint.position, _playerSpawnpoint.rotation, transform);
```

Above, the player is instantiated, using the playerPrefab prefab (set in the Inspector) and the position and rotation of the _playerSpawnpoint Transform. Notice that we also set the parent of the object to be instantiated here. If you do not parent a newly instantiated object like this, due to how Unity deals with initializing our merged core and level Scenes the new GameObject will be instantly destroyed by the engine as soon as the game starts (is this a bug? I have no idea, but this was the only way to stop Unity eating my players!).

```
                // grab a reference to the player script through the
new transform we just instantiated
                BlasterPlayer _aPlayerScript =
_thePlayer.GetComponent<BlasterPlayer>();

                // assign ID to this player from the player list
                _aPlayerScript.SetPlayerDetails( _playerInfo[i].id );

                _playerScripts.Add(_aPlayerScript);
                if(i==0)
                        _thePlayerScript = _aPlayerScript;
        }
```

Next, we set the ID number of our player on its BlasterPlayer Component to match up with the ID from the BaseUserManager player List. To do this, we start out by getting a reference to BlasterPlayer with GetComponent(), above, to hold in the locally scoped _playerScript variable. It is locally scoped because we only need it temporarily, during the set up.

With _playerScript in place, SetPlayerDetails() is called and we pass in the ID number from the _playerInfo List. _playerScript is then added to the _playerScripts List so that we always keep a List of players in the game – making access to their BlasterPlayer Components convenient.

To finish this function, if this is the first player we assume that is the player we will follow with the Camera and track the score and lives values of, so we check if the loop variable i is equal to zero and, if it is, grab a reference to this player's BlasterPlayer Component (in _aPlayerScript) and store it in _thePlayerScript.

The curly bracket at the end of the code above signifies the end of the loop (looping through the List of UserData objects in _playerInfo).

```
                // set the score display
                _uiManager.UpdateScoreUI(_thePlayerScript.
GetScore());

                _uiManager.UpdateLivesUI(_thePlayerScript.
GetLives());

                BaseCameraController theCam =
FindObjectOfType<BaseCameraController>();
                _theCam.SetTarget(_thePlayerScript.transform);

                // clear out the object..
                _playerInfo = null;
        }
```

Above, we update the score, and live user interface displays by calling their respective functions in the BlasterUIManager class (see Section 12.2.6 for a breakdown of that script). To get the values we use GetScore() and GetLives() functions on the _thePlayerScript (BlastPlayer class) object.

We need to tell the Camera script what to follow here, too, and we get to it by setting up a locally scoped variable theCam of type BaseCameraController and then use FindObjectsOfType() to get Unity to go off and search for it. With a reference set up in theCam, we can call BaseCameraController.SetTarget() and pass in the target of our player's Transform.

The last line of CreatePlayers() sets the temporary List we made, _playerInfo, to null. Just to make sure that we do not incur any garbage collection from it at the start of the game.

```
public void RegisterEnemy()
{
        enemyCounter++;
}
```

When an enemy is added to the game, the BlasterEnemyBot script will call the above RegisterEnemy() function. We keep a count of how many enemies there are, in the variable enemyCounter, so we can tell when they have all been destroyed and it is time to move on to the next level.

```
public void EnemyDestroyed()
{
        // before reacting to a player destroyed, we should
check that we're still in game playing mode
        if (currentGameState != Game.State.gamePlaying)
                return;

        enemyCounter--;
        _thePlayerScript.AddScore(150);
        UpdateUIScore(_thePlayerScript.GetScore());

        if (enemyCounter <= 0)
                SetTargetState(Game.State.levelEnding);
}
```

Enemies hit by projectiles will call the above EnemyDestroyed() function. We kick it off by making sure that the game is still in the Game.State.gamePlaying state and, if we find it is in any other state than that, we drop out. This prevents any collisions being registered either before or after the game has started.

As mentioned above, we keep a count of how many enemies there are in the variable enemyCounter. When one gets destroyed, we decrement enemyCounter by one.

The next job is call a function named EnemyHit in the BlasterPlayer class. EnemyHit() will award the player with score. With the score updated, we then call on the function UpdateUIScore, passing in _thePlayerScript.GetScore() as a parameter. UpdateUIScore will take that parameter and display it on screen as a score value. BlasterPlayer.GetScore() will return an integer containing that player's current score.

Next, we check to see if the level has finished by seeing if enemyCounter is less than or equal to zero. If it is, we know that all of the bots have been destroyed and it must be time to move to the next level so SetTargetState() gets called to set the new target state to Game.State.levelEnding.

```
public void UpdateUIScore(int theScore)
{
        _uiManager.UpdateScoreUI(theScore);
}
```

We will look at the BlasterUIManager class in detail in Section 12.2.6 of this chapter. Above, we call BlasterUIManager.UpdateScoreUI() and pass it the score that was passed into this function as its parameter. BlasterUIManager will update the on-screen score display.

```
        public void PlayerDestroyed()
        {
                // before reacting to a player destroyed, we should
check that we're still in game playing mode
                if (currentGameState != Game.State.gamePlaying)
                        return;
```

Above, PlayerDestroyed() will be called by the BlasterPlayer class. If the game is in a different state to Game.State.gamePlaying then we drop out right away, since we only want to register player death while the game is running.

```
                if ( _thePlayerScript.GetLives() <= 0)
                        SetTargetState(Game.State.gameEnding);
                else
                        SetTargetState(Game.State.restartingLevel); }
        }
```

When the player has been destroyed, there are two ways it can go. If they have any lives left, the level will be restarted. If they have no lives left, the game needs to end.

Above, we use the GetLives() function to see if there are lives left, then SetTargetState() sets the target game states to either Game.State.gameEnding or Game.State.restartingLevel.

```
        public void NextLevel()
        {
                // increase the current level counter in the
LevelVars static variable, so that the levelloader can use it later
                LevelVars.currentLevel++;

                // check to see which level we're on
                if (LevelVars.currentLevel == 4)
                {
                        // they finished the game!
                        Invoke("LoadGameCompleteScene", 1f);
                }
                else
                {
                        Debug.Log("LOADING NEXT LEVEL..");
                        // game isn't completed yet, so..
                        // load the sceneLoader scene (which will
load the next level)..
                        SceneManager.
LoadScene("blaster_sceneLoader");
                }
        }
```

When all of the enemies have been destroyed, the LevelEnding() function calls the function above, NextLevel() to progress the player and initiate loading the next level.

The first thing it does is to increase the currentLevel value held in our LevelVars class. This will be used to form the filename of the next level, so we need to be sure that the value of currentLevel never goes above the number of levels we have made in Scenes otherwise it will produce an error. We can currentLevel at 4, for this game. If you use this project as a template for your own games you will need to adjust this number accordingly, otherwise your game will always end after level 3!

If the currentLevel is 4, the code above makes an Invoke() call to LoadGameCompleteScene one second from now. In the example game, LoadGameCompleteScene simply loads the main menu and ends the game but if you use this project, you can make it load a nice congratulations message or a big finale – anything you like, really!

If the currentLevel is not 4 (less than 4, since we will never get any higher due to this if statement) then we need to load the next level. As LevelVars is already set up and we have already increased its currentLevel value, all we need to do is use SceneManager.LoadScene() to load the loader Scene – blaster_sceneLoader – to load and start the next level.

```
void CallFadeOut()
{
        _fader.FadeOut();
}
```

The CallFadeOut() function is used to call out to the ScreenAndAudioFader Component to fade out the Scene to black. It will be called when the game has ended, or when the level has finished, and we are about to load the next one.

```
//-------------------------------------------------------------------------------

// GAME STATE FUNCTIONS (CALLED BY THE UPDATETARGETSTATE    /
UPDATECURRENTSTATE FUNCTIONS)
```

The functions below all override virtual functions from the base BaseGameManager class. They are called by the BaseGameManager class at the beginning of game states. We looked at the BaseGameManager class in Chapter 3, Section 3.2.1., so look at that if you need more information on where these are called exactly.

```
public override void Loaded()
{
        Init();
        OnLoaded.Invoke();
}
```

Above, when the core Scene has loaded, we call the Init() function and invoke a UnityEvent named OnLoaded. The UnityEvents are there so that you can easily hook in other scripts to react to game state changes without dependencies. In the example game, any UnityEvents we do use are used to tell the user interface to hide or show Canvases such as the get ready message or game over.

```
public override void LevelStarting()
{
        OnLevelStarting.Invoke();
        Invoke("LevelStarted", 5f);
}
```

LevelStarting() calls our OnLevelStarting UnityEvent then schedules a call to the LevelStarted() function. At this point, our player has been told to get ready and we give them this 5 second delay to ready themselves.

```
public override void LevelStarted()
{
        OnLevelStarted.Invoke();

        // now we find all the enemy spawners
        GameObject[] _spawners =
GameObject.FindGameObjectsWithTag("EnemySpawner");
```

Above, LevelStarted() is responsible for getting the game going. The first step to accomplish this is to find all of the enemy spawners in the Scene with FindGameObjectsWithTag() passing in the string EnemySpawner. The enemy spawner prefab used in all the levels has its tag set to EnemySpawner so that this function can easily find them. FindGameObjectsWithTag() returns an array of GameObjects we can now iterate through:

```
            // next, iterate through the list of enemy spawners
and send a message to start their spawn timers
            for (int i = 0; i < _spawners.Length; i++)
            {
                    _spawners[i].SendMessage("StartSpawnTimer");
            }
```

One by one, each spawner has a message sent to it in the loop above, which runs the StartSpawnTimer() function in the Spawner class.

```
            // level is started now, so we can move on to
'playing' state
            SetTargetState(Game.State.gamePlaying);
    }
```

The last line of LevelStarted() sets the target game state to Game.State.game-Playing – signifying that the game is afoot.

```
    public override void LevelEnding()
    {
            OnLevelEnding.Invoke();

            // play level complete sound
            _soundComponent.PlaySoundByIndex(1);

            Invoke("CallFadeOut", 4f);
            Invoke("NextLevel", 6f);
    }
```

Earlier above, the in EnemyDestroyed() function, we set the target state to Game.State.levelEnding when the enemyCounter reached zero to indicate that all of the enemies had been destroyed for this level. The LevelEnding() function above is called as we enter that state and need to begin to move on to the next level.

LevelEnding() starts by invoking the OnLevelEnding UnityEvent. It then plays a sound using the BaseSoundController – the sound in the array on our sound controller, at index 1, is a simple sound effect to signify that the level has been complete.

To finish up, we schedule a call to the CallFadeOut() function (fading out the entire screen to black before loading) in 4 seconds, followed by a call to NextLevel() – the function that will do the actual level progression and loading – in 6 seconds, to give the fader time to do its thing before starting the load.

```
    public override void GameEnding()
    {
            OnGameEnding.Invoke();

            // play level complete sound
            _soundComponent.PlaySoundByIndex(0);

            Invoke("CallFadeOut", 2f);
            Invoke("GameEnded", 3f);
    }
```

You may be used to the pattern now – each of these functions calls it corresponding UnityEvent. Above, it is the OnGameEnding event.

We play a little sound at the end of the game to let the player know that things did not go so well, and the game is over. _soundComponent.PlaySoundByIndex() passes in 0 to the BaseSoundController Component as the sound to play.

CallFadeOut() gets a scheduled call next, in 2 seconds time, to fade out the Scene. Then, we get a scheduled call to GameEnded() to load the main menu and quit the game in 3 seconds.

```
public override void GameEnded()
{
        OnGameEnded.Invoke();
        LoadMainMenu();
}
```

GameEnded() calls its UnityEvent, then on to LoadMainMenu(). The LoadMainMenu() function will show up below, toward the end of this C# script.

```
public override void RestartLevel()
{
        Invoke("CallFadeOut", 2f);
        Invoke("LoadSceneLoaderToRestart", 4f);
}
```

RestartLevel() does just that by calling CallFadeOut() to darken the Scene in 3 seconds, then it schedules a call to LoadSceneLoaderToRestart() for 4 seconds' time.

```
void LoadSceneLoaderToRestart()
{
        SceneManager.LoadScene("blaster_sceneLoader");
}
```

Since the LevelVars class still has the values set up for loading the same level we are already on, all we do to have it restart is to reload the Scene loader. LoadeSceneLoaderToRestart(), above, uses SceneManager.LoadScene() to tell Unity to load blaster_sceneLoader.

```
void LoadMainMenu()
{
        SceneManager.LoadScene("blaster_menu");
}
void LoadGameCompleteScene()
{
        SceneManager.LoadScene("blaster_menu");
}
}
```

The final two functions of the BlasterGameManager class use SceneManager to load the blaster_menu Scene. LoadGameCompleteScene() is provided for you to customize should you use this project as a template. This is where you should put your celebration for completing the entire game or loading of another Scene to congratulate your player or something like that.

15.3.2 The BlasterPlayer Class

The BlasterPlayer class is a sort of glue between the Components and game logic. All of the movement of the player is taken care of by a separate Component, the

BasePlayerCharacterController (which we will cover in the next section of this book, in 12.2.4). It is also the place where we look to get player input for the fire button and tell the weapon system in StandardSlotWeaponController to fire.

It begins.

```
using UnityEngine;
using GPC;
public class BlasterPlayer : BasePlayerStatsController
{
        public LayerMask projectileLayerMask;
        public Transform explosionPrefab;
        [Header("Respawn")]
        public GameObject playerAvatarParent;
        public float respawnTime = 2f;
        public BasePlayerCharacterController _controller;
        [Header("Weapon")]
        public StandardSlotWeaponController _weaponControl;
        public bool allowedToFire = true;
```

BlasterPlayer derives from BasePlayerStatsController, which provides a bridge between BaseUserManager and the player by accessing and storing data about the player such as lives and score values.

```
        public override void Init()
        {
                base.Init();
                SetHealth(1);

                _TR = transform;
                _controller =
GetComponent<BasePlayerCharacterController>();
        }
```

We call base.Init() to run the Init() function of BasePlayerStatsController, the class this one derives from, so that the player data is set up and ready to go before – on the next line – setting the player's health level to 1. When a player's health reaches zero, they lose a life. We set the health level to 1 because this game uses a lives system rather than health, and we want them to lose a life as soon as they are hit not after reducing a health level first.

Above, we grab a quick reference the Transform for this player and then use GetComponent() to find the BasePlayerCharacterController Component (the script that will be handling movement of the player) and store that into a variable named _controller so we can access it further down.

```
        void Update()
        {
                if (_controller._inputController.Fire1)
                        _weaponControl.Fire();
        }
```

The BasePlayerCharacterController class has a variable in it named _input-Controller that links to a BaseInputController Component attached to the player. BaseInputController provides the input from the user to the movement system, but we can also tap into it for other input such as (above) the fire button. Here, we access BaseInputController via _controller.inputController and check to see if its Fire1 Boolean variable is true. If it is, we can pass the message on to the weapon system. We use the ref held in _weaponControl here to call StandardSlotWeaponController.Fire().

```
        public void OnCollisionEnter(Collision collider)
        {
                if (IsInLayerMask(collider.gameObject.layer,
projectileLayerMask) && !_controller.isRespawning)
                {
```

Unity's collision system will automatically call the OnCollisionEnter() function above, where we can identify what it was that collided with the player and react to it. To do this, we start out by comparing the layer of the Collider that hit the player to the projectileLayerMask. This will tell us if the player has been hit by a projectile from an enemy.

BasePlayerStatsController, the class this class derives from, in turn derives from ExtendedCustomMonoBehaviour. ExtendedCustomMonoBehaviour provides a function named IsInLayerMask(), which can be used to find out if a specified layer fall within a LayerMask (which is a collection of layers). To use IsInLayerMask, we pass in the layer you want to check as the first parameter and the LayerMask as the second. Above, we pass in the Collider's GameObject's layer to look for and the projectileLayerMask LayerMask as the LayerMask to look at.

When the player dies, before respawning the player object is hidden but it still exists in the game world and can still receive collision events. It is for this reason that we make sure the player is not respawning by checking against _controller.isRespawning.

```
                ReduceHealth(1);

                if (GetHealth() <= 0)
                {
                        Instantiate(explosionPrefab, _TR.position,
_TR.rotation);

                        // need to respawn, or reload the current
level here.. life lost!
                        PlayerDestroyed();
                }
        }
}
```

If we know the Collider that hit the player is a projectile and we are not respawning, we go ahead and reduce the player's health stat by 1. Below that, we take a look at GetHealth() to see if it is less or equal to 0. Since the player only has one health in this game, one hit has the effect of killing the player instantly. If you want to make the player have more than one chance before getting destroyed by a projectile, you could change the SetHealth() statement in the Init() function near the top of the class.

If GetHealth() says the health level is less or equal to 0, Instantiate creates an explosion effect in the Scene, courtesy of the explosionPrefab prefab and positioned at the player's Transform position and rotation. We then call on the PlayerDestroyed() function to deal with the next steps:

```
        void PlayerDestroyed()
        {
                _controller.isRespawning = true;

                // hide the avatar / visual representation of a
player!
```

```
            playerAvatarParent.SetActive(false);

            // reduce this player's lives by 1
            ReduceLives(1);

            // tell game manager that the player was destroyed
            BlasterGameManager.instance.PlayerDestroyed();
        }

}
```

Above, when PlayerDestroyed() is called we first set a flag _controller.isRe-spawning to avoid registering any more projectile hits/health losses and/or dupli-cate respawn calls. playerAvatarParent is a variable containing the GameObject above our players avatar in the Hierarchy, and here we call SetActive() on it to make it inactive in the Scene. This will hide the parent GameObject and any child objects, too, so the entire player should become invisible the player. As the player has been destroyed, we call ReduceLives() (all stats functions like this are in that BasePlayerStatsController class, by the way!) and finally call out to the BlasterGameManager instance to register the player destruction with it. BlasterGameManager will then take care of reloading the Scene to reset the game state and restart the level.

15.3.3 Enemy Bots and the BlasterEnemyBot Class

When it comes to inheritance, there is a three class chain leading up to BlasterEnemyBot:

BlasterEnemyBot>BaseEnemyStatsController>BaseAIController>ExtendedCustomMonoBehaviour.

BaseAIController is a class full of utility functions for dealing with AI, such as waypoint management, and movement. On its own, it does not do anything until we tell it what to do. BaseEnemyStatsController is the equivalent of Bae PlayerStatsController only for enemies. It holds information about the enemy's health, score, and name and can be expanded to hold any information you like. BlasterEnemyBot.cs brings BaseEnemyStatsController and BaseAIController together, to form the AI for our enemy bot.

The inherited classes means that BlasterEnemyBot is a relatively small script which derives from AIBotController, as described in Chapter 10, Section 10.4, of this book:

```
using UnityEngine;
using GPC;

public class BlasterEnemyBot : AIBotController
{
        [Header("Game specific")]
        public bool isRespawning;
        public bool isBoss;

        [Header("Weapons and hits")]
        public BaseEnemyWeaponController _weaponController;
        public LayerMask projectileLayerMask;
        public Transform _explosionPrefab;

        public override void Start()
        {
                Init();
        }
```

```
public override void Init()
{
        base.Init();
        // now get on and chase it!
        SetAIState(AIStates.AIState.chasing_target);
}
```

Above, we override BaseAIController's Start() function with this one. It calls the Init() function to get set up. Init() calls its base class equivalent then sets the AI's state to AI.States.AIState.chasing_target so that our bots will start moving right away.

```
public override void Update()
{
        base.Update();
}
```

We only need the base class to update, so that's all we do here.

```
public void OnCollisionEnter(Collision collider)
{
        if (IsInLayerMask(collider.gameObject.layer,
projectileLayerMask))
        {
                ReduceHealth(1);
                if (GetHealth() <= 0)
                {
                        Instantiate(_explosionPrefab,
_TR.position, _TR.rotation);
        BlasterGameManager.instance.EnemyDestroyed();
                        Destroy(gameObject);
                }
        }
}
```

Above, when OnCollisionEnter() gets called by the engine, we check to see if it is a projectile hitting the bot. If it is, health is reduced by 1 and there's a check to see if our enemy health is depleted. If the health is at (or below) 0, explosion-Prefab is instantiated at our position. BlasterGameManager's instance gets informed of the enemy demise via EnemyDestroyed() and then we use Unity's Destroy() function to remove the enemy GameObject from the Scene.

15.3.4 Weapons and Projectiles

Our EnemyBot prefab uses two Components for its weapons system. Those are; AI Weapon Controller and a Standard Slot Controller. The Standard Slot Controller is the system provided as part of the framework for dealing with weapons – we use the exact same Component on the player. It is the AI Weapon Controller that accesses StandardSlotController to tell it when to fire.

The main weapon (a prefab named Blaster_1) has a cylinder that looks like a weapon with a single Component attached to it – BaseWeaponScript – and it contains a reference to a projectile named Blast that will be instantiated whenever it fires. For more on the weapon system, see Chapter 7.

15.3.5 User Interface

The UI script derives from BaseUIDataManager, the standard UI script shown in Chapter 10. The BaseUIDataManager declares several common variables and provides some basic functions to deal with them:

```
using UnityEngine.UI;
using GPC;
public class BlasterUIManager : CanvasManager
{
        public Text scoreText;
        public Text highText;
        public Text livesText;

        void Start()
        {
                // hide all ui canvas
                HideAll();
        }

        public void ShowGetReadyUI()
        {
                // here we delay showing the get ready message just
so it flows nicer
                Invoke("ShowGetReady", 1f);
        }


        void ShowGetReady()
        {
                ShowCanvas(0);
        }
        public void HideGetReadyUI()
        {
                HideCanvas(0);
        }
        public void ShowGameOverUI()
        {
                ShowCanvas(1);
        }
        public void ShowGameUI()
        {
                ShowCanvas(2);
        }
        public void HideGameUI()
        {
                HideCanvas(2);
        }
        public void ShowLevelComplete()
        {
                ShowCanvas(3);
        }
        public void HideLevelComplete()
        {
                HideCanvas(3);
        }
        public void UpdateScoreUI(int anAmount)
        {
                scoreText.text = "SCORE " + anAmount.ToString("D6");
        }
        public void UpdateHighScoreUI(int anAmount)
        {
                highText.text = "HIGHSCORE " + anAmount.ToString("D6");
        }
        public void UpdateLivesUI(int anAmount)
        {
                livesText.text = "LIVES " + anAmount.ToString();
        }
}
```

■ 15.4 Level Scenes

Level Scenes contain spawners for the enemies and any environment for that level.

15.4.1 Spawning Enemies

The Spawner class derives from BaseTimedSpawner, which is a class used for automatically spawning another prefab and deleting itself once the prefab has been added to the Scene. The idea is that you add Spawner (or a derivative of it) as a Component to a cube primitive object in your Scene. The cube acts as a visual guide, just so you can easily gauge where your prefab will be spawning. At run-time, the cubes Renderer is disabled by the script, making it invisible, before the prefab is spawned and the original spawner GameObject destroyed.

Spawner also allows you to set a randomized delay time so that spawning may be staggered to avoid everything spawning in at the exact same time. Spawner.cs was covered in Chapter 5, Section 5.8.1, in this book but in this chapter, we will look at the derived version of it used specifically for this game. That is, the Spawner class.

BlasterTimedSpawner gets its behavior from BaseTimedSpawner. Essentially, the function of this script to register an enemy whenever one is spawned by the regular BaseTimedSpawner code.

```
using GPC;
public class BlasterTimedSpawner : BaseTimedSpawner
{
        public override void Start()
        {
                // do everything the base script does
                base.Start();
                // tell gamemanager about this enemy
                RegisterEnemy();
        }

        void RegisterEnemy()
        {
                // make sure we have a game manager before doing
anything here
                if (BlasterGameManager.instance == null)
                {
                        Invoke("RegisterEnemy", 0.1f);
                        return;
                }

                // at the start of the game, we need to register
this spawner as an enemy before it has spawned
                // so that we have an initial enemy count right away
                BlasterGameManager.instance.RegisterEnemy();
        }
}
```

Above, we override the Start() function of BaseTimedSpawner so that we can call RegisterEnemy() at the start of the game. We still need BaseTimedSpawner to do its set up, so base.Start() is called too.

The RegisterEnemy() function starts by checking that the BlasterGame Manager instance has been created – this is to prevent our script from trying to access the Game Manager before it has been added to the Scene and initialized properly. Since the level Scene and core Scene is loaded separately and merged, it may sometimes be necessary to do things like this when trying to avoid errors due to the odd way that Scenes are initialized by the engine.

If we do not find BlasterGameManager, Invoke() is used to try this function again in 0.1 seconds, then we drop out. This function will repeat call itself until BlasterGameManager is ready.

Finally, BlasterGameManager's instance gets a call to its RegisterEnemy() script, which you may remember from earlier in this chapter just keeps count of how many enemies there are in the Scene so it can count how many are destroyed and know when all of the bots are destroyed and the level has been completed.

Index

X

x axis, 18, 21–22, 36, 65, 112, 117, 167–168, 173, 203, 233

Y

y axis, 18, 65, 78, 79, 104, 106, 111, 114, 117, 121, 167–168, 173, 203, 233, 249–250

yield return null, 5, 6, 92, 152–153, 192–193, 213–215
yield statements, 6

Z

z axis, 79, 104, 106, 112, 114, 132, 167, 173, 203, 233

Printed in the United States
By Bookmasters